RELUCTANT HOSTS: EUROPE AND ITS REFUGEES

Research in Ethnic Relations Series

The New Helots
Migrants in the International Division of Labour
Robin Cohen

Black Radicalism and the Politics of De-industrialisation
The Hidden History of Indian Foundry Workers
Mark Duffield

The Ghetto and the Underclass
Essays on Race and Social Policy
John Rex

The Politics of Community
The Bangladeshi Community in East London
John Eade

Race and Borough Politics
Frank Reeves

Ethnic Minority Housing: Explanations and Policies
Philip Sarre, Deborah Phillips and Richard Skellington

Reluctant Hosts: Europe and its Refugees

Edited by
DANIÈLE JOLY
Research Fellow, Centre for Research in Ethnic Relations
University of Warwick
and
ROBIN COHEN
Professor of Sociology and Director, Centre for Research in Ethnic Relations
University of Warwick

Avebury

Aldershot · Brookfield USA · Hong Kong · Singapore · Sydney

Published by
Avebury
Gower Publishing Company Limited
Gower House
Croft Road
Aldershot
Hants GU11 3HR
England

Gower Publishing Company
Old Post Road
Brookfield
Vermont 05036
USA

ISBN 0-566-07106-1

Printed in Great Britain by
Billing & Sons Ltd, Worcester

CONTENTS

REPORTS AND DOCUMENTS

ACKNOWLEDGEMENTS

The material in this book was assembled from revised papers delivered at a conference convened by the Centre for Research in Ethnic Relations at the University of Warwick in October 1987.

The conference was innovative in that the principal organiser, Danièle Joly, with the help of Gustavo Jara, sought to include policy-makers, officers in voluntary agencies and academics with an interest in the field in one meeting. She also was determined, whatever the language difficulties, to make the conference as representative of European countries as possible. A good spread of delegates appeared from Scandinavia, southern and northern Europe - and we were disappointed only in the lack of representation from Italy.

Our deliberations were made possible by using funds allocated by the Economic and Social Research Council (UK) to the Centre for Research in Ethnic Relations. As usual, the Centre's administrative and support staff responded loyally to various demands made on them. In particular, we have to thank Charlotte Wellington for taking the principal role in administering the conference. Lynda Hemsley, Gurbaksh Hundal and, above all, Rose Goodwin, word-processed the papers and chapters with their customary efficiency and good humour.

Gustavo Jara translated Ana Vasquez's paper and acted as a simultaneous translator on the day. Selina Cohen copy-edited the material and rendered Euro-language into a more elegant version of the Queen's English. Our anglophone contributors also profited from her eagle eye for grammatical and logical slips. John Wrench, as Series Editor and Sarah Sutton, at Gower Publications, also gave valuable help. To all these colleagues we offer our warm thanks.

We would like to apologise to Dr Jonathan Schwartz of the Institute of Cultural Sociology at the University of Copenhagen, for inadvertently using a similar title to his own book, *Reluctant Hosts: Denmark's Reception of Guest Workers,* published by Akademisk Forlag, Copenhagen, in 1985. Only after the publicity for this book had been sent out, were we able to see his book, which we are happy to commend to our readers. We thank him for his colleagial attitude and understanding.

Danièle Joly and Robin Cohen
University of Warwick

THE CONTRIBUTORS

Jochen Blaschke is a Fellow of the Berlin Institute for Comparative Social Research and also teaches political science at the Free University of Berlin. He writes on various aspects of ethnic group mobilisation and formation as well as on issues of comparative politics. His latest books are: *Volk, Nation, Interner Kolonialismus, Ethnizität: Konzepte zur politischen Soziologie regionalistischer Bewegungen in Westeuropa* (1983) and *Die Türkische Ökonomie in Berlin* (1988).

Jacques Chonchol is Director of the Institut de Hautes Etudes de l'Amerique Latine at the University of Paris III, and was formerly Minister of Agriculture in President Allende's government in Chile. He is interested in problems of third world development, particularly rural development. Among his publications are: *Paysans à venir: les sociétiés rurales du Tiers Monde* (1986) and *Le Défi Alimentaire: le Faim dans le Monde* (1987).

Robin Cohen is Director of the Centre for Research in Ethnic Relations and Professor of Sociology at Warwick. He writes mainly on international migration, labour and third world issues. His latest books are: *Endgame in South Africa?* (1986, 1987, 1988); *Popular Struggles in South Africa* (coedited, 1988) and *The New Helots: Migrants in the International Division of Labour* (issued in this series, 1987, and by Gower as a paperback, 1988).

Maria José Santa Cruz Robles works in the Ministry of Labour & Social Security in Madrid, Spain. She was one of the people responsible for the special programme run by the Spanish Ministry of Labour between 1979 and 1982 to settle South East Asian refugees in Spain.

Andreas Germershausen is a social anthropologist working at the Berlin Institute for Comparative Social Research. He has conducted various studies on the global refugee crisis. His latest publication is *Flucht und Asyl*, Berlin, 1988 (co-edited with Wolf-Dieter Narr).

Tomas Hammar is Director of Stockholm University's Centre for Research in International Migration and Ethnic Relations, and Associate Professor of Political Science. His research interests include political participation, the rights of aliens, naturalisation and citizenship, regulation of international migration and refugee and immigrant policy. He is the editor of *European Immigration Policy*, Cambridge, 1985.

Danièle Joly is Research Fellow at the Centre for Research in Ethnic Relations, University of Warwick. She obtained her higher degrees from the Sorbonne and Aston. She is co-editor of a Gower book titled *Immigrant Associations in Europe* (1987) and is currently writing on Islam in Birmingham, while completing various projects on refugees.

Maria Cruz Jordana worked for many years as a social worker in a number of National Health hospitals in Spain. She holds a university degree in history and is presently in charge of the Spanish government's refugee resettlement programme at CESSAR.

Diana Kay is Research Fellow in the Research Unit on Racism and Migration, Department of Sociology, University of Glasgow. Her recent research includes a study of the experiences of Chilean men and women in exile in Scotland, published as *Chileans in Exile* (1987). She is currently researching post-war British government policy towards the recruitment of 'displaced persons' for British industries.

Eszter Körmendi is a well-known Danish research psychologist. She has been Director of several research programmes on minority questions funded by the Danish National Institute of Social Research. Her interests include a concern with the conditions facing ethnic minorities and the study of attitudes towards minorities on the part of the majority population. She has published widely in Danish, a recent edited volume being *Flygtninge og indvandrerpolitiek i Norden* (1987).

Anders Lange is Research Associate at the Centre for Research in International Migration and Ethnic Relations and Reader in Educational Psychology at the University of Stockholm. His research deals mainly with ethnic and social identity, social psychological aspects of ethnic relations and theoretical aspects of international migration and cross-cultural research. He has published a number of reports in these fields, which are available from the Stockholm Centre.

Ragnar Naess is a researcher at the Work Research Institute in Oslo. He writes mainly on international migration, the situation of labour migrants in their working life and on refugee issues. His latest papers are titled 'Being an Alevi Muslim in Norway and Central Anatolia' (1988) and 'Newcomers: Migrants, Refugees and Asylum-seekers and the Consequences for Norwegian Internationalism' (1987).

Erik Pedersen is Chief Surgeon at the Fakse County Hospital near Copenhagen. He was a member of the Amnesty International Medical Advisory Board and a member of the board of the Rehabilitation Centre for Torture Victims in Copenhagen. He has served on medical missions to Zaire, Vietnam and South Korea.

Alan Phillips was Deputy Director of the British Refugee Council where he worked primarily on Information and Policy towards refugees in the UK and internationally. He has recently assumed a position as General Secretary of the Minority Rights Group. His publications include *British Aid for Overseas Students* (1980) and *Training and Employment Provision for Refugees in Europe*.

Philip Rudge is General Secretary of the European Consultation on Refugees and Exiles whose secretariat is based in London. He worked from 1977–83 as Reorientation Adviser to the World University Service (UK), specialising in training Latin American academics in exile in Britain. From 1972–6, he worked as a British Council/ODA Technical Assistance Officer on an educational development programme in Laos, South East Asia.

Lorenzo Sanchez Pardo is a social worker. He has worked in various areas in the Spanish social services and has lectured at the official school for social workers in Madrid. Over the past three years he has been more specifically concerned with refugee problems, first with them Red Cross and now with CESSAR.

Robert Sayers is Head of the Refugees Section of the Ministry of Welfare, Health and Cultural Affairs in the Government of the Netherlands. he formerly was concerned with welfare policies for ethnic minorities in the same ministry.

Robin Schneider is a social anthropologist. He lived in Central America from 1980 to 1983 and conducted fieldwork among Lowland Indians. From 1984–86 he was Head of the section concerned with Middle Eastern Refugees for a West German-based human rights organisation. At present he is lecturer in sociology at the University of Hannover. His latest books are: *Rama: Lowland Indians of the Nicaraguan Atlantic Cost* (1987) and *Zum Beispeil Flüchtlinge*.

Ana Maria Silva has recently been appointed as Head of the Social Security service in a subdivision of Greater Lisbon. For the previous ten years she worked with refugees and asylum-seekers in a special government section. She also has wide academic interests, having contributed papers on *Cultural Change in Guinea-Bissau* and *The Resettlement and Professional Training of the Former Portuguese African Settlers*.

Walter Stöckli is Head of the Legal Service of the Swiss Central Office for Aid to Refugees (SFH) and also works for the United Nations High Commission for Refugees (UNHCR) as a consultant for Swiss refugee and asylum matters. He is the Chief Editor of ASYL, a magazine for lawyers and practitioners specialising in the asylum field.

Anna Vasquez is a researcher at the Centre National de Recherche Scientifique (CNRS) in France. She works in the Social Psychology Laboratory from where she has studied the exiled Latin Amercian community and the proceses of transculturation undergone during long-term exile. Her latest publications are: 'Les avatars de "l'identité culturelle" étudiée chez des exilés politiques', *L'Homme et la Société* (1987) and *Exils Latino-américains: la malédiction d'Ulysse* (edited with A M Uraujo, 1988).

LIST OF ACRONYMS

ADWG	Anti-Deportation Working Group (UK)
AMA	Association of Metropolitan Authorities (UK)
BCAR	British Council for Aid to Refugees (UK)
BRC	British Refugee Council (UK)
CAHAR	Committee of experts on the legal aspects of territorial asylum, refugees and stateless persons
CARITAS	Catholic Relief Organisation (Portugal, Spain, Switzerland)
CDU	Christian Democratic Union (West Germany)
CEAR	Spanish Commission for Refugee Aid (Spain)
CEIFO	Centre for Research in International Migration & Ethnic Relations (Sweden)
CESSAR	State Refugee Social Service Centre (Spain)
CIDE	Centro de Investigación y Desarrollo de la Educación (Chile)
CRSS	Centro Regional de Segurança Social de Lisboa (Portugal)
CSU	Christian Social Union (West Germany)
DAR	Délégué aux Réfugiés (Switzerland)
DHSS	Department of Health & Social Security (UK)
DRC	Danish Refugee Council
DSAR	Direcçao dos Serviços de Apoio e Reinstalaçao / Divisao de Apoio a Refugiados (Portugal)
ECRE	European Consultation on Refugees & Exiles (UK)
EEC	European Economic Community
FASIC	Fundación de Ayuda Social de las Iglesias Cristianas
FDP	Free Democratic Party (West Germany)
EPCP	European Programme to Combat Poverty
FILOR	Fond pour l'installation locale de Refugiés (France)
IAD	Immigration Act Detainee (UK)
IATA	International Air Transport Association
ICAO	International Civil Aviation Organisation
IRCT	International Rehabilitation Centre for Torture Victims
ISAR	International Social Service (Switzerland)
JCRV	Joint Committee for Refugees from Vietnam (UK)
JCWI	Joint Council for the Welfare of Immigrants (UK)
KSSE	Kurdish Students Society of Europe (West Germany)
MCVA	Midlands Vietnamese Community Association (UK)
MP	Member of Parliament (UK)
MSC	Manpower Services Commission (UK)
NAVF	Norwegian Research Fund for the Humanities (Norway)
NGO	Non-Governmental Organisation
OSAR	Central Office for Aid to Refugees (Switzerland)
PRT	Prison Reform Trust (UK)

RCT	Rehabilitation Centre for Torture Victims (Denmark)
RFCE	Resettlement Fund of the Council of Europe
RLE	Refused Leave to Enter (UK)
SCF	Save the Children Fund (UK)
SEA	Secondary Examination Area (UK)
SFH	Swiss Central Office for Aid to Refugees
UK	United Kingdom
UKIAS	United Kingdom Immigration Advisory Service
UN	United Nations
UNHCR	United Nations High Commission for Refugees
WUS	World University Service
WUWM	Section for Refugee Welfare & Housing of Minorities (Netherlands)
YMCA	Young Men's Christian Association
ZDWF	Zentrale Dokumentationsstelle der Freien Wohlfahrtspflege für Flüchtlinge (West Germany)

PREFACE

Jacques Chonchol

It is an honour to have been asked to write the Preface to this book on research into how various European governments and non-governmental organisations approach their refugee problems. As both a refugee and an academic myself, I have a personal as well as a professional interest in research into the various policies different governments adopt in resettling their refugees.

The research contained here covers a wide range of situations and basically focuses on the refugees' cultural and social integration into the host society, their problems associated with finding employment and the kinds of difficulties they face if or when they eventually return to their home countries. These various problems are, in effect, the instruments of our research.

The actual nature of the refugee problem has, however, changed quite substantially since the Second World War. During and immediately after this period most of the refugees were themselves Europeans displaced by the war itself or by its political aftermath, when the international frontiers of many countries were changed and the cold war set in. The civil war in Spain also generated large numbers of European refugees. Since the 1960s, however, the pattern in Europe has changed and the majority of the refugees now come from the countries of the third world, especially from Asia, Latin America and Africa.

At present there are an estimated 600,000 refugees in Europe, with significant concentrations in the UK, France and Germany. Given that there are approximately 10 million refugees in the world as a whole, the proportion in Europe is very small and should be easy to integrate. The difficulty, however, arises less from the size of the refugee population as from the fact that its arrival happened to coincide with economic crises in many European countries.

It is necessary to realise, however, that it is not only the refugees living in Europe who are affected by Europe's economic problems, but also those in other parts of the world with which European countries have relations. For example, international bodies like the European Community (EEC) can influence refugees in places as far afield as Central America.

Although I believe that this is a useful area for research, I think that it is vitally important to examine problems, not only in terms of their present implications, but also with regard to the future. If we project from now to the year 2000 – which is not very far off – and think in terms of the growth of the population and the prolongation of the international economic crisis, we begin to suspect that future years will bring a considerable increase in the numbers of refugees. The United Nations' demographic projection from

1980 to the year 2000 forecasts an increase in the world's population from 3,400 million to 5,000 million. In other words, within a period of only 20 years, the existing population is expected to increase by a further 1,600 million people.

Within the context of international tension between the super-powers, numerous local political conflicts and the continuation of a worldwide economic crisis, the refugee problem is hardly likely to subside. It has now become a crucial factor in decisions about how to face the world's problems.

As I see it, there are three kinds of refugees. First, there are of course the political refugees, or political exiles, who are forced to flee because they are being persecuted by those who control the governments in their countries. Included in this category are those refugees who have been displaced by various kinds of political conflict - whether open war between countries or civil war within a country. Guerrilla warfare and counter-insurgency create yet another kind of political refugee, often seen in Africa and Central America, in which people without any direct association with the conflict are displaced from their usual places of residence. The peasants in El Salvador and in other Central American countries are such examples.

Second, are what I would call the politico-economic refugees, in other words, the victims of economic crises aggravated by political circumstances. The initial cause of the problem could be a general economic crisis, a specific politico-economic crisis, or even a drought. Whatever it is, the victims tend to be displaced minorities who are often forced by the juxtaposition of economic and political factors to move from their original place of residence in order to survive.

And finally, there are the refugees created as a direct result of an economic crisis. These economic refugees are frequently created by the very policies the governments implement to tackle the crisis - policies that are more often than not exported from abroad. What immediately springs to mind in this context are some of the policies the International Monetary Fund has recommended to third world governments in an attempt to correct foreign trade imbalances or to check inflation, but which have in fact made the internal situation much worse and consequently created even more refugees.

One thus faces three main problem areas, each of which may well compound the kinds of difficulties the world is likely to face 30 years from now.

For the first group - the political exiles - I think the solution lies in Europe's tradition of democracy and of granting asylum, especially given the relatively low numbers involved. Since the war various laws have been introduced to make this easier. For example, international treaties such as the Geneva Convention allow us, at least within Europe, to treat political refugees fairly well. The one obstacle to this solution, however, lies in the development of terrorism, which has provided governments with an excuse to close their borders. Another problem and one which has continued for a good many years is that of the refugee camps. The situation in the Palestinian camps, for example, dates back to the formation of Israel, but the international community is still no closer to resolving it. The Vietnamese camps are another painful reminder of political strife, as are the large numbers of Haitians who fled from the Duvalier regime to seek refuge in camps in the United States. One is left with the distinct impression that the problem is not being dealt with effectively and could become even worse, especially if one bears in mind the situation in Somalia. Europe and the international community have a responsibility to try and solve it.

The politico-economic refugees, however, raise even more serious problems, for as this population increases so too do the problems of immigration and the enormous pressures of trying to find employment. In this matter I think it is important to reflect on the responsibilities of governments of European and other developed countries, especially the United States and the Soviet Union. After all, these governments are responsible for having developed the kinds of international policies that tend to increase the numbers of refugees in the third world; there is no doubt that many of these refugees stem directly from super-power attempts to influence certain parts of the world. Whatever people might say about it, the situation in Lebanon and the Middle East is undoubtedly sustained by a conflict between the super-powers. Arms sales and the development of the arms race also of course increase tension and conflict in the third world.

And finally, the fact that the situation as a whole is further aggravated by the practice of export subsidies, protectionism and the like, demonstrates that European countries and the rest of the developed world (especially the United States) are directly or indirectly responsible for heightening these problems and for the existence of economic refugees.

These highly complex problems, which include political, economic, social and psychological aspects, all need to be more systematically and widely researched within the framework of a multi-disciplinary approach. In my opinion, there should be at least three broad lines to this research.

The first should look at the real causes of the refugee problem in different parts of the world. There are different situations and not everything can be explained in the same way. Therefore, although the research must be of a general nature, it must also be linked to specific circumstances.

The second needs to look at ways of reducing the kinds of pressures brought by the newly displaced people. Whether one likes it or not, the arrival of people in another country or area creates problems, particularly if the countries of origin have very different cultures and historical backgrounds. For example, the initial arrival of Italian and Polish workers in France created a considerable amount of conflict within the country, but today, a generation or two later, they have become part of France and are as French as anybody else. It is necessary to accept that, although in the long term refugees are usually beneficial to the host country, when newcomers first arrive they do create imbalances and problems which are often met by a resurgence of racism and widespread rejection of foreigners.

And the third should try to establish how to bring about the quick and effective integration of people who decide to stay in a particular country. This is a particularly important field of research, not only because of the valuable contribution it can make to our social knowledge, but also because it enables us to exert some influence over public opinion and to help formulate policies to find solutions to these kinds of problems. This book will have fulfilled its purpose if it goes some way towards illuminating these three problem areas.

1 INTRODUCTION: THE 'NEW REFUGEES' OF EUROPE

Robin Cohen & Danièle Joly

Although the movement of refugees is an age-old phenomenon occurring, for example, through the clash of ancient rival war parties or the movement of nomadic peoples, it is only in the twentieth century that the issue has been politicised and internationalised - by media attention, inter-state rivalries and the adoption of legal instruments and protocols (Bettati 1987).

Europe has been at the centre of these developments, both as a refugee-producing and as a refugee-receiving region. While many European politicians now represent their countries as stable entities being assaulted by an unstable outside world, for most of the last 100 years the boot was on the other foot. Not only did the New World receive vast numbers of European immigrants, fleeing from poverty and social oppression, but Europe itself became a swirling vortex of unsettled peoples. White Russian émigrés fled the 1917 Revolution, Jews and political dissenters the rise of the Nazis, Republican supporters the triumph of Franco. The Second World War itself created many major population shifts, while the accession of the Communists to state power in Eastern Europe accelerated the drift to the rapidly expanding industrialised economies of the West of Europe.

The first international law applying to refugees and asylum-seekers was drafted by Europeans for other Europeans. For example, the 'Nansen passport' was granted to the Russian émigrés, while the 1951 Geneva Convention originally applied only to post-1945 displaced Europeans. What proved more universal was the Convention's definition of a refugee - 'persons who are outside their country because of a well-founded fear of persecution for reasons of race, religion, nationality, membership of a particular social group or political opinion'.

This definition was retained in the Bellagio Protocol (1967), signed by nearly 100 countries. The Protocol removed the geographical and temporal limitations of the 1951 Convention, thus extending it to all refugees. This modification was a reflection of changes in the world situation whereby refugees were being engendered everywhere, not least in the third world. The underlying causes of this phenomenon include the decolonisation process, the struggle for spheres of influence between big powers, the involvement of imperialist countries with local class contradictions and the conflict of interests in the third world. Military coups succeeded one another in Latin America, while inter-communal violence, civil wars and revolutions shook Africa and much of Asia during the last forty years.

The 'New Refugees'

Although the majority of third world refugees were 'regionalised', in that they usually settled in countries neighbouring their homelands, noticeable numbers have reached the shores of Europe. As a report for the Independent Commission on International Humanitarian Issues (ICIHI 1986: 33) puts it:

> In the 1970s a new phenomenon emerged. Refugees from the crisis areas of Africa, Asia and Latin America began to move in increasing numbers to the industrialised countries ... the arrival of many refugees from geographically and culturally distant areas constituted an unprecedented challenge to the legal machinery and conscience of the receiving countries. The refugee problem, previously regarded as a factor in east-west relations, now has a north-south dimension added to it.

The volume and effects of the refugee crisis have been amplified because, in response to nationalist and protectionist pressures in the industrialised countries, they coincided with a reduction in aid and social investment programmes to the third world. These pressures became most insistent precisely at the moment when many poor countries had their economic and environmental resources stretched to the limit. Increased energy costs, more expensive imports, political instability and lower commodity prices all placed a number of third world countries in a position where they were unable to respond effectively to the devastations wrought by famine, war and drought.

Mass exoduses from the wastelands resulted, with the European countries receiving a mere fraction of the total involved. The special character of post-1970 refugees has led to the expression 'new refugees', who are distinct from traditional refugees in that, as one author suggests, they are 'culturally and ethnically different from their hosts; they come from less-developed countries, at a different stage of development from that of the host, and they are likely to lack kin and potential support groups in their country of resettlement' (Stein 1981: 330). Another important datum is that the new refugees happened to come at a time when Europe was in the process of restricting the entrance of third world immigrants brought over during the economic boom of the 1950s and early 1960s.[1]

Refugees are subject to a different regime from that of immigrants both in respect of admission and settlement. Little theoretical work has been developed to understand the differences and similarities of refugees and immigrants. We shall outline a few essential aspects which particularly affect settlement. Kunz's 'kinetic' model attempts to analyse refugees and immigrants within the framework of a traditional pull-push paradigm. This mode of explanation is limited by the general critique that may be directed at explanations rooted in subjective and personal opinions of collective phenomena.[2] As a starting point, however, we can cite Kunz's opinion that, whether they be 'anticipatory' or 'emergency' refugees, the main factor that determines their flight is the 'push–pressure' aspect, thus distinguishing them from most migrants who are 'pulled'. As Kunz (1973: 130) explains:

> With a different past and with motivations at variance with those affecting voluntary migrants, the refugee moves from his homeland to the country of his settlement against his will. He is a distinct social type ... It is the reluctance to uproot oneself, and the absence of positive original motivations to settle elsewhere, which characterises all refugee decisions and distinguishes the refugee from the voluntary migrants.

The unwillingness of refugees to leave crucially effects their settlement in the receiving country. Most refugees will tend to look backwards and do not have a project for the future in their new abode (Guillon 1988); in practice this may lead to resisting settlement and finding adaptation more difficult (Vernant 1953).

These problems are compounded by the often traumatic circumstances of their migration which may cause psychological resistance to the adopting of new cultural and behavioural norms (Reid and Strong 1987) – depicted in this book in Vasquez's account of Chilean exiles in France. Such a situation is aggravated by the shock of functioning in Europe's markedly different society and culture. In this respect they are not unlike third world immigrants, but the cultural discrepancy will tend to be greater for refugees as they often cannot choose their destination and therefore have less chance of settling in a country with historical and cultural links with their homeland.

The question of returning home is also perceived differently by immigrants and refugees. Immigrants cherish the myth of return but in the final analysis the decision to go home remains within their control, however difficult it may prove. For refugees, the possibility of returning home is less feasible, in that they are barred from it by the turn of events in their homeland, but also more certain in that they perceive the situation back home as temporary. This has been evidenced by the mass returns of refugees to countries like Greece and Argentina after the fall of the dictatorship. These characteristics have led some to argue that refugees more than other migrants need to keep links with their homeland (Nettleton 1984) and must have the right 'not to assimilate' and 'to be politically active' on issues concerning their country of origin.

Immigrants and Refugees in Europe

Despite these differences, refugees share with immigrants the fate of being 'moved to the very bottom of the socio–economic scale' (Cuny 1979: 339). The two groups suffer from similar disadvantages in housing, general standards of living, educational opportunities and language learning. Both immigrants and refugees are also the target of racism, discrimination and hostility on the part of the receiving society, as most of them are different in appearance from European population groups and generally come from distant third world cultures.

Nowadays the issue of refugees has become very topical in Europe, not only because their numbers have increased but also because media and governments have brought them to the fore. The latter are expressing their concern and quote statistics on asylum–seekers to account for the restrictive measures they have taken, individually and collectively. In October 1986, a meeting of the 12 Ministers of the Interior created an *ad hoc* group to examine 'the measures to be taken to reach a common policy in order to stop the abusive use of the right to asylum' (Commission Européenne 1988). In the meantime, the Commission is preparing a directive on refugees while members of the European Parliament have produced reports and resolutions on this question. These are a few of the actions designed to prepare for the 1992 abolition of national borders within the EEC.

However, the semi–hysteria displayed by governments and media seems disproportionate to the actual numbers of refugees in Western Europe. These constitute only 0.17 per cent (720,000) of the European population,[3] and a small share of the refugee population settled in the third world, including 12 million in Africa, Asia and Latin America (*Le Monde*, 28 June 1988). The UNHCR and the Council of Europe have produced extensive documents and numerous resolutions to counter the initiatives of European governments.

In practice, the percentage of successful applications for asylum ('good–quality applications' say government officials) keeps decreasing and a narrowing down of the notion of refugee occurs. As a newspaper report put it, 'the spirit of the Geneva Convention is not respected any more' (*Le Monde*, 19 April 1988). In the wake of these developments, new 'categories' of refugees arise, such as the 'refugees in orbit' pushed on from country to country and *de facto* refugees (Costa Lascoux 1988; Council of Europe, 1975). The latter are often allowed to stay in Europe on humanitarian grounds under a variety of statuses, such as the 'B status' in Nordic countries or 'exceptional leave to remain' in Britain. They enjoy a less favourable status than Convention refugees and are not entitled to the same social benefits and assistance towards settlement.

Procedures for the admission of refugees vary greatly throughout Europe, as does the rate of successful applications (Vetter 1986: 31).[4] Funding devoted to them follows the same motley pattern.[5] But the most outstanding discrepancies are those affecting the structures set up to manage refugee reception and settlement. European countries do not seem to have learned as yet from one another's experience of resettling refugees. Moreover, most European states have also proved incapable of developing settlement policies that draw lessons from past experience with earlier waves of refugees. *Ad hoc* and precipitate measures are taken to respond to each intake of refugees because the refugee phenomenon is consistently treated as a transient one, as Vetter's report (1987: 13–14) to the European Parliament confirms:

> In all the countries visited by the rapporteur the influx of asylum-seekers is seen as a short-term phenomenon. There is no forward-looking consideration of how the refugee problem in Europe and elsewhere can be solved in a properly humane manner. Nor have there been any attempts within the framework of the European Community to take positive action to deal with the refugee problem. Even after the entry of larger groups of refugees at the end of the seventies, no preventative measures were taken to provide arrangements for their reception and integration.

By bringing together experiences and research across Europe, the editors hope that this book can make a contribution to a better understanding of the patterns of refugee admissions, reception and settlement.

The Role of the State and Local Government

One of the major themes pursued by our contributors is the role of the state in the admission of refugees and its role, together with local authorities, in their settlement. The pictures presented in our articles and documents are mostly drawn by government officials and social workers and, for this reason, provide unusually clear 'insider' accounts of the workings of the system. For example, Sayers (Chapter 2), as head of the refugees section in the relevant ministry in the Netherlands, is able to provide an authoritative account of how refugees and asylum-seekers are selected and recognised. This is followed by a description of the 'in-house model', which the Dutch authorities developed to deal with issues such as reorientation, training, housing, the involvement of the local municipalities, and the health and welfare needs of the new arrivals.

Our Iberian contributors depict a similar governmental concern, though with one major difference. Unlike the Netherlands, where the main voluntary agency (the Dutch Refugee Association) pulled out of a cooperative arrangement with the ministry, in both Portugal and Spain the respective ministries run their reception and settlement programmes in close association with religious and secular voluntary agencies and with the United Nations High Commission for Refugees (UNHCR). In the case of Portugal, as Silva shows (Report & Document I), the government had experienced a recent and massive refugee wave in the form of 600,000 returnees from the former Portuguese colonies in Africa, thus permitting 'a valuable body of experience and professional know-how' to be accumulated.

Spain, however, had more historical experience in creating refugees (particularly in the civil war period) than in receiving them, at least until unsettled conditions in Latin America generated a considerable volume of Spanish-speaking refugees and asylum-seekers. As Jordana and Pardo recount (Report & Document II), the existence of a shared language and, perhaps in a more remote sense a common cultural tradition, led to a relatively easy process of integration by the Latin Americans, though difficulties were reported in respect of competition with the local population over housing and employment.

The Spanish authorities had greater difficulty wrestling with the much smaller numbers admitted from South East Asia late in 1979. This contingent, mainly of Laotians and Vietnamese, were pre-selected from the camps in Hong Kong, the Philippines and Thailand, but, as Santa Cruz demonstrates (Chapter 4), the careful planning of the authorities broke down in subtle ways. Some selected refugees pulled out when they received offers from other countries where their relatives had settled; women were resistant to learning Spanish; men turned down the first jobs on offer. Moreover, the policy of dispersal relied too much on the goodwill of local authorities and violated the tendency of the South East Asians to cluster together for mutual support. More positively, Santa Cruz found no evidence of hostility to the newcomers from the Spanish trade union movement over the issue of job competition. On the contrary, 'trade unions, political parties and private people showed solidarity and understanding in every case.'

The policy of dispersing refugees (or immigrants for that matter) to a number of cities and local authorities raises both ethical and practical problems. Those who argue in favour of this policy point to the avoidance of ghettos, the reduced likelihood of triggering a backlash from the local population and the spreading of the impact and cost of the new arrivals in respect of housing, employment and welfare support. On the other hand, there is an intrinsic violation of the principle of freedom of movement in instructing people where they have to live, a violation made all the more poignant by the fact that refugees may be the victims of state directives of a similar kind. As Hammar and Lange illustrate (Report & Document IV), the issue is also a practical one for the Swedish authorities. Though the Swedish researchers have yet to report the results of their investigation, the answer to the politicians' policy dilemmas seems to lie in gauging the point where a sufficient critical mass of refugees can be assembled to permit cultural solidarity and the provision of specialist services (language support, education and welfare), but not so large a mass as to inhibit the processes of integration or trigger a revanchist lurch into xenophobia or racism by the local population.

It is undoubtedly this fear that lies at the heart of the relatively modest programmes for refugee admission adopted by all European governments. As our contributors show, the numbers involved in quota, emergency or special admissions programmes are quite limited. Moreover, despite the alarmist noises made from time to time by sections of the press and right-wing politicians, the numbers of asylum-seekers trying to find recognition in European countries is also, with the exception of West Germany, quite low – in absolute terms and certainly in relation to the enormous numbers of refugees in third world countries (*see* Table 1.1).

Table 1.1 Asylum-seekers in Europe, 1984-6

	1984	*1985*	*1986*	*Total*	*No.per million*
Sweden	11,300	15,000	15,000	41,300	4,975
Denmark	4,300	8,700	9,300	22,300	4,370
Switzerland	7,400	9,700	8,500	25,600	4,000
W Germany	34,400	73,900	99,700	208,000	3,350
Austria	7,400	6,700	8,700	22,800	2,965
Belgium	4,000	6,300	7,500	17,800	1,780
France	16,100	28,900	26,300	71,300	1,310
Holland	2,600	5,700	5,900	14,200	990
Norway	400	800	2,700	3,900	945
Britain	3,900	5,500	3,900	13,300	240

Source: British Refugee Council, 1987

If a small and poor European country such as Portugal can absorb 600,000 returnees from Africa in a short space of time and without noticeable trauma, the only conclusion we can draw from the much smaller figures of asylum-seekers involved in other, richer countries, is that the cultural and ethnic backgrounds of the refugees have acted as a major disincentive to the recognition of their plight. European governments *have* held out a hand of friendship and *have* voted funds for admission and resettlement schemes. But the hands have been held half-stretched and the purse strings have only been fractionally opened. In short, European governments are reluctant hosts, barely fulfilling their international obligations and barely recognising the humanitarian values that purportedly underlie their own democratic constitutions.

Relations between the State and Voluntary Agencies

In addition to their caution on the issue of admission, European governments have also displayed their reluctant welcome to refugees by seeking to 'download' the issue of resettlement to voluntary agencies. In the Netherlands, as we have seen, this proved impossible and the ministry was forced to set up settlement programmes itself.

In other European countries, the churches, human rights organisations, solidarity groups and groups hitherto concerned with immigrant questions have become centrally involved in refugee issues. Occasionally more specialised services are offered - as in the case of the Copenhagen Rehabilitation Centre for Torture Victims (Report & Document VI), a medical facility half-funded by the Danish state and the Nordic Council, with the other half coming from private sources. Originally established to treat tortured prisoners of conscience, the Centre now finds similar symptoms occurring amongst refugees.

The linking of private and public sector funds is often undertaken, as in Britain, by some kind of umbrella organisation (in this case the British Refugee Council) which co-ordinates joint approaches to governments, local authorities and international agencies. In the case of Denmark, described by Körmendi (Chapter 3), the Danish Refugee Council (DRC), an umbrella organisation for 12 humanitarian relief organisations, has the main responsibility for the 18 months immediately after admission and before the local authorities are meant to absorb the refugees into their normal administrative and welfare systems. However, the 'fit' between the systems administered by the local authorities and the DRC was poor and the level of cooperation 'tokenistic, resulting in a 'certain antagonism within and between the systems'.

The Vietnamese refugees who settled in Birmingham also found their fates subject to countervailing systemic demands, with the additional complication that, under the rubric of 'community support', the English tradition of enthusiastic amateurism was given full rein. As Joly (Chapter 6) reveals, the functional tasks of admission, resettlement, training and employment creation were overlaid by geographical fiefdoms carved out by the different voluntary agencies. The Midlands was designated the territory of the 'the Ockenden Venture', a body that became more professionalised and reasonably effective – but at the cost of losing the support of the principal body of the Vietnamese themselves, the Midlands Vietnamese Community Association (MVCA). Though self-organisation may be regarded as a positive sign of cultural adaptation, the difficulty that many government and local authority bodies had in dealing exclusively with the MVCA was that, despite being the *most* representative organisation, the MVCA was none the less biassed in favour of South Vietnamese, older Vietnamese and those who wanted to return to the old capitalist order of South Vietnam.

Both Körmendi and Joly point to the minefield of overlapping authority and legitimacy between and within governments, local authorities, refugee organisations and voluntary agencies. But even if there is a fair degree of muddle, the predominant intentions are benign. Stöckli, on the other hand (Report & Document III), describes a situation that arose in Switzerland when conflict between voluntary agencies and government reached a more critical point. Under such circumstances, 'the conflict is less about how much the government spends on helping refugees as it is about the effect this has on Switzerland's internal political climate'. The Swiss example illustrates what possible political consequences can arise from the conflation of the period when labour immigration ended and the asylum-seekers, mainly of third world origins, began to arrive. For the Swiss citizens, 'overforeignisation' is the common fear, irrespective of how the foreigners are legally defined or differently motivated. As Stöckli implies, for a Swiss politician to set his face against successive plebiscites on this question is to invite political oblivion.

The Politics of Refugee Exclusion and Detention

The political sensitivities of any programme designed to admit or to resettle refugees is a theme addressed in three further contributions.

Naess (Chapter 5), writing on Norway, finds areas of conflict between government and voluntary agencies similar to those in the Netherlands, Switzerland and the UK. The conflict in Norway reached such a pitch, however, that the Norwegian Red Cross threatened to close its refugee reception facility altogether rather than continue to be used as a means of enabling the government to avoid its public responsibilities. Unlike other European countries, the Norwegian government cannot even plausibly plead poverty – with substantial oil revenues, Norway is one of the most prosperous countries in the world with one of the lowest rates of unemployment. Instead, government and conservative commentators and politicians have promoted a discussion about the 'cultural' homogeneity of Norway and the limits to how many third world refugees could be accommodated in such a society. As in other European countries, Norwegian government questions the authenticity of asylum-seekers' claims and have sought to label them as not being 'real' refugees. As Naess shows, the debate in Norway is particularly oblique as the liberal and social democratic traditions of the country make it necessary, even for the most right-wing politicians, to distance themselves from Nazism, apartheid and the lack of civil liberties in the pre-1964 US south. Culture rather than biology is thus deployed to discriminate and exclude.

The West Germans have an even heavier heritage of the past to escape, as Schneider reminds us (Chapter 12). The deportation of Kurds and Palestinians back to civil-war situations and the Minister of the Interior's warnings that the constitutional provisions for the asylum of politically persecuted persons have to be annulled, cannot but evoke memories of the Nazi past. As in the war period, 'the alien' and the fugitive have become a source of fear and an object for intimidation rather than sympathy and concern. The more liberal traditions of the state whose very foundations Mühlmann (1962) sees as rooted in the right to sanctuary, have been overwhelmed by orchestrated images of the 'hordes' who are supposedly 'flooding', 'swamping' and 'pushing back the Germans'.

Even where, as in the UK, there is a positive history of accepting refugees (the Huguenots and those escaping Nazi Germany made notable contributions to Britain's economic and cultural welfare), the authorities have responded in a similar manner to their German counterparts in respect of third world asylum-seekers. Indeed, the number of asylum-seekers applying for recognition in Britain is *much smaller* in Britain relative to the population than in any other European country (*see* Table 1.1). Moreover, as Cohen (Chapter 11) shows, reaching British shores with a good case for being considered a 'Convention' (i.e. recognised) refugee, does not mean that this case will be accepted by the British authorities. On the contrary, deportation, return to a 'third country' (which an asylum-seeker had passed through), or detention, are the common outcomes. Home Office officials are adamant that a tough policy provides a deterrent effect to those who are deemed to intend to violate Britain's immigration laws. The reasons for (and effects of) this policy on 'Immigration Act Detainees' and asylum-seekers are the subject of Cohen's study.

Who are the Refugees?

Aside from the analysis of the state, its governing ideologies and policies, and its relations with voluntary bodies, of great interest to a number of our contributors is a detailed sociological or social psychological analysis of the refugees themselves. It has already been suggested that part of the state's and host population's reactions to the influx of third world refugees was the attempt to assuage the right-wing and populist sentiments that became agitated during the period of labour immigration – roughly from 1945–75 (*see* Cohen 1987).

Such popular reactions are particularly manifested against refugees who are phenotypically different from the indigenous population, such as the Kurds and Yezidis in West Germany described by Blaschke (Chapter 7). Both groups are strongly driven by a sense of nationalism-in-exile, a powerful bond which helps both in group cohesion and self-organisation. Kurds also form uncomfortable links with the wider Turkish migrant community, with whom they are identified by the general populace and with whom they may also share the common religion of Islam. However, the Turkish right-wing and many of the Turkish community in Germany are fiercely opposed to Kurdish 'separatism', so, like the Yezidis who suffer political persecution in Turkey, the Kurdish community often finds itself without much support from the German state, churches or the larger Turkish community.

Although dealing with refugees and exiles who are generally closer in appearance to their European hosts, both Vazquez (Chapter 9), on Chileans in France, and Kay (Chapter 8), on Chileans in Scotland, find high levels of alienation. Some of the difficulties arise from the differences in the social institutions of the new country or in the perceptions, or rather misperceptions, of how they are supposed to work. But neither contributor loads all the problems onto the faults of the host society. On the contrary, Vasquez, a distinguished exile herself, sees an inner turmoil whereby adaptation, or what she calls 'transculturation', can itself be perceived as a betrayal of the country the exiles have left. To adapt too fully is to reject one's past and in rejecting one's past one is also denying the possibilities of progressive change in, and a return to, Chile.

Kay draws attention to differentiating the exile experience by gender (as well as by class). The subordinate occupational and domestic positions of her sample of interviewees *in Chile* 'were carried into exile largely unexamined'. Males, particularly more class-privileged males, initially lost their social power, but professional women – cushioned by domestic servants in Chile – also found it a continual strain to try to combine a public and private life. In the new environment a 'power struggle' occurred to renegotiate the terms of the gender order. Though subtle shifts in the gender order took place, particularly in the home, Kay concludes by suggesting that the superordinate public and political role of the men was reasserted largely because women were not prepared to press their case to the point of a coherent and public oppositional stance.

European Initiatives and Perspectives

The contributions to this book stand as the first major attempt to study the 'new refugees' of Europe and the policies constructed to deal with their admission, reception, settlement and exclusion. As such, the chapters and documents provide valuable comparative information. But what was striking to us as the organisers of the conference, and may well strike the readers of this book, is the extraordinary simultaneity and similarity of the responses at the level of the policies of European governments. Formally, they differ in political traditions and the political hue of their current governments (from socialist to 'Thatcherite'). They find it difficult to decide whether to belong to a common political or economic association – and bicker endlessly about lamb imports, agricultural subsidies, monetary policy and the potential shape of a possible political union.

Yet apparently a uniform policy on third world asylum-seekers has quietly emerged or been shaped outside the clamour of the public forums. It *has been shaped* in the bodies portrayed in Rudge's contribution (Report & Document VII), some of which, like the Trevi and Schengen Groups, are barely known to the general European public. It *has emerged* because of the broad similarity of political conditions facing European governments – the growth of a populist right-wing inside each country and the emergence of a global crisis in the generation of a third world refugee population.

To combat current trends in the management of the refugee crisis, or even to propose some coherent alternative proposals, needs a new research agenda and a set of proposals that will both evoke the best traditions of the European states and protect the rights of the newcomers. At least in the case of West Germany, Germershausen (Report & Document V) surveys the old research agenda and proposes a new one. Many of his observations, however, have a wider European import.

Phillips's proposals in Chapter 10 are explicitly European in scope. Drawing on the deliberations of the European Programme to Combat Poverty, Phillips argues for the centrality of employment as the best means to aid the resettlement of refugees. He is of course conscious that this looks like waving a red rag at the populist bull – what greater incitement could there be to reactionary sentiments than a supposed job threat. None the less, his arguments may carry a great deal of weight even with unsympathetic officials – not all European countries have a high unemployment rate and in a number of countries the rate is falling; labour segmentation will insulate the indigenous population from the effects of refugee employment; employment for some is in any case not a zero-sum game for others; finally the cost of welfare programmes will be greatly reduced by early employment. These are the arguments for his case on *realpolitik* grounds; there is also a strong case for arguing that generating employment (or the means of self-employment) may be an effective way of welcoming refugees at the personal and cultural level.

Our final document, drawn up by the European Consultation on Refugees & Exiles (Report & Document VIII), is a considered but trenchant set of proposals by the most representative groups of voluntary agencies. It suggests numerous ways in which European governments and agencies might respond more creatively to the increased number of asylum applications in recent years without violating either the fundamental values of their constitutions or the spirit (and one suspects also sometimes the letter) of the international agreements to which they are signatories. Without endorsing any of the detailed proposals, we are happy to reproduce the document as both a thoughtful and persuasive point of departure from the present impasse in which European governments find themselves.

Conclusion

As editors of this collection we were conscious that many of the fundamental building blocks of research on the 'new refugees' of Europe had not yet been put into place. This remains the case, but such is the urgency of the problem we are addressing that we felt a volume that was broadly representative of all the major European countries was essential, even at this early stage of research. We also considered it a distinct advantage to work closely with practitioners (government and voluntary agencies) who shared their experiences in a common forum with the few European academics working on the theme.

The conclusions we derive are fourfold. First, conditions in the third world suggest that the numbers of refugees produced there are unlikely to decline. Neighbouring third world countries have borne the brunt of the resettlement of displaced and refugee populations – so far the European contribution has been modest. It may be that the number of refugees engendered by the interlocking environmental, economic and political crises in the third world can be stabilised. But this requires a massive injection of development aid, emergency assistance, the renegotiation of crippling debts and the lifting of commodity prices to levels which would act as an real incentive to increased productivity. Indeed, such a 'development package' may be insufficient – ultimately the whole relationship between industrialised and third world countries may require a re-evaluation of the whole relationship between industrialised and third world countries. This is no place to pursue this argument in detail. Suffice it to say that there is simply no evidence that European governments have grasped, or wish to grasp, the scale and complexity of the problem.

Instead, and this is our second principal conclusion, European governments have bowed down, largely passively, to internal right-wing pressures. They have tried to draw an impermeable barrier around themselves – detaining and deporting asylum-seekers, attempting to prevent refugees reaching European borders, offloading immigration controls to airlines, shipping agents and travel companies, and grudgingly funding the work of voluntary agencies involved in resettlement programmes. The European Community looks more and more like a gilded cage with the Ministers of the Interior bracing and painting the bars. It is clear that European govenments are primarily concerned with 'the security of the state' and immigration controls. Indeed in official circles immigration controls are closely identified with 'the security of the state'. Soulier (1987: 14) convincingly argues that this preoccupation stands in direct opposition to the protection and extension of democratic and human rights. In support of this proposition, he quotes (loc. cit.) Charles Pasqua, the French Minister of the Interior, who declared unambiguously that 'la démocratie s'arrête où commence l'Etat' [democracy ends where the state begins]..

Our third conclusion must therefore be a gloomy one. At the level of official European institutions and national government we see little of the generosity of spirit that will be required to allow Europe to make a significant and long-lasting contribution to the solution of the world's refugee crisis.

For a defence of the right to asylum one needs to look beyond the political level to some organised sections of civil society. For example, in France the Campagne Nationale pour le Droit d'Asile, active in the period January to October 1986, brought together many non-governmental organisations in defence of the refugee. In Britain, the trade unions actively pressed for the acceptance of Chilean refugees during the 1970s, while all over Europe the churches have sought to protect asylum-seekers from deportation and the exercise of unbridled state power. Other voluntary agencies, partly represented in this book, point a humane and not too costly way forward. We were also much encouraged by the sensitive and caring attitude of many European officials working to implement refugee admission and resettlement programmes - some of these perspicacious individuals are represented in this book.

Our fourth conclusion is therefore more positive. Despite the growth of xenophobia in Europe, humanitarian initiatives at the level of civil society can influence public opinion and create a climate in which sympathetic officials can exercise their discretionary power in an altruistic direction. The 'new refugees' can provide a strength and a depth to European culture and economic advancement, just as other refugees have done in past. They offer new skills, a commitment to entrepreneurship and self-improvement and, above all, a window onto different but exciting and creative cultural milieux. As European citizens we would be foolish to turn our backs on this kind of enrichment in favour of the dessicated and impoverished vision of the future enunciated by many European politicians.

Notes

1. Laws limiting immigration appeared in 1968 and 1971 in Britain, in the early 1970s in Switzerland, in 1973 in West Germany, and in 1974 in Belgium, France and the Netherlands.
2. See Cohen (1987: 34–42) for a critique of established theory and a review of alternative theories of migration, including 'involuntary' migration.
3. Rudge (1986) suggests that the number of refugees may indeed be even less than these official figures indicate.
4. 'If the percentages of applicants recognised as refugees, for example, in 1982 in Denmark, the Federal Republic of Germany and France are compared, the difference can be as much as 50 per cent. The Federal Republic reecognised only 6.8 per cent of refugees in that year, Denmark 48 per cent and France 56 per cent.' (Vetter 1987: 31).
5. Measured in the common European Currency Unit (ECU), government expenditure in 1985 on refugees and asylum-seekers was as follows: West Germany - 952 million ECU; France - 145 million ECU; Denmark - 107 million ECU (refugees only); Italy - 19.3 million ECU; Belgium - 7.5 million ECU; Spain - 7.3 million ECU (asylum-seekers only); UK - 0.8 million ECU (plus wage and administrative costs of refugee welfare organisations).

2 RESETTLING REFUGEES: THE DUTCH MODEL

Robert Sayers

Introduction

Until mid-May 1981, the Dutch Refugee Association, using funds supplied for the purpose by the Ministry of Welfare, Health & Cultural Affairs, was responsible for the reception and guidance of refugees and asylum-seekers.

In May 1981, however, the association announced that it no longer wished to take on this responsibility. Consequently, the then Minister for Cultural Affairs, Recreation & Social Welfare decided that the Ministry itself should take over this task and the Working Party for Refugees & Housing of Minorities, later called the Section for Refugee Welfare & Housing of Minorities (WUWM), was set up in August 1981. It was charged with organising, in the very short term, the reception, introduction, social orientation and subsequent welfare of refugees and their families. The WUWM consisted of two departments, one dealing with all aspects of policy, the other with financial affairs, data management and housing.

In 1985 the Ministry of Welfare, Health & Cultural Affairs reorganised its welfare division. A new section was created for refugee reception, a special task section set up for housing invited refugees and a Staff Bureau for Financial & Economic Affairs established to take care of the financial implications of resettlement.

A motion supported by Evenhuis-Van Essen formed the basis of the Ministry's 'in-house model' for receiving refugees. To prevent the refugees becoming institutionalised (which may occur if they stay too long in the main reception centre) and also because the Ministry needed to consider the financial implications of the whole reception process, a model was chosen which kept the refugees at the reception centre for as short a time as possible before housing them in their permanent places of residence. Hence the name 'in-house model'.

The 'in-house model' is designed to encourage refugees to function independently in Dutch society and, to this end, they are located, as soon as is feasibly possible after their arrival, in the municipality in which they are expected to remain. An attempt is also made, where desirable, to house all the members of a group in the same municipality and to ensure that they receive the most intensive reception, introduction and social orientation that it is possible to provide.

The rate and extent to which these aims can be achieved depend largely on whether or not it is possible to prepare for the arrival of the refugees in advance and on what instruments are available for implementing the reception model. The basic means include the availability of a central reception centre, the preferential provision of state housing, and the existence of regulations for the provision of refugee facilities.

The reception centre is for the exclusive use of refugees who have been invited to the Netherlands by the government (and their relatives who may arrive later) and for the Vietnamese boat-people. Preferential state housing and refugee facilities, however, are also extended to asylum-seekers who have come to the Netherlands of their own accord and have been granted refugee status (A-status) and to people with an entitlement to asylum (B-status).

The aim is to achieve a quick, smooth transition in which the refugees' initial reception, housing and subsequent settlement in the municipalities form an integrated whole and in which there is a gradual transfer of responsibility (during which there is constant consultation) from central government to the municipalities. By the time all the various government grants have been withdrawn, the refugees have become residents of the Netherlands and are entitled to exactly the same facilities as any other Dutch citizen.

In the early stages of its implementation the Interministerial Coordination Committee on Policy for Minorities met regularly to discuss what form the new policy should take, including who should be admitted, who should be entitled to use the reception facilities and how refugees should be received. (These points are discussed in greater detail below.)

Quota and Funding Problems

Whenever the refugee situation in certain parts of the world has warranted it, the Dutch government has always been willing to contribute to the international effort to relieve human suffering by bringing a number of refugees to the Netherlands on an ad hoc basis. This has been done in response to requests from the UNHCR in Geneva, which acts as the international coordinator in such matters.

Between September 1973 and July 1976, the Council of Ministers was called upon no less than 12 times to come to a decision about admitting various groups of refugees. Because of this recurrent need to make ad hoc decisions, the Council of Ministers asked the then Interministerial Committee on Refugees to produce a document on long-term policy. This led to the 1977 regulations empowering the Interministerial Committee on Refugees to make recommendations to the various ministers responsible for inviting groups of refugees to the Netherlands. On the basis of past figures, it was expected that 200 individual asylum-seekers would be admitted each year and recognised either as refugees (A-status) or persons entitled to asylum (B-status). It was also expected that 550 refugees would be invited annually to settle in the Netherlands. The financial provision for a maximum of 750 refugees per year was called the budgetary quota.

Certain developments occurred over the years following the introduction of the regulations which led to the quota being exceeded and which made it difficult to invite groups of refugees. There was, for example, the completely new group of Vietnamese boat-people, whose arrival brought a steady increase in the number of Vietnamese coming to the Netherlands to rejoin their families, as well as an annual rise in the number of individual asylum-seekers coming to the Netherlands on their own initiative.

The regulations had to be amended. The Interministerial Coordination Committee on Policy for Minorities made some recommendations concerning the quota and funding and their advice was accepted by the Cabinet. Provisions were made, as from 1984, to accommodate an annual quota of up to 250 refugees who were to be invited to settle in the Netherlands over and above the individual asylum-seekers (estimated at 800) and the Vietnamese boat-people and their families (estimated at a total of 250). In an attempt to prevent the number qualifying for admission in this way being affected by other factors, the government undertook to admit the latter categories on condition they met certain criteria.

The quota of 250 people who were to be invited to settle in the Netherlands was to fall into three categories, namely the 'contingents', which consisted of up to 200 refugees who were to be brought over in groups; 'emergency cases', i.e. a maximum of ten individuals in dire distress who could no longer stay where they were; and a total of 40 'disabled refugees', which included any relatives accompanying them, who were unable to acquire treatment in their present place of residence. (This was in accordance with the criteria set out in the UNHCR's 'Ten or More Plan'.) In January 1987, however, the annual quota was increased to 500 invited refugees, of which 400 places were set aside for contingents, 80 for disabled refugees and 20 for emergency cases. This was over and above the 200 family reunion cases, the 100 Vietnamese boat-people and the 1,000 individual refugees brought in under the budgetary quota.

The UNHCR in Geneva is expected to draw the Dutch government's attention to any refugees who may qualify for an invitation under any one of these three categories, but since 1984 most of the refugees have come into the country solely on the initiative of the Dutch government.

The level and manner of financing the reception, orientation and social integration of these categories of refugees were also adjusted under the new quota regulations and it ceased to be necessary to sort out financial problems several times a year - at least for the duration of the Cabinet's term of office. The regulations came into operation on 1 January 1984. Appendix I lists the sums of money involved in policy for refugees and persons entitled to asylum since that date.

The 'In-House Model': Preparations

The admission of asylum-seekers who come to the Netherlands of their own accord and subsequently apply for (and are granted or refused) refugee or asylum status is not the responsibility of the Ministry of Welfare, Health & Cultural Affairs. This group can benefit from preferential state housing and refugee facilities only after being granted the necessary status. The account given in this section of the preparations for the arrival of refugees therefore applies only to invited refugees who are accommodated in a central reception centre, to the Vietnamese boat-people and to refugees who come to the Netherlands to be reunited with their families.

Preparations for inviting refugees to the Netherlands are made by a sub-committee of the Interministerial Coordination Committee on Policy for Minorities. Basically, when the UNHCR in Geneva issues its request to receive refugees, the committee draws up recommendations for consideration by the ministers and state secretaries concerned.

The size of the group, the country of origin and the language of the refugees are important factors in reaching a decision. The availability of space in the reception centre and the group's expected time of arrival are also taken into account. Once these facts have been established, preparations for the actual reception can begin.

These include collecting background information about the group, or groups, of refugees in question; renting a reception centre if there is insufficient space at the existing centre; engaging new personnel if necessary; translating the language and introduction programmes into the language of the group; choosing potential municipalities where the refugees can ultimately be housed and discussing this with the various municipal councils; and compiling a programme for use during the initial reception stage which is geared to the particular needs of the group in question.

Practically all the staff of the WUWM are involved in these preparations. Since time is usually short and the various activities need to be closely coordinated, a roster has been worked out for the staff. It lays out the lines of communication and stipulates, on a day-to-day basis, what tasks must be performed by whom and which members of staff bear what responsibility. The roster is useful not only because it enables the existing staff to know exactly what is expected of them, but also because it quickly points to the most efficient way of employing new personnel.

Central Reception

Because the period the refugees spend in a central reception centre has been reduced to a maximum of three months and because the number of refugees arriving each year can fairly accurately be estimated at 500, the required reception capacity can be determined with reasonable accuracy. At present one reception centre (Apeldoorn, in the east of the country) is being used. It consists of a main building and several annexes, the latter being in full or partial use according to the number of beds required and the different groups of refugees. The work of the reception centre is carried out by a permanent staff consisting of social workers, a reception officer, a Vietnamese interpreter, two language consultants, three languages teachers and a creche supervisor.

If the size and nationality of the group concerned and the nature and gravity of its anticipated problems warrant it, extra personnel may be engaged on a temporary basis. A liaison officer acts as intermediary between the reception centre and the policy department and between the reception centre and the municipality in which the refugees will be housed. A WUWM central reception coordinator supervises the whole operation.

During the first few days at the centre, which to some extent provide an opportunity for the refugees to unwind, their various particulars are recorded and medical examinations carried out at the Ministry's own refugee health centre.

While at the reception centre, the refugees receive a subsistence allowance equivalent in value to a national assistance benefit.

During this period, the refugee schoolchildren attend an 'international link course', for which a special teacher is appointed. Shortly after their arrival, refugees over the age of 16 start Dutch language lessons and classes to help them find their bearings in the strange society in which they have come to live. This is done with the help of an information package that has been especially adapted to the needs of the group. Dutch language classes start at the beginning of their second full week in the Netherlands. Use is made of the language and introduction programme *Zeg nu Zelf* (Now Say it Yourself), which has been specially compiled for this purpose. The aim of the programme is to give refugees a basic knowledge of Dutch society and the Dutch language, so that they can cope with common everyday situations. It may be summed up as 'social self-sufficiency'. The programme consists of an intensive six-week course of 25 periods a week, during which information is given about those aspects of Dutch society with which the refugees come into direct contact. The programme also gives them a basic knowledge of the spoken language in these situations. Themes include: introductions, the market, shops, the post office, the bank, public transport and the health service.

At the conclusion of the programme refugees are usually housed in a municipality. If permanent housing cannot yet be provided for them, they stay in the centre. After a week's break they begin a six-week continuation course of 25 periods per week, dealing with: living in a house, the Dutch weather, budgeting, education, work, leisure pursuits and traffic.

If it is already known in which municipality the group will settle, the refugees are told about the various aspects of its housing and reception. The people from the municipality who will be involved in receiving the refugees may also participate in the programme at the centre to ensure that the transition from the reception centre to the municipality goes as smoothly as possible.

Once the transition is made, the WUWM passes the refugees' particulars on to the municipality concerned, including data on education and health.

Preferential State Housing

Under this scheme, 10 per cent of all newly-built government-subsidised dwellings are set aside annually to accommodate particular groups specified by the Minister of Housing, Physical Planning & the Environment. Though much of this is intended for housing civil servants on special duties, the Ministry of Welfare, Health & Cultural Affairs is supposed to implement the scheme for the benefit of minorities and about 5 per cent is reserved for housing refugees and asylum-seekers.

The search for suitable accommodation for invited refugees takes place, if possible, before their arrival in the Netherlands. In the case of family reunification, the WUWM contacts the municipality to ask whether the previously allocated dwelling is large enough to accommodate the whole family. If it is, the family can be quickly reunited, and the municipality is subsequently informed of this in writing. If the dwelling is too small for the whole family, the municipality is asked to put the refugees already living there onto a special housing waiting list. The newly-arrived relatives then remain at the centre until the whole family can be permanently housed.

Refugees or asylum-seekers who come to the Netherlands of their own accord can apply for accommodation under the preferential state housing scheme as soon as they are granted the necessary status.

The refugees' housing preferences are taken into account as much as possible. The speed with which they can be housed depends on what accommodation is available in a particular place.

Refugee Facilities

Upon arrival in the Netherlands refugees and asylum-seekers find themselves in a completely new environment. They are at a considerable disadvantage compared with other residents and are unable to take immediate advantage of the provisions available to them. The first reception period is meant to alleviate this initial disadvantage, but there is still a need for further help in the municipalities in which they settle. There is a definite need for a reception programme in the municipalities through which to introduce and socially orient the refugees to their new environment. This should include language classes, social guidance, the services of an interpreter, help from host families and regular meetings at which the refugees can be given information and help. Since the government realised that there was little or no chance of the municipalities, from their own financial resources, being able to finance such a programme, it agreed to provide extra facilities and funds for this purpose.

Hence, as from 1 January 1985, the refugee facilities became absorbed into the government's 'minorities grant scheme', although without any change being made in the level of grants allocated or in the nature of the activities funded. The scheme was for the benefit of both refugees invited to the Netherlands by the government and of asylum-seekers who had come to the Netherlands on their own initiative and been awarded A- or B-status.

Under the scheme, a single government grant of 5,000 guilders is made for each refugee/asylum-seeker. If at the end of the initial reception programme, which may take about a year, there is a demonstrable need for further social guidance, a second payment of 1,000 guilders per refugee may be made.

In January 1987, the government's minorities grant scheme and the refugee facilities regulations were subsumed under a single Welfare Act.

A municipality receiving between 30 and 90 refugees at more or less the same time may be designated a nuclear municipality, meaning that it is required to submit a reception plan to the Ministry stating that it has sufficient accommodation available and explaining how and by whom the reception, introduction and social orientation of the refugees will be carried out. The government grant is then set at 6,000 guilders for each of the first ten refugees. The Welfare Act also provides for a contribution to be made towards loss of rent when a dwelling intended for a refugee remains unoccupied for a short period at the Ministry's request. There are two more facilities available to refugees staying at a government reception centre. First, a furnishing grant for refugees unable to meet their furnishing costs themselves. This is necessary because the municipalities cannot be expected to bear the costs of furnishing the houses themselves, yet the National Assistance Act stipulates that the house must be furnished before the occupants take up residence in the municipality. The municipality gives the refugees a payment, part of which must be refunded in accordance with the National Standardisation Decree, and then receives a non repayable government grant equivalent to that sum. Second, a government grant is also provided in the form of a commutation fee to cover costs incurred by the municipality in making a dwelling ready for use.

The 'In-House Model' in Action

When the Ministry assumed responsibility for the refugees' initial reception in August 1981, the Dutch Refugee Association agreed to find accommodation as quickly as possible (and in any case before the end of the year) for the refugees who were still in reception centres at that time. Unfortunately it was unable to do this in every case, with the result that, on 1 January 1982, the Ministry had to take over responsibility for the previous groups as well as the new arrivals and this somewhat slowed down the whole housing programme. Moreover, it was having to cope with the sudden arrival of the Vietnamese boat-people at the same time as it was trying to set up an entirely new organisation. As a result, implementation of the new model, especially with regard to its stipulation that the stay in the reception centre should not exceed three months, had to be delayed until the end of 1982. During this time the number of reception centres was reduced from 37 to three. Then, from 1 April 1983, with the reduction in the number of boat-people, it was necessary to keep only one centre open.

The refugee facilities were introduced in March 1982, but took effect retrospectively from 1 January. Until then, use had been made of a number of interim measures, but from the beginning the reception of refugees, once they were definitely housed, had been undertaken by the municipalities in question. This aspect of the 'in-house model' was therefore achieved from the very start.

The success of the 'in-house model' could be said to depend on several factors: (1) the arrival of (groups of) refugees must be phased and capable of being pre-planned; (2) during the period in the reception centre nothing must prevent the refugees from moving on quickly to the municipalities; (3) there must be sufficient accommodation available in the municipalities at the right time to house a group or several single persons; and (4) municipalities must be willing and able to assume responsibility for the refugees' reception, introduction and social orientation.

We shall now examine these factors in the light of recent experience.

Invited Refugees

Ideally, the size of the group and the exact time of its arrival should be known well in advance, so that the necessary accommodation, personnel and costs can be worked out with reasonable accuracy and language lessons and introductory activities prepared. Roughly speaking, a period of three months is required for the entire preparation. However, it is often difficult to predict exactly when the various categories of refugees will arrive and, in some cases, the real size and composition of the group. Nevertheless, with the concerted efforts of all concerned, refugees can usually be moved to their permanent place of residence within the three-month time limit. As the amount of effort required varies from one category to another, each category is discussed separately.

Contingents

The annual maximum quota of 200 is mainly made up of contingents. The nature, composition and size of the group invited to the Netherlands is, however, basically determined by the UNHCR in Geneva.

The idea is to bring contingents to the Netherlands in several separate groups which are spread out over the year. There is usually a fairly long interval (approximately four to eight months) between the relevant ministers agreeing to invite the refugees and the actual arrival of the group. This is because, to avoid the possibility of losing selected refugees to another country, the final selection only takes place after the decision to invite the refugees has already been made. Consequently, the actual size of the group and the composition of its families are sometimes known only a month before arrival. The group is usually smaller than originally expected, but none the less preparations must be started as early as possible. Enough beds must be reserved, new personnel (often an interpreter) engaged and future housing sought.

It sometimes happens that when everything is ready, the refugees' arrival is delayed for a considerable length of time. This causes difficulties in that new personnel are engaged on six-monthly contracts and reserve dwellings may stand empty for so long that the time limit for loss of rent is exceeded. If, on the other hand, the municipality gives the house to someone else, the search for accommodation has to begin all over again. All this sometimes incurs extra cost and may result in the three-month time limit being exceeded.

Whether or not refugees are housed in groups depends on the nature of the group. A contingent of Vietnamese refugees from the South East Asian camps, for instance, nearly always consists of people who have relatives in the Netherlands and therefore wish to live as near to them as possible. Where feasible, a check is made beforehand to ascertain whether this is practicable in view of the available accommodation. Refugees without relatives in the Netherlands are, if possible, housed in nuclear municipalities.

Of the early contingents invited to the Netherlands, there were 50 Vietnamese in 1981, 100 Poles in 1982 and 75 Vietnamese in 1983. They arrived in several groups of various sizes and, as most of them had relatives or acquaintances in the Netherlands, were housed in various locations throughout the country. On average they spent 3.2 months in the reception centre.

Disabled People

When the policy document on quota and funding problems was published, it was also decided that disabled refugees who could receive no further treatment in the country in which they were living or elsewhere in that region, could be invited to the Netherlands.

Although under the Ten or More Plan the UNHCR does not require countries to admit disabled people every year, it has now been decided to offer this opportunity in future, because the Netherlands is prepared to make an extra effort for this vulnerable category of refugees. Because of their disability, it is expected that such refugees will often be accompanied by their immediate family or other relatives, all of whom are included in the sub-quota of 40 people.

In order to ensure that reception and housing proceed as smoothly as possible, the Ministry of Welfare, Health & Cultural Affairs has laid down several additional criteria. The basic principle in the selection of disabled people is that they should be capable of being received, rehabilitated and integrated in the Netherlands. They are most likely to be taken in if their handicap is physical,. if they do not require lengthy residential care or hospital nursing and require no special provisions in the reception centre or in the accommodation provided for them in the municipalities. To achieve the general aim for refugees – to become independent as quickly as possible – at least as fully as is feasible, it is stipulated that the disabled person should not, if possible, come to the Netherlands alone but should be part of a family, with whom they can share a house. Nevertheless, unattached disabled people who already have relatives in the Netherlands or whose situation is particularly tragic do still stand a chance of being selected.

As with the contingents, disabled refugees tend to arrive later than would be ideal with regard to planning and preparation. Attempts are made to place them in municipalities in which other refugees of the same nationality are already settled and, to make best use of the municipality's reception facilities, the authorities prefer to accommodate them at the same time as a group. Unfortunately, however, this is sometimes made impossible by the disabled person having to undergo surgery while still at the reception centre.

Between 1981 and 1983, the Ministry of Welfare, Health & Cultural Affairs received 34 disabled people and their families into the Netherlands. Their average stay in the reception centre was two and a half months.

Emergency Cases

A maximum of ten emergency cases are allowed to be invited to the Netherlands each year. All these are individuals in need of immediate assistance and about whom a swift decision has to be made. As a result it is practically impossible to plan their reception. The situation is further complicated by the fact that they come from all parts of the world and that it is usually difficult to find an interpreter who can be engaged on an hourly basis who is able or willing to travel regularly to the centre. As most of the emergency cases have no relatives in the Netherlands and invariably come in small units, housing presents no problems.

Vietnamese Boat–People

Since 1979 the government has undertaken to admit Vietnamese boat–people who are rescued at sea by ships sailing under the Dutch flag. They have to enter the Netherlands within three months of landing at a nearby port of call.

This means that the exact number of Vietnamese boat–people to be admitted cannot be planned in advance and explains why this group of refugees is excluded from the quota. Also, since the number of boat–people rescued at sea and brought to the Netherlands has fallen considerably (1,118 in 1979, 930 in 1980, 831 in 1981, 360 in 1982 and 119 in 1983), the arrival of an occasional group no longer presents any real problems, especially since the authorities have almost three months in which to prepare for their arrival and to find accommodation for them. As most boat–people prefer to be housed together and it is easier for municipalities to organise a reception programme for a group rather than a single person, they are invariably housed in a nuclear municipality, the choice of which is determined mainly by the size of the group and the accommodation required.

Several municipalities are visited in an attempt to select the most suitable housing and a decision is usually made about their ultimate place of residence before they actually arrive. There is also enough time to assemble the right number of beds and to engage the appropriate support staff for the reception centre.

Appendix II shows how many groups of boat-people have been admitted since the central reception was taken over by the Ministry of Welfare, Health & Cultural Affairs, when and in what municipalities they were settled and the average length of their stay in the reception centre.

Family Reunion

Almost immediately after arriving in the Netherlands, practically all refugees, including the Vietnamese boat-people, file petitions for permission to have their families reunited with them. The petitions are considered by the Minister of Justice and may or may not be granted. There is never any difficulty about relatives in the South East Asian camps being allowed to come to the Netherlands.

Organising family reunions with relatives from Vietnam is a different matter altogether. The relatives need to obtain exit permits from the Vietnamese authorities, for which they sometimes have to wait for years. On other occasions, the relatives merely fail to arrive on the plane on which they have been booked. Vietnamese refugees in the Netherlands who wait for long periods for their relatives, occasionally in vain, are subjected to enormous pressures which sometimes prevent them from integrating into Dutch society.

It is difficult to plan in advance for the reception of relatives from Vietnam, for the Dutch authorities are only notified of their impending arrival a fortnight (at most, and sometimes just a few days) before they arrive. Nevertheless, as family reunions take place throughout the year and an estimated 100 to 150 relatives are expected to arrive, the WUWM employs a Vietnamese interpreter on a permanent basis. Normally no difficulties occur in the reception centre, which is probably partly because the refugees arrive in small groups.

Problems sometimes arise, however, when it comes to finding permanent accommodation. Only a few refugees are able to accommodate their newly-arrived relatives in their existing houses and this means that a larger house has to be found. Ideally this should be in the same area, for the refugees who have already lived in the Netherlands for some time are usually already working or studying in or near their places of residence and have their children settled in local schools. When new housing has to be found, the refugees often have to stay in the reception centre for longer than three months if there is no suitable accommodation available in the municipality under the preferential state housing scheme.

In 1981, when the Ministry of Welfare, Health & Cultural Affairs assumed responsibility for the reception of refugees, 205 people came to the Netherlands to be reunited with their families. In 1982, this figure was 136 and in 1983, it was 188, with an average stay in the reception centre of 2.3 months.

The Reception Centre

Several different groups of refugees with a varying assortment of nationalities are likely to be occupying the reception centre at any given point in time. In one particular year, for example, it housed refugees of six different nationalities – Vietnamese, Cambodian, Laotian, Chilean, Polish and Ugandan – during which there was continual overlap.

As newcomers arrive almost weekly to be reunited with their families, it is unavoidable that groups should merge in the course of their reception and guidance. Dividing the refugees into classes for instruction, for instance, requires a certain amount of ingenuity. Differences in cultural background may lead to conflict, but this only, however, becomes apparent in exceptional circumstances. Usually it can be avoided by wise and thoughtful guidance.

An extremely flexible form of organisation and a great deal of improvisational ability on the part of the staff ensure that activities at the reception centre are carried out efficiently. The staff are required to cope with situations as they arise and to adapt their methods to suit the needs of the different groups.

The social workers are responsible for attending to the refugees' personal affairs, for detecting and solving problems at an early stage and for generally advancing their interests. The reception officer deals with all the material aspects of the reception, from settling the refugees into their rooms and arranging doctors' visits, to informing them of when they have to leave. The interpreter is responsible for all spoken and written translation work and also provides an indispensable service as the purveyor of useful information. The creche supervisor, who is in charge of baby and child care and looks after the toddlers and pre-school children, is also responsible for identifying dietary deficiencies, mental handicaps, cases of neglect and disease and sometimes, even, for establishing a child's correct age. The language teachers are in charge of teaching the language and introduction programmes and, sometimes, also the continuation programme. Since they have most contact with the refugees, the teachers are usually the ones who detect problems at an early stage and notify the social workers. The language consultants are in charge of the construction and continual adjustment of the language course. Before a 'new' nationality group arrives, they ensure that an adapted language and introduction programme is ready for their use. Their programme is now available in Vietnamese, Sino-Vietnamese, Cambodian, Laotian, Iranian, Afghan (Bari), Polish, Spanish and English. Besides advising the language teachers, the language consultants are being asked more and more frequently (by municipalities and private people) for advice and information. The municipalities are especially eager for such information, for they want the language classes that form part of their reception programme to link up with the tuition the refugees received at the reception centre.

All the activities at the reception centre are geared towards helping the refugees cope with any everyday situation they may encounter once their three-month stay has ended. When they move to their permanent accommodation they are expected to be able to live more or less independently in their own homes, doing their own shopping, dealing with money and making themselves understood. Naturally individual results vary, but, on the whole, they can usually manage reasonably well by the time they are properly settled.

Although this can, theoretically, be achieved within the three-month time limit, difficulties do sometimes arise in the reception centre during preparations for the permanent settlement of some categories of refugees.

Although people coming to the Netherlands to rejoin their families are generally housed with them as quickly as possible, often within a few days of arrival, in some cases there is insufficient room in the existing accommodation and it becomes necessary to apply for a new house. This problem usually arises in municipalities in which few or no new houses are being built and the refugees are having to wait for a property to become vacant. This, especially in the case of a large family, may take a long time. How long the refugees stay in the reception centre will then depend entirely on the cooperation and resources of the municipality.

As it is sometimes two or three years before a family is reunited, there is a fairly high incidence of marital breakdown. When this happens, placement with the family, even if possible, is considered inadvisable. Working towards a reconciliation takes time and it is only once this has been effected that a cautious start can be made to settle the family permanently.

Unattached minors, who are principally Vietnamese, constitute a separate problem. An organisation called *De Opbouw*, which is subsidised by the Ministry of Justice, acts as their guardian. The guardianship procedure usually takes a few weeks, after which *De Opbouw* bows out until the host municipality is known and the regional social worker can establish contact with his or her future charges. In consultation with the reception centre's staff, who have often already done some preparatory work, *De Opbouw* contacts municipal staff and tries to arrange some kind of supervised accommodation or foster homes for its wards. Unfortunately it is sometimes impossible to find accommodation in the same municipality as the others who had been at the reception centre with the young people. It also sometimes takes much longer to settle the youngsters in the municipality, which means they cannot participate with the others in the municipality's reception programme.

Reception in the Municipalities

Not only does the Ministry have to be resourceful and coordinate its own activities, but must also ensure that there is proper cooperation between itself and the various municipal departments. For example, the housing department, usually in consultation with various housing corporations, provides the actual accommodation, but the municipal social services are responsible for furnishing the houses and getting them ready for occupation. Either the welfare department or the municipal social services recruit host families to help the refugees in their daily lives during the initial settling-in period and several professional staff are also usually engaged. The welfare or education department prepares the language and introduction classes, while the education department is responsible for providing education for school-age children.

If the municipality wishes, it can receive help with all these activities from the reception centre. This is also (though to a lesser extent) possible when the reception in the municipality is well under way. As the Ministry's various bureaux are usually represented on the local advisory committees, any obstacles or difficulties that arise are reported to the WUWM, which, in turn, tries to find a solution. The major municipalities also organise regular meetings at which to air and discuss their mutual problems and this enables them to benefit from each other's experiences. The meetings are usually attended by the people from the municipalities responsible for coordinating the refugees' reception and, depending on the topic for discussion, by one or more of the language teachers, a social worker and/or a municipal social services representative.

These meetings have shown that, in terms of social guidance, the main role is played by the host families, for it is they who help the refugees on a day-to-day basis. In the main municipalities, both the host families and the refugees can enlist the help of a member of staff from the municipal social services or from among the general social workers, whose services are often found to be indispensable, sometimes even for several years. The general social workers eventually take over sole responsibility for the refugees.

For refugees above school-leaving age, nearly all the large municipalities offer an integrated package of language and introductory activities. This includes 400 hours of language teaching (480 for illiterate refugees) over a period of no less than one year and no more than two. For the many refugees for whom this is insufficient, financial help for extra lessons is available from a fund set aside to provide educational facilities for ethnic minorities. Although most municipalities employ trained personnel for their language and introductory activities, they also rely heavily on voluntary help. The choice in this respect is the municipality's.

School-age refugees are educated at ordinary schools and on international link courses. If the group is large enough, the Ministry of Education & Science makes extra facilities available to 'priority target schools'.

For the education of adult refugees, the municipalities sometimes turn to occupational orientation and training centres and, to a lesser extent, to adult vocational training centres.

From various municipal reports, proceedings of meetings in the larger municipalities and the Ministry's general day-to-day discussions with municipality staff, it is obvious that the municipalities (especially those that have received one or more groups) take their responsibilities towards the refugees very seriously and try hard to do their work as well as possible. One of the advantages of housing refugees in groups is that it enables some of the funds set aside for refugee facilities to be used for hiring trained staff to help with their reception. The municipalities are not, however, always able to accommodate invited refugees in groups, which is a pity because it is impossible to set up special facilities for one or two families. Such refugees have to make do with the existing facilities, which some municipalities are better than others at providing. Certainly, given the amount of money available for refugee facilities, these municipalities need to show considerable resourcefulness as they are usually unable to afford professional help. The most the Ministry of Welfare, Health & Cultural Affairs can usually offer them is sound information and advice based on the experiences of other municipalities.

Refugees and asylum-seekers who come to the Netherlands of their own accord often fail to claim the financial help to which they are entitled under the provisions of the Welfare Act. The Dutch Refugee Association is trying to ensure that more refugees and asylum-seekers take advantage of this facility.

Since there is enormous variation in the skills, experiences and educational levels of refugees and asylum-seekers arriving in the Netherlands, the extent to which they benefit from the municipal programmes naturally differs from one individual to another. What is considered an adequate government grant for one person can prove inadequate for another. It should also be borne in mind that the grant is only an average sum, with children and even babies, who do not need language lessons, being allocated the same amounts.

Subsidised Welfare Work

Although central government and the municipal authorities are responsible for the success of the reception as a whole, this does not mean that private organisations have no (further) part to play. The national guardianship organisation, *De Opbouw*, and some local organisations have already been mentioned, but several government-subsidised national bodies are also involved in various stages of the reception. These fall into three different categories.

First is the Foundation for Refugee Reception Projects, which employs some of the staff at the reception centre and is in charge of the language and introduction programme, work in the creche and all interpreting duties that cannot be performed by the full-time Vietnamese interpreter. The Ministry also enlists the Foundation's help when there is a temporary increase in the centre's workload. The WUWM's central reception coordinator is ultimately responsible for the Foundation's activities.

Second is the reorganised Dutch Refugee Association which, since the government took over the reception of refugees, has become an efficient support organisation to which the municipal authorities and local organisations can turn for help and advice once the refugees are settled in their permanent homes and facing the full impact of living in a strange country.

The Dutch Refugee Association receives a government subsidy for its work in advising, mediating, providing information, increasing specialised knowledge and supporting voluntary workers. How much the association is asked to assist in the reception of refugees in the municipalities depends on how much help the local authorities wish to receive. On the whole they need more help with refugees and asylum-seekers who have come to the Netherlands on their own, for the WUWM and the Foundation for Refugee Reception Projects deal with most queries about those who have come by invitation and been to the reception centre.

And third are the national refugee organisations which often play a part in the introduction programme at the reception centre and, if necessary, give the staff background information about the refugees staying there.

Welfare Policy

After the first stage (reception, introduction and social orientation) most refugees and asylum-seekers are more or less ready to manage on their own and the extra attention they have been receiving from social workers and host families is gradually decreased. Because general organisations have usually been involved in their reception from the very beginning, and therefore policy for certain aspects of their welfare has kept pace with policy for the target group as a whole, most of the refugees have a good chance of eventually becoming acclimatised.

The longer the refugees stay in the Netherlands, the more aware they become of their position in the country, of what opportunities await them and of what difficulties they are likely to encounter. How they deal with this process depends largely on their individual backgrounds, the circumstances under which they had to flee and the impression made on them by the initial reception, introduction and social orientation.

Although the refugees' legal and housing position can be described as good, their employment situation is usually less encouraging. They also have special emotional problems to deal with – homesickness, anxieties about relatives left behind or impending family reunions, memories of traumatic experiences before or during their flight and unresolved mourning.

After the initial period of intensive activity, many refugees are in danger of slipping into a state of isolation. It is important to ensure that they are not cut adrift too abruptly after their intensive reception, especially as this is the time when psycho-social problems are most likely to emerge. They need a framework within which to meet one another, a context with opportunities to develop and to become more self-sufficient.

The point at which refugees begin to realise where they fit into Dutch society varies from one individual (or group) to another, but sometime during the second stage of their settlement practically all of them begin to feel a need to meet compatriots, to organise their own activities and sometimes even to join forces to improve their position in the society. Cultural and social activities, whether confined to the refugees or directed towards the society at large, can play an important part in helping refugees achieve a more equal position in the society.

As it takes rather a large number of participants to form an organisation and as the refugees and asylum-seekers tend to be scattered all over the country, there are relatively few subsidised national refugee organisations. Included among those that do exist are the Project Group for Latin-American Refugees, the Association of Vietnamese Refugees in the Netherlands, the Community of Sino-Vietnamese Refugees in the Netherlands and the Association of Ethiopians in the Netherlands. Moreover, the subsidy is only available for a limited period because, with new groups of refugees being admitted every year, the money is often transferred from national activities to the more specific demands of the new arrivals. Unless the budget is increased each year, refugees who have been living in the Netherlands for some years are bound to receive a decreasing share of the subsidy for their national activities.

Despite the small number of refugees at the municipal level, they too have a need for their own activities and it would be unwise to allow everything to come to an abrupt end, especially after such intensive activity during their early years in the Netherlands. They should be given the opportunity to play an active part in improving their position in the local community. As the government was responsible for admitting the refugees, so too should it be responsible for providing funds at the local level during the second stage of settlement. A government grant towards the costs of promoting the emancipation, participation and cultural enjoyment of refugees and asylum-seekers is helpful, even if only for a limited period of time.

An appropriate complement to the 'in-house model' has been a diminishing grant (a first payment of 5,000 guilders, a second of 1,000 and a third of 875), for which the municipalities could apply on behalf of each refugee who completed the initial reception programme. (In recent years the threefold grant has been scrapped and all payments standardised at 875 guilders.) This government grant, which augments the funds provided by municipalities from their ordinary resources, means that from the beginning of the initial reception onwards, for a period of five or six years, the government provides the municipalities with extra funds to support and promote the settlement of refugees.

The refugees' already existing national organisations could help the process along by stressing the importance of these activities to the municipalities concerned. The Dutch Refugee Association could supply the municipalities with relevant information and encourage local organisations to help the refugees set up and implement their activities. The Dutch Refugee Association could also play a part in encouraging the appropriate authorities to organise advanced courses for refugees who wish to upgrade their specialisms. The refugees' own national organisations have an important part to play in getting refugee organisations established in the municipalities and in submitting applications for grants to municipal councils.

Finally, there is the question of 'after-care' provisions to help solve the special and complex problems peculiar to refugees and connected, for instance, with their experiences before and during the flight from their country, the fact that they are usually forced to leave (close) relatives behind and that (at least in the foreseeable future) they have no prospect of returning home. Since the refugees usually discuss such problems with people in their direct environment, attempts are made to ensure that the appropriate general practitioners, social workers, municipal officers, etc., are in possession of the relevant background information. The same function is also performed by the Refugees' Health Centre, run by the Ministry of Welfare, Health & Cultural Affairs, which employs three doctors and three medical social workers for the purpose. In the last resort they can be asked to give direct assistance, as can the mobile social workers employed by the WUWM.

Summary and Conclusions

In accordance with the policy document on quota and funding problems, a maximum of 250 refugees per year are invited to the Netherlands. A further allowance of 250 is made for people coming to rejoin their families and Vietnamese boat-people. Finally, it is assumed that each year 800 of those who come to the Netherlands of their own accord will receive permission to remain as A-status refugees or B-status asylum-seekers. Activities are planned and finances made available on the basis of this figure of 1,300 refugees and asylum-seekers. Ever since the Dutch Refugee Association announced it was no longer willing to organise the reception of invited refugees, these activities have been run by the government's Ministry of Welfare, Health & Cultural Affairs and start, in the case of invited refugees, in the main reception centre. They are subsequently continued by the municipalities in which the refugees are settled. Refugees and asylum-seekers who come to the Netherlands on their own initiative have access only to the municipal activities.

The reception, introduction and social orientation of refugees is based on an 'in-house model' designed to encourage refugees and asylum-seekers to function independently in Dutch society as quickly as possible. The features of the model are: reception for a maximum of three months in a main reception centre (available only to invited refugees); housing under a preferential state housing scheme; and, since 1 January 1985, the incorporation of refugee facilities in the government's minorities grant scheme. The government issues a grant of 5,000 guilders to each refugee and 6,000 guilders for the first ten refugees housed in groups in a 'nuclear municipality'. If a group of more than 30 refugees is housed at the same time in a municipality, the bonus is 10,000 guilders.

Once the initial reception in the reception centre and/or municipality is over, several additional provisions are available to refugees and asylum-seekers. For example, the municipality can receive a government grant of 1,000 guilders per refugee for continued social guidance and, for a few years, the municipality can claim a diminishing grant from the government of 500, 250 and 125 guilders respectively for cultural activities especially geared towards promoting the emancipation, participation and enjoyment of refugees and asylum-seekers.

The aim is to effect a smooth transition whereby, after several years of intensive government and municipal involvement, the refugees, in consultation with the authorities, gradually assume responsibility for their own lives. At the end of the process they are considered to be ordinary residents of the Netherlands, for whom all provisions are evenly and equally available. Subsidised welfare bodies also play a part in the process. For example, the Foundation for Refugee Reception Projects employs some of the staff in the main reception centre; the Dutch Refugee Association will, on request, give the municipalities advice and information on how to organise the reception of refugees; and the refugees' own national organisations help refugees and asylum-seekers become acclimatised to the Netherlands by organising various cultural and social activities.

Several conditions must be met if the in-house model's objectives are to be achieved. For instance, the invited refugees' arrival must, as far as possible, be phased and pre-planned; nothing should prevent them from moving on promptly from the reception centre to their new homes; and the municipalities must be able and willing to provide enough accommodation on time and to accept responsibility for the refugees' reception.

It has usually been possible to meet these conditions. The three-month limit has rarely has been exceeded and enough municipalities have been prepared to undertake the reception procedures. Preferential state housing for minorities has been indispensable in this respect, as have the refugee facilities.

After the first few difficult years, a fairly satisfactory situation has evolved within the constraints of the available resources. There is considerable cooperation between the central and municipal authorities and a number of private initiatives have been incorporated into the process.

Appendix 2.1: Financial breakdown of expenditure for refugee policy in the Netherlands

	guilders
Basic reception costs (number of beds, personnel and activities) in reception centre	2.29m
Cost of bringing 250 quota refugees and of keeping and clothing them	2.28m
Cost of bringing 250 Vietnamese boat-people, and subsequently their relatives and of keeping and clothing them	2.28m
Government grants for 800 individual refugees and people entitled to asylum and for 500 invited refugees	10.40m
Cost of staffing and WUWM activities	1.90m
Cost of staffing and activities of the Refugees' Health Centre	1.25m
Subsidy to the Dutch Refugee Association	2.15m
Welfare activities of and for refugees/asylum-seekers at local level	1.60m
Total	**24.65m**

Note: Half the total above will be met by the Ministry of Development Cooperation.

Appendix 2.2: First reception and housing of boat-people since 1981

Year	Number of persons	Day of arrival	Housing period	No. of persons	Nuclear municipality	Central reception
1981	60	20-08-81	Sept/Nov '81	60	Hoorn	1.8
	36	03-09-81	Sept/Dec '81	32	Hoorn	1.6
	33	29-10-81	June '82	26	Veldhoven	8.3
	99	16-11-81	Apr/July '82	74	Hoorn	6.1
			Febr/June '82	19	Spijkenisse	4.6
	99	03-12-81	Jan/May '82	29	Spijkenisse	2.7
			Feb/June '82	66	Groningen	2.3
	65	14-12-81	Feb/July '82	17	Hoorn	5.4
			Apr/July '82	33	Heerlen	4.8
1982	94	07-01-82	May/Dec '82	87	Nieuwegein	6.1
	66	18-01-82	July/Aug '82	45	Alkmaar	4.2
	50	01-03-82	Sept/Nov '82	38	Zwolle	7.9
	22	16-03-82	Sept/Nov '82	20	Zwolle	7.1
	70	27-05-82	Nov/Dec '82	64	Den Bosch	6.1
	30	02-09-82	Dec '82	30	Smallingerland	2.9
1983	43	24-03-83	June '83	41	Alkmaar	2.4
	48	12-10-83	Jan '84	45	Nijmegen	3.2
	23	23-11-83	Feb '84	22	Purmerend	2.9

Note 1 The column marked 'Central reception' indicates the length of stay in months

2 In 1981 36 Vietnamese boat-people were individually housed compared to 98 in 1982 and 6 in 1983.

3 REFUGEES IN DENMARK

Eszter Körmendi

Introduction

For its size, Denmark has received an unusually large number of refugees in the last few years. The influx was unexpected and the Danish authorities normally in charge of handling the reception of refugees and their subsequent integration into Danish society were quite unprepared. Within just a few years, there was a tenfold increase in the number of refugees for whom the way had now to be paved. A parallel increase occurred in the number of local authorities that had to become involved in this work. From a modest task, involving very few municipalities, the work of integrating refugees developed into a nation–wide concern involving almost all Denmark's 275 local authorities.

Denmark has a relatively clear division of labour in its refugee policy. Certain authorities are responsible when the application for asylum is under consideration; others take over during the phase when the refugee is being prepared for entry into Danish society, while yet others continue the work after the integration phase is over.

At a time when the workload increases dramatically and unexpectedly, it is natural to focus on the lines of communication and cooperation as well as the frictions that exist between the various authorities involved in refugee work.

This chapter briefly describes Danish refugee policy and the main results of a study of the short–term integration work. The study deals with the problems of communication and coordination between the organisations responsible for ensuring that the goal of Denmark's official integration policy is achieved.

Danish Refugee Policy

Legislation

On 1 January 1987, there were 128,000 foreign nationals in Denmark. This figure represents 2.2 per cent of the Danish population and is somewhat lower than the proportion of foreigners in many Western European countries. A large number of these foreign nationals – approximately 55,000 – are citizens of the Nordic countries, Western Europe and North America. Of the remainder, the great majority have come to Denmark as immigrant workers or their dependents.

Refugees constitute only a fraction of the foreign nationals in Denmark. Of the approximate 28,000 persons who in the last 30 years have found asylum in Denmark, more than 50 per cent have arrived since the autumn of 1984.

In 1983, a new Foreigner Law was passed which, in many respects, merely confirmed what Denmark had been practising for years. The law's definition of the term 'refugee' is broader than the commitments made by Denmark under the 1951 UN Convention. The law gives both Convention and *de facto* refugees the legal right to obtain a residence permit in Denmark.

The prerequisites for an entitlement to asylum in Denmark are regulated by the key provisions of the Foreigner Law, namely articles 7 and 8. First, in accordance with these provisions a residence permit is granted to individuals covered by the 1951 Convention (relating to the status of refugees) and to those not covered by the Convention but having equally weighty reasons for not wishing to return to their country of nationality. Second, a residence permit may be granted to foreigners arriving in Denmark in consultation with the United Nations High Commissioner for Refugees (UNHCR). The Foreigner Law, based on Denmark's signing of the 1951 Convention and the 1967 Protocol, is worded in such a way as to ensure that individuals who fulfill the Convention conditions have a legal claim to residence in the country. Its main objective is to give legal and physical protection to individuals who for reasons of race, religion, nationality, membership of a particular social group or political opinion are unable, or, through fear of persecution unwilling, to avail themselves of the protection of the country of their nationality.

Refugees who are granted asylum according to the provisions of article 7, paragraph 1, are called Convention (or C–status) refugees. As a rule, C–status is accorded to refugees covered by paragraph 8, who must fulfill the (formal) condition that they have arrived in Denmark as part of an agreement with the UNHCR or another similar international agreement.

Refugees who are granted asylum in accordance with article 7, paragraph 2, of the Foreigner Law are termed *de facto* (or F–status) refugees. In the vast majority of cases refugees with either C– or F–status have the same legal status. Refugees who travel to Denmark to seek asylum on their own are termed spontaneous refugees, whilst those who come to Denmark as part of various international treaties are called quota refugees. Previously, all applicants for asylum were entitled to reside in Denmark while their applications were being considered. Since an amendment to the Foreigner Law in October 1986, however, a preliminary investigation is made at the frontier to determine whether or not applicants for asylum should be permitted to enter the country. The decision depends on whether they possess proper travel documents (passports and visas) and on whether they come from a country that places them in a 'de facto situation of security', which in practice means a country that has signed the Geneva Convention. If it is deemed that the applicant has no need, for reasons of security, to enter Denmark and seek asylum on the spot, he is refused admission at the frontier, but then an application may be resubmitted through representation at a Danish consulate abroad.

Foreigners denied refugee status may apply for a residence permit (according to article 9 of the Foreigner Law) if they 'find themselves in such a situation that compelling reasons of a humanitarian nature make out a strong case for accepting the application'. Even although these persons are not refugees within the meaning of the Foreigner Law, they are offered the same integration programme as C- or F-status refugees.

The decision to grant a residence permit (asylum) and hence refugee status is initially made by the Directorate for Aliens of the Ministry of Justice, but if the Directorate rejects the application, an appeal can be made to the Danish Refugee Board. The Board's decisions are final.

Post-War Refugee Policies

Since the end of the Second World War, Denmark has received about 28,000 refugees over and above the large number of German displaced persons, who came to the country for a short time towards the end of the war.

The decision to receive and integrate refugees into Danish society in an organised and orderly manner dates back to 1956 when, in the wake of the Hungarian uprising, Denmark took in 1,500 refugees. On that occasion several humanitarian organisations joined together to found the Danish Refugee Council (DRC), which was given the task of coping with these and later refugees. Today the DRC serves as an umbrella organisation for 12 humanitarian relief agencies. According to its statutes, the DRC's tasks are national, international and informational.

It defines its national purpose as being 'in accordance with humanitarian principles to offer assistance in integrating refugees into Denmark' and, since the early 1960s, all national integration expenses, (including social welfare and administrative costs), have been met by the Ministry of Social Affairs. This somewhat unusual setup means then that a sizeable and expensive publicly-financed task is, at least for the present, carried out by a private, humanitarian relief agency.

Table 3.1 shows the major national groups received into Denmark between 1956 and 1986. Up until 1984, almost all refugees were invited by the government (quota refugees); before 1979, a separate decision had to be taken at government level each time the frontiers were opened to a new group of refugees.

After 1979, entry permits were regularly granted to 500 refugees annually. In principle, the 500 permits were reserved both for the refugees who came as part of an agreement with the UNHCR (quota refugees) and for individuals who applied for refuge in Denmark on their own initiative (spontaneous refugees). To this number were added the Vietnamese boat people picked up by Danish ships.

Over the years the Danes have been responsive to the international emergencies that produced new floods of refugees. Table 3.2 shows how many refugees were transferred to the care of the DRC between 1979 and 1986.

Table 3.1: Refugees received into Denmark from 1956 until 1 August 1987

Hungary	1,500	(1956–)
Czechoslavakia	500	(1968–)
Poland	4,200	(1969–)
Uganda	160	(1972–)
Chile	800	(1973–)
Vietnam	3,700	(1975–)
Iran	6,100	(1984–)
Iraq	1,100	(1985–)
Sri Lanka	3,000	(1985–)
Stateless Palestinians	3,100	(1986–)
Others (30 countries)	4,600	
Total	**28,760**	

Table 3.2: Number of refugees turned over to the care of the DRC 1979–1986

1979	1,100
1980	890
1981	830
1982	810
1983	689
1984	1,200
1985	8,698
1986	9,299

In the autumn of 1984 the number of spontaneous refugees rose sharply, with this rise continuing through 1985 and 1986 until the autumn of 1986, when the amended Foreigner Law came into effect. The marked increase was only partially connected with the passage in 1983 of a new law granting applicants for asylum the right to remain in the country while their case was under consideration. Other European countries noted similar increases in the numbers of registered applicants during that period. As more and more European countries gradually introduced restricted legislation to make it more difficult for applicants to gain admission, the pressures on the more liberal countries increased. Rumours that amendments to the Danish Foreigner Law would take effect in the autumn of 1986, led to a final and very sizeable rise in the number of applicants in the late summer of 1986. Table 3.3 shows the distribution by different refugee categories of the intake of applicants for asylum and refugees.

Table 3.3: No. of applicants for asylum and refugees 1983–86

	1983	*1984*	*1985*	*1986*
Applicants for asylum	332	4,312	8,698	9,299
Refugees:				
spontaneous	198	909	6,272	6,375
quota	312	168	230	258
boat people	179	123	7	130
Total refugees	**689**	**1,200**	**6,509**	**6,763**

There is no direct correlation between the number of applicants and the number of refugees in any one year. In the first place it takes time – often a very long time – to consider an application for asylum and, secondly, not all applicants obtain refugee status.

The period between the autumn of 1984 and 1986 not only brought what for Denmark was a marked increase in the number of refugees and applicants for asylum, but also a radical change in their composition. Whilst up until 1984 Denmark had taken its refugees mainly from Eastern Europe and Vietnam, in 1985 the great majority came from the Middle East, especially Iran. In 1986 the composition of the applicants for asylum changed once more. The two largest groups in that year were stateless Palestinians and Tamils. During those years a much smaller, but still for Denmark sizeable, group arrived from Eastern Europe, especially Poland.

Since the amendment to the Foreigner Law, the number of applicants for asylum has dropped sharply. Until 1 August 1987, approximately 1,000 persons have sought asylum in Denmark. It has been proposed that the amendment (which covered a year) be extended, but that the quota be raised from 250 to 1,500. This figure includes quota refugees and persons who are expected to get a residence permit in Denmark by virtue of the Foreigner Law's provision for family reunification.

In 1987, approximately 1,200 people obtained residence permits on the basis of family reunification with refugees already residing in Denmark. If the bill is passed, it can be expected that in 1988 Denmark will grant residence permits to approximately 3,000–3,500 people, including family reunifications.

Reception and Integration of Refugees

There is a relatively clear-cut division of labour in refugee policy. The Directorate for Aliens is responsible while applications for asylum are being considered. As soon as the residence permit has been granted, the DRC, a private humanitarian organisation, must 'on behalf of the state' offer and carry out a programme of reception and integration averaging 18 months. After this period, the necessary work of assistance is continued by the same public authorities responsible for other foreigners and Danish nationals. This means that the work begun by the DRC will be taken over and carried on by the local authorities.

An applicant's or refugee's progress through the system is divided into three fairly distinct phases:

(a) The pre–asylum phase

The period from the applicant's entry into Denmark until the asylum question has been decided is called the pre–asylum phase. During this period the Directorate for Aliens is ultimately responsible for the welfare of the applicants, who are permitted to remain in the country until their cases have been decided. The Ministry of Justice allows the Danish Red Cross to handle some of the more practical matters, especially those associated with housing and maintenance. Applicants for asylum are housed in asylum centres and, in addition to board and lodging, are given a small weekly allowance. They are not entitled to work or to put their children into the Danish school system. The Danish Red Cross offers them 30 hours of instruction in Danish. The waiting time in the asylum centres varies, depending on the work load and the applicant's own circumstances. Consideration of a case now usually takes about three months, during which all expenses are covered by the state.

(b) The integration phase

Once the applicants for asylum receive their residence permits they are immediately transferred to the care of the DRC, which has the main responsibility for their welfare during the integration phase, which averages about 18 months. Though providing maintenance and offering language instruction and counselling, the DRC attempts to assure the refugees' subsequent integration into Danish society. As a rule, the refugees, who are attached to a county integration centre, are temporarily quartered in collective housing, with a view to adopting more permanent, individual living arrangements later in the integration phase. Under the terms of the Social Assistance Act, refugees are given the same treatment with respect to public relief as nationals. Residence and labour permits are issued upon the granting of asylum. Refugee status normally gives full access to the Danish educational system. Expenses during the integration phase are paid for by the state; in 1984 these amounted to 177 million Danish kroner and to 915 million in 1986, with the total amount of public social expenditure in 1986 being 130,449 million Danish kroner.

(c) The subsequent phase

After the integration phase, public responsibility for refugees falls into the hands of whatever authority, according to general statutory provisions, is charged with that responsibility. Few refugees are able to provide for themselves at the end of the integration phase, which means that after 18 months they are entitled to the same social benefits and services as any other citizens unable to provide for themselves for any length of time. Like other citizens (both nationals and foreigners), they receive these benefits through their local branch of the social services department.

The Transfer from the DRC to the Local Community

Background and purpose of the study

In addition to offering physical and legal protection, refugee work in Denmark is geared towards providing the support and remedial action necessary to ensure that the refugees are able to participate in society on an equal footing with the Danish population. The object, in other words, is to start a process of functional integration, entailing a gradual and harmonious adjustment to Danish society, while at the same time preserving their original cultural and ethnic identities. The main task is to equip the refugees with such linguistic, occupational and educational skills as will enable them to use their own resources and competence for shaping their careers and lives in the receiving country.

Over the past 30 years, the period during which refugee work was firmly established in Denmark, neither the laws nor the authorities who carried out the day-to-day practical work of integration, ever questioned the overall aim of achieving equality between national and new citizens.

Very little is known, however, about how far and in what areas integration work in Denmark can be said to have achieved its objectives. This is probably mainly because, until 1984, from a socio-economic viewpoint, the task was relatively modest. It was only when the influx of spontaneous refugees gathered momentum from the autumn of 1984 that interest in the practical implementation of the integration work and its different aspects and methods came to the fore in Denmark.

The National Institute of Social Research has now initiated several studies with a view to identifying both the short- and the long-term effects of the integration work. The first of these, the one under discussion here, looks at the transfer from the DRC to the local community, in other words, at a limited but important phase of the integration process when, after an 18-month period of massive investment of resources, the refugees begin their entry into Danish society. This is the phase when, from the viewpoint of the receiving authorities, the refugees should be able to stand on their own feet and be eligible for the same payments and have the same obligations as national and other immigrant categories. From its short-range view of the integration process, this study sought to shed light on the problems of communication and coordination faced by those who carry out the daily work of integrating the refugee into Danish society.

Until 1984, very few municipalities (and these were mainly in the larger cities) had any refugees on public assistance and there was therefore little opportunity for them to learn about this kind of practical social work. The great increase in the number of refugees made it necessary to change the geographical distribution policies and many local authorities, without any previous knowledge, became involved in the work of trying to distribute the refugees evenly across the country.

One reason why this particular phase in the process is considered important from a socio-political standpoint is because of the high hopes attached to it. As I mentioned earlier, the main obstacles to starting a life with about the same type and range of assistance accorded to the country's own citizens are by then expected (though nowhere explicitly stated) to have been cleared away and refugees' claims on local social services needing to be no greater than those of any other rehabilitee.

Another reason for focusing on the transfer from one support system to another lies in the social conditions pertaining at the time of the large intake of spontaneous refugees, for, despite a rise in employment from the autumn of 1982 to the autumn of 1984, unemployment was still considerable; few resources were available for providing educational opportunities and the housing shortage was creating considerable concern.

Finally, another important consideration derives from the fact that social work, whether in integrating refugees or solving a range of other problems, receives an indispensable lift from personal involvement and public support. Many years of experience in integrating refugees into Danish society has shown that, without wide popular support, the chances of success are greatly reduced. And, with the exceptionally large intake of refugees during this period, the climate facing the newcomers was much cooler than that experienced by earlier refugee groups.

Study Methods and Materials

The study consisted of two parts. The first was based on a postal questionnaire addressed to the social services departments in the 103 (of Denmark's 275) local authorities with refugees in their care during the period from 1 January to 30 September 1986. The data also include responses to another postal questionnaire completed by the managers of the DRC's 13 country centres.

The second was based on qualitative interviews in four selected local communities (Helsingor, Herning, Odense, and Nykobing Falster). Its aim was to describe and analyse the 'transfer' in its total setting, including local conditions surrounding the work of handing over and receiving the refugees. Staff as well as representatives from management in both systems were interviewed. Also interviewed were a small number of refugees in each community and a group of people connected with the local refugee work.

Findings

Inter-organisational cooperation before the transfer of refugees to local communities

The two bodies handling integration are supposed to work as a team to provide ready information about the possible transfer of refugees to the area, which is essential for local authority planning. The study shows that satisfactory cooperation in this field had not yet been established with all local authorities during the survey period. There is a need both for earlier and for fuller information. There were problems of communication particularly with regard to the refugees' permanent domicile in the area.

The authorities also need to cooperate on individual cases. If the work already begun while the refugees are in the care of the DRC is to continue without interrupting the integration process, the refugees and the local authorities must know about each other and should preferably also become personally acquainted. Although all refugees receive information about the community in which they are being permanently housed, not all local authorities are given any advance information about the particular refugees being transferred to their care. The study shows that two thirds of the local authorities receive information about individual cases, usually about two months before the transfer. A few local authorities, mostly in the metropolitan areas, had no contact at all with the DRC before the transfer. This, however, was mainly because it is so difficult to find permanent housing for refugees in the metropolitan areas that it tends to be allocated as soon as it becomes available, thus preventing the cooperation with the receiving community from being initiated at the proper time.

Once the first contacts have been made, the two authorities will tend to enter into an ongoing dialogue, usually by telephone. The social services only participated in meetings about individual refugees still in the care of the DRC in 28 per cent of the communities. None of the parties involved found the relationship entirely satisfactory, for the heavy workload and lack of resources made it difficult to establish personal contact.

The frequent failure of local authority social workers to become personally acquainted with the refugees may be one reason why refugees are less 'integrated' than expected. Language problems are often greater than anticipated and the refugees' educational and occupational plans frequently have to be changed more than once.

Both organisations consider it desirable to expand cooperation before the transfer; two thirds of the local authorities and a corresponding number of centre managers state that there is a need for such an expansion.

Refugee work by the local authorities

The study shows that when the refugees are handed into their care most local authorities proceed to take over the task of integration in a rather traditional manner.

In just over four fifths of the communities with refugees in their care during the survey period, cases were handled in the customary way. In only 15 per cent of the communities was the work carried out by especially interested or especially qualified personnel. These communities all had relatively large numbers of refugees. A small number of the communities announced that they had plans to employ more highly-qualified personnel.

The lack of any proper preparation for the special demands of refugee work is hardly surprising considering that, in 80 per cent of the local authorities, the staff employed to undertake this work are without any kind of previous training. This lack of professionalism is not, however, limited to the local authorities. Many case workers in both the DRC and the local departments of the four selected communities were thrown into their work without any kind of introduction or training. The study shows that there are far too few courses available for case workers and other staff to learn about refugee conditions and cultural barriers, as well as insufficient practical help in applying this knowledge to their daily work in preparing for the transfer. Of course, some experience is gained along the way, but changes in the cultural and socio-economic composition of the refugee groups and the comparatively large turnover of personnel in the organisations necessitate a more systematic accumulation of experience. This need is accentuated by the Danish practice of transferring refugees from one organisation to another. The fact that only slightly more than half the local authorities use interpreters during counselling, demonstrates that, at least until the time of the survey, the authorities had failed to recognise that refugee work requires exceptional measures. That most of those who do not use an interpreter see no need for one, probably reflects their own lack of experience rather than the unlikely scenario that most refugees can overcome the language barrier in 18 months.

Over the past few years, slightly more than half the local authorities have needed to refer refugees for psychological treatment. Although between 10 and 15 per cent of the refugee population typically requires such treatment, very few of the communities have access to health authorities capable of alleviating the particular kinds of problems encountered by refugees. There is every indication that the need will increase with the rise in the numbers of transfers.

At the time of the survey, very little headway had been made in acquainting the refugees with their local communities and vice versa. This can partly be accounted for by the survey being conducted early on in the transfer, but there was none the less hardly anything available in the way of useful printed matter, meetings or other forms of discourse whereby either the refugees or members of the receiving community could learn about one another. The local newspaper is the most popular vehicle for conveying information, yet fewer than 15 per cent of the local authorities use it to inform the inhabitants about the refugees.

Cooperation in the handover to the local authority

By and large the local authorities carry on the integration plans started while the refugee is in the care of the DRC. Several of the local government case workers admitted in interview, however, that they often followed the plans merely because they had no time to reassess the situation, even when they thought it necessary. The need for a reassessment often comes from the refugees themselves wanting to change their educational or occupational plans. In some cases the change is necessary because of a refugee's ignorance of Danish or lack of motivation, in others it is because the educational programme is too difficult for the refugee to follow.

The study shows that the help of educational and occupational counsellors could usefully be enlisted earlier on in the process; that there is a need for closer cooperation with language schools to allow for the experience of language teachers to be taken into account; and that more attention should be paid to the refugee's own wishes and motivations.

Although the DRC's official responsibilities cease once the transfer is completed, 86 per cent of the local authorities continue to liaise with the DRC after the transfer, often by means of informal casework contacts or a brief telephone–call. But even at this stage there is usually little time to exchange more than the barest practical details. Approximately half the local authorities and 70 per cent of the centre managers mentioned that they would have preferred to have had more cooperation during this period.

Barriers to further cooperation

Staff in both organisations were having to cope with heavy workloads and tight schedules throughout the survey period. They were too rushed to do their work properly and were having to resort to quick superficial solutions. As a result, cooperation tended to be somewhat tokenistic and information received frequently failed to reach the proper channels. Not surprisingly, this generated certain antagonisms both within and between the systems.

The local authorities saw the main problems as follows:

- information about general conditions relating to the area and especially plans for settling the refugees was being received too late;

- the local authorities had too little influence in setting up the plans for integration and rehabilitation which they had to implement and finance;

- there was insufficient time for personal contacts between the case workers in the two systems.

- there was a lack of knowledge about social work with refugees; and

- the heavy workloads were making personnel spend too much time on administration instead of with the refugees.

From the DRC's point of view, the main problems are:

- difficulties finding permanent housing for refugees in many municipalities through lack of local political support;

- the failure of many local authorities to recognise the need for new and occasionally costly measures in integration work;

- an absence of specialists in this field in the local administrations; and

- lack of time and resources in both systems for establishing personal contacts.

The lack of an effective housing policy was considered an important cause for concern by both types of organisation, for, without such a policy it is impossible to ensure that refugees can get permanent accommodation within a reasonable period of time, or that they can be evenly distributed geographically.

Just as there is considerable overlap in identifying what factors prevent the teamwork from running smoothly, so too are there many points of agreement between the different types of organisation on how best to overcome these obstacles. For example, there is general agreement that the 18–month transfer deadline is impractical and that it should be replaced by a gradual or staged transfer in which the refugee keeps in touch with both organisations for a shorter or longer period.

The refugees' view of the transfer

Over the years the transfer between the two administrative systems has been surrounded by a considerable amount of myth–making. In certain contexts is has even been described as a trauma. The study shows that there is, however, no real basis for this particular myth.

Interviews with selected refugee groups in all four geographical areas showed that, unlike the administrators, the refugees do not consider the transfer a particularly significant turning point. Family, housing, education, work and financial factors have a far more important bearing on how the refugees perceive their situation than under what system they are being administered.

The ethnic and national backgrounds of the refugees are also far less decisive than local conditions in determining how well or badly the transfer is accomplished. Important among local conditions are the standard of housing, the provision of places at day–care centres and other institutions, opportunities for on–the–job training and the availability of regular jobs, as well as what kind of reception the refugees are given by the local population.

All these factors add to the complexity of the administrative work associated with the transfer from either the DRC's local centre or the social services department. The fact that the system is simply not equipped to cope with such wide–ranging socio–economic problems and mental attitudes merely reinforces the need for a 'changeover'.

The DRC has grown from a small organisation working alongside a few large local authorities into a nationwide operation working with 225 of Denmark's 275 local authorities. The massive and sudden increase in the number of refugees and, consequently, the DRC's workload, has meant that new and unfamiliar paths have had to be trodden, which is bound to engender a certain and understandable sense of insecurity among all parties concerned. Some of the difficulties the organisations encountered in cooperating and coordinating their tasks were undoubtedly exacerbated by the newness of the situation at the time of the survey. Now that both parties have had a great deal more experience, many of these problems are likely to have been ironed out.

None the less, the successful integration of refugees does require and can be achieved only if certain social resources are made available. These not only include concrete resources like housing, jobs and educational opportunities, but also the local population's recognition of the refugee's need for protection and security and its backing of the public authorities' integration initiatives. Unfortunately, in Denmark, over the past few years insufficient resources have been made available to these areas.

The relatively large numbers of refugees received by Denmark during 1984–86 are now entering Danish society. Their chances of integration depend on whether Danish society – despite other pressing claims – can mobilise enough resources and direct enough innovative thinking into developing new working methods, removing the various administrative barriers and influencing public opinion in a deliberate and goal-directed manner.

Danish Attitudes to Refugees

In the autumn of 1985, when there was a relatively high influx of applicants for asylum in Denmark, the Danish National Institute of Social Research carried out a study of public attitudes to the country's refugee policy and to refugees in general, in which a representative segment of the adult population (2,000 people between the ages of 16 and 99) was interviewed by telephone.

The results showed that the majority of the respondents were unhappy about the policy Denmark was adopting towards refugees at that time; 51 per cent thought that Denmark accepted more refugees than other countries in proportion to its population and 55 per cent thought that this amount was excessive. Only one third supported the current policy; the remainder all thought that it was too easy for refugees to enter Denmark.

The debate on refugees in Denmark has tended to focus on a few key themes, one of which is an assertion that the new refugees are not 'real' refugees, but have come to Denmark either for reason of convenience or because certain Middle Eastern countries want to export their surplus populations. The study showed, however, that the majority of Danes (84 per cent) do not subscribe to this theory, but believe that most refugees come to Denmark because their lives or security are threatened at home. Only 11 per cent disagreed wholly or partly.

Another key theme in the refugee debate concerns the so-called cultural gap, the question of whether the Islamic background of so many of the more recent refugees will sooner or later come to represent a threat to Danish civilisation. This view was also largely rejected, with only 12 per cent of the population seeing the refugees' cultural background as a potential threat to their identity as Danes. Two thirds, however, did fear that the refugees' presence made it more difficult to control international terrorism, from which Denmark had largely been spared.

Yet another theme focuses on the economy and the question of whether Denmark can afford to take in refugees, or whether it might be at the cost of creating social conditions in Denmark as bad as those in the refugees' own countries of origin. In 1985 these worries were shared by 15 per cent of the Danish population, but with as many as 80 per cent feeling that we ought to have sufficient resources to help others.

But there is a difference between subscribing to humanitarian and democratic principles, in theory, and sharing scarce resources with strangers who seek protection, in practic. As many as 44 per cent of the respondents gave the reason for so many refugees coming to Denmark as a desire on their part to share Denmark's high standard of living. One third of the population thought that most refugees really came to Denmark to get an education or a job. The study, which also surveyed attitudes to immigrant workers, somewhat surprisingly revealed that in 1985 the public was more favourably disposed to immigrants than to refugees, even although the immigrants had quite blatantly come to Denmark to take advantage of the economic boom. In the survey, 13 per cent of the sample placed immigrants in the least desirable category, whereas 19 per cent placed refugees in that category.

Antagonism towards aliens, whether immigrants or refugees, was most pronounced among those aged 60 or over, but the study also revealed that negative attitudes were relatively common in those aged under 25 and that in this group such attitudes were on the increase during 1984/5.

No comparable surveys of public attitudes to refugees have been made since 1985. The Danes have changed their refugee policy, however, which has resulted in a drastic decline in the intake of applicants for asylum. But refugees and refugee policies are still hotly–debated social issues, with the silent majority being alleged to support anti–refugee viewpoints. I mentioned earlier in this chapter that this claim was a myth in 1985. Developments since then make it highly improbable that the myth is any more likely to be true now than it was then.

4 REFUGEES FROM SOUTH–EAST ASIA IN SPAIN: THE CHALLENGE OF HOPE

Maria José Santa Cruz Robles

Introduction

During a special conference held in Geneva in July 1979, the Spanish government decided to make a gesture towards human and international solidarity and agreed to receive several groups of refugees from south–east Asia (totalling approximately 1,000 people).

To plan the reception, settlement and integration of the refugees, the Ministry of Foreign Affairs set up a working committee under the presidency of one of its ambassadors. The members of the committee included representatives of the various Ministries (Interior Home Office, Health & Social Security, Justice, and Labour), as well as representatives of the United Nations High Commission for Refugees (UNHCR) in Spain and of various voluntary agencies (such as the Red Cross and CARITAS).

In August 1979, the committee laid down the criteria for receiving the refugees and set up a programme for their initial integration into Spanish society, in which the various departments and voluntary agencies were allocated different roles and duties.

It was agreed that, because of the difficulties of handling, looking after and finding lodgings for 1,000 people, the reception would take place in four groups (each of approximately 250 people) and that it would be extended into 1980. It was also agreed to keep the different ethnic groups apart, to have the first two groups made up of Laotians and the second two of Vietnamese.

The Ministry of Labour took responsibility for coordinating the programme, for finding a suitable place for accommodating the refugees during the early initial period of adaptation, as well as for implementing a programme for it.

The programme undertook to organise the selection and reception of the refugees, an initial health examination, any administration pertaining to their documentation and/or professional classification, Spanish language classes, the refugees' eventual distribution around the various provinces and the follow up of results.

Initial Reception and Settlement

Selection

The refugees were selected from camps in Ubon (Thailand), Palawan (the Philippines) and Hong Kong by a commission containing one representative from the Ministry of Foreign Affairs and two from the Ministry of Labour. Among the criteria taken into account in the selection process, which included interviews with all prospective refugees and their families, were family status, working skills and experience, educational level attained, motivation, adaptability and personality. Selection was aimed more towards finding refugees who would fit into the groups and get along with each other, rather than towards finding those with the highest score in the various criteria being measured.

At the beginning, refugees were selected from all the refugee camps, but the system began to break down somewhat as time passed (especially with the third and fourth groups) because pre-selected refugees were being accepted by other countries to which they had also applied. Some refugees would pull out at the last minute on the grounds that they did not want to come to Spain because they were expecting to be accepted by other countries where they had relatives. Others had to be turned down because they developed diseases after the pre-selection had been made. The strict selection made by the Spanish commission began to lose strength and the third and fourth groups consequently failed to meet the established criteria.

Reception

The first group (54 families with 248 members) arrived at Madrid airport on 20 December 1979. They were immediately given suitable clothing and introduced to the media, after which they were taken to their new lodgings in San Rafael, in one of the Ministry of Labour's holiday residences about 70 kilometres from Madrid.

The second group arrived at Santiago de Compostela airport and were accommodated in a similar residence in Panjon (Pontevedra). Again, they comprised 54 families with 248 members. Both groups were of Laotians from the camps of Ubon and Nonkai in Thailand.

The third group, Vietnamese nationals from the distribution camps in Hong Kong, was made up of 66 families with 276 members. They arrived on 2 October 1980 and were housed in a residence at La Línea de la Concepción (Cádiz).

The fourth group, of Vietnamese from the camps in Manila, consisted of 30 families with 96 members. They arrived on 4 October 1980 and were also housed at La Línea de la Concepción, but were transferred to another residence in Baños de Montemayor (Cáceres) on 24 October, when it became evident that the two groups were unable to get along together, mainly because of their different social and ethnic origins. Those from Hong Kong were ethnically mainly Chinese, whereas those from Manila were all Vietnamese.

Activities in the Residences

The first week was spent on a series of preliminary activities, such as carrying out medical examinations, sorting out documentation, distributing suitable clothing, filling in various files and entering useful information for the individuals and their families. Then, with the help of interpreters and with a view to finding suitable jobs for the refugees, a team of experts in occupational classification and orientation began to conduct personal interviews to establish the refugees' working skills, vocations and interests, and to acquire information about their previous employment and educational backgrounds.

To provide the refugees with a preliminary introduction to the receiving country, a document was drafted and translated into Laotian and Vietnamese, which outlined the various legal aspects of the refugees' situation and gave general information about different points of interest, such as working conditions, unemployment, social security, climate and national customs.

Spanish language classes, which were held in the residences, were taught by a team of specialists from the Employment Institute with the help of some unemployed teachers. The adult classes were designed to give the refugees sufficient Spanish to survive and, to achieve greater homogeneity, members of a family were (in so far as this was educationally possible) placed in the same group. Athough a kindergarten was provided to allow women with children to join the classes, the attendance of wives was disappointingly low.

The mornings were devoted to classes (using a direct, audio-lingual method with visual aids) and the afternoons and evenings to complementary activities such as informal talks, social events and extra classes for those either having difficulty keeping up with the morning classes or sufficiently advanced to start on written work. Various recreational activities, excursions and even an occasional show were also provided.

Children of school age were split into two groups; one for the six to ten-year olds and the other for those aged between 11 and 14. The younger children were taught by social workers and the others by primary school teachers. Being a somewhat smaller group, the children at the Baños de Montemayor residence were found places in the public primary school.

Settlement

When the initial reception and period in the residences ended, the families were distributed around Spain. This provincial distribution, which was carried out in accordance with government guidelines, took into account each refugee's professional profile and the availability of employment and housing in the respective provinces.

Local authorities, local governments and provincial labour delegates were the main sources through which employment was sought. The provincial departments responsible for housing supplied information about possibilities of obtaining council houses. The provincial branches of the Ministry of Education were approached about the children's schooling. Employers' organisations, trade unions, neighbourhood associations and voluntary agencies were also informed about the scope of the programme. Television and radio supplied general information about the arrival of the refugees and the main purposes of the programme.

During the first term of their residence in the country, the refugees were informed about what government help was available to them in areas such as housing, feeding and medical care. The intention was to give a rented house to each family, as well as a first job to the head of each family. Stipulations for employing refugees were similar to those pertaining to foreign workers, except that for refugees the national employment situation did not have to be taken into account. The work permit was granted at the same time as the residence permit, namely when the contract was signed.

The families were told that they would lose the government's help if they turned down a job offer, but that they were none the less legally free to do so and to look for a job or a house anywhere in the country. They were, however, strongly advised to accept their first job offer, partly because it allowed them to take advantage of the social security benefits, but mainly because the authorities felt that it would be much easier for them to become integrated into Spanish society if they were working. Although this advice was not always heeded, the government did in fact continue to help them.

Each family was given a file in which its medical records, family history, information about working skills, as well as a language teacher's report and description of teaching methods, were entered. They were given some money for their settling-in expenses and, for any of those who already had a house, furniture was also available.

To facilitate the settlement, groups of three or four families, between which various affinities, relationships and friendships had developed, were sent to the same province.

The families of the first group eventually settled in 21 different provinces. They travelled to their destinations in four successive batches, with the first leaving two and a half months after arrival and the last a month later.

Haste, inexperience and perhaps too much confidence in the goodwill of the local authorities and population, led to the first group being settled before any proper research had been undertaken into employment and housing prospects. This caused some problems in a few of the provinces, with families being frustrated by unanticipated delays.

Some family heads already had jobs to go to when they departed for their destinations. These had either been processed through the programme's head office in Madrid, or employers had taken the initiative themselves and got in touch with those responsible. In some cases, employers even went to the residences to interview the jobseekers and to provide them with information about the conditions and salaries of prospective jobs. Occasionally a contract was signed during the interview, but more often than not this was postponed until after a period of adjustment.

The responsibility for housing, feeding and finding work for those who were travelling without a definite job to go to was assumed, in collaboration with the provincial labour delegate and the programme's head office in Madrid, by the government authorities in the province in which they expected to settle.

The second group stayed in Panjon (Pontevedra) for about two months, after which the families were sent to 18 provinces, in some cases to join relatives who had come with the first group.

From the experience of the previous group, it was decided not to send families to the provinces of their choice until a definite job had been found for them to go to. This decision proved to be correct, for most of them were working within six months of their arrival. Unfortunately the residence had to be vacated two months after the group arrived, which was a pity, for their settlement would have been perfect had they had one more month in the centre.

The overall planning of the second group's settlement was helped considerably by the experience of the previous group. Staff from the programme's head office were sent to the residence to meet the refugees personally, to help in the selection of candidates for jobs that had been offered, to set up contacts with interested employers who preferred to conduct their own interviews, and to play a general advisory role.

The problems encountered by the first group were mainly caused by lack of planning and the failure to provide jobs, for there was a lot of support at a number of different levels, from provincial and local authorities, voluntary agencies and even the population at large. With the second group, all the arrangements were made to provide jobs and to secure offers from national employers, but the local authorities were less forthcoming in their support and, in some cases, were clearly reluctant to cooperate at all.

After one year, the first two groups comprised 101 families with 156 members. Of these, 59 families were established in houses and 93 people were working.

The refugees of the third and fourth groups, all of whom were Vietnamese, remained in the residences for about three and a half months. The third group was distributed among 24 provinces and the fourth group (of 30 families with 95 members) among nine.

As with the second group, attempts were made to find out what jobs and accommodation were available and staff from the programme's head office were used to process the offers and to set up contacts between the refugees and their prospective employers.

By the time the last two groups were settled, certain patterns had begun to emerge. For example, in those provinces in which jobs were readily available and/or previous groups had settled down without any difficulty, the local authorities willingly accepted new families. In other provinces, however, especially those with high rates of unemployment, the local authorities were reluctant to take in new families on the grounds that it was impossible to guarantee that they would find either work or housing and that they feared the refugees would be rejected by the local population. Under such circumstances the committee would approach the Red Cross to take care of the needs of these families until their problems could be solved.

There is no doubt that fewer jobs were offered to the third and fourth groups than to the others and that employers began to adopt very much stricter selection criteria once they had experienced refugees from previous groups abandoning their jobs as soon as they became frustrated.

Comments on Selection, Reception, the Period in Residence and Settlement

As I mentioned earlier, the refugees were selected at the beginning of the programme and their arrival scheduled to take place in four groups. The procedure was somewhat undermined when many of the selected refugees decided against coming to Spain and the numbers in the groups had to be made up with refugees who had been neither interviewed nor selected. For this reason, the groups were less homogeneous than might have been desirable, especially the third and fourth groups, which contained a wide range of social and cultural backgrounds and, consequently, refugees with very different prospects.

In addition, it soon became clear when the refugees were interviewed at the reception residences that much of the personal information they had given in the refugee camps during the pre-selection phase was untrue and that, in their desperation to leave the camps as soon as possible, many of them had lied. For example, because Spain had decided to restrict its intake to families, a number of single people had declared that they were members of a particular family, but then requested to be associated with a quite different family once they got to Spain.

When they were first selected, the refugees had promised to accept any job that could be offered, but later on, in the residences, even although it was proving so difficult to find suitable work for them, they became far more particular about what jobs they would and would not accept.

The first few days were spent trying to find out what skills and previous experience the refugees had so that they could be appropriately placed in future jobs. The information was collected through personal interviews with the head of each family and other members of working age. After that, they were grouped according to their existing occupational skills, as well as their potential for other work should they acquire the necessary training.

Generally speaking, the orientation process was useful. There were problems, however, with communications between the refugees and the members of the commission being seriously hampered by the refugees' inability to speak Spanish and the need to use interpreters. Other problems arose because the refugees took it for granted that, since at the beginning they had been asked what kind of work they would like to do, such jobs and no others would be offered to them in Spain. It was, however, impossible to satisfy every refugee's aspirations, especially since in many cases they had insufficient experience or training to qualify for the kinds of jobs for which they had asked and this did, in some cases, make integration more difficult.

Spanish classes were held for approximately two months (less for those who had to travel long distances to their places of settlement) and the refugees (especially the women, due to shyness or old age) tended to start their lives in Spain with an insufficient knowledge of the language to engage in everyday working or social relationships. This meant that they had difficultly fitting into their neighbourhoods and would instead spend all their time at home with the children.

The period in the residences was surprisingly harmonious, with refugees, teachers and social workers spending far more time together than planned; it was a period of reciprocity and understanding which perhaps concealed some of the difficulties and hardships of real life in Spain. It may even have contained an element of paternalism.

To avoid creating further problems in the light of the difficult employment situation in the country, it was thought best to send an average of only three or four families to each province. This would also prevent the formation of ghettoes. There were, however, other problems, of which perhaps the most important was that families felt so isolated that they sometimes even abandoned their houses and jobs in an attempt to move closer to one another.

The initial enthusiasm with which the programme was launched soon evaporated and the responsibility for solving the refugees' problems was left to those who felt personally engaged, who were able to muster some assistance from voluntary agencies such as CARITAS, but who mainly had to rely on the help and goodwill of neighbours. Very few of the local settlement committees, which delegates from the various departments and voluntary agencies, such as the Red Cross and CARITAS, had agreed to set up to deal with problems arising in settling the families, ever actually materialised.

Community Adjustment and Development

It should be noted, however, that the team in charge of the reception and preparation for settlement carried out its job with enthusiasm and great energy. Its members lived with the refugees and grew to know and to love them. The refugees' problems became their problems and they made every effort to understand them despite the cultural and language barriers. They advised them on every conceivable aspect of life in Spain, but, despite such dedication, the integration of the refugees was less successful than they had hoped it would be.

There were several reasons for this. For a start, the great cultural divide between the two societies had perhaps been underestimated and it had been asking too much to expect them to adopt Spanish customs and a Spanish way of life. It was basically a failure on both sides: the Spaniards misunderstood them and they, on their part, were often unwilling to cooperate.

Because of the high level of unemployment in the country, the team were anxious in case there were complaints from the trade unions about refugees being given preference over Spaniards on the job market, but this fear was proved groundless. Nobody complained, on the contrary, trade unions, political parties and private people showed solidarity and understanding in every case.

Problems with provincial settlement arose only when the people responsible failed to take a proper interest in what they were doing, either because they expected the government to take charge or because they thought that giving the refugees food and shelter was sufficient. In some cases, they managed to secure employment for a refugee at the level of a 'favour', but this was a mistake, for such practices can lead to exploitation.

The economic crisis and rates of unemployment in the province were constantly used as excuses for bad management. Many provinces shared the same problems, yet in those where proper provisions were made for the settlement, integration always went well and with minimal cost. Employers' reports about the refugees were usually positive. They adapted well and worked hard.

Certain problems arose in the first and second groups through so many of the offers being for agricultural jobs. These did not usually work out well because the refugees, apart from finding it difficult to live in isolated places, were unused to modern techniques and to the hardships of working in the field. They had been unable to accomplish their ambitions as quickly as they had hoped and, as a result, had felt frustrated and cheated.

In those provinces in which committees were organised with help from voluntary agencies to keep in close touch with the families and to deal with their problems, once their job and housing situation had been resolved, there were no further problems in the settlement. Integration was complete and lasting; these families are now very much a part of the community, they maintain normal relationships with their neighbours and there are even some mixed marriages.

But this was by no means the usual pattern. There are obviously several different aspects to the problem, but one of them is that Spain, by tradition, has been the refuge for Latin Americans and therefore had no previous experience of taking in refugees from an Asian culture. Although those responsible for the reception and settlement did have valuable help along the way from UNHCR translators and some volunteers from Laos and Vietnam, they were basically having to learn as they went along. In addition, the numbers involved were low and this also made it difficult considering there was no established colony to lend them support.

Both these factors made it difficult for them to settle in Spain. They felt lonely and, even although no family was ever sent to a province on its own, the jobs were sometimes in distant villages and this made the families feel isolated, especially since their knowledge of the language was insufficient for any real communication with their neighbours.

It was interesting that no leaders emerged and that the refugees never developed enough group consciousness to solve their own problems, but instead waited passively for the government to help. Both Laotians and Vietnamese are by nature outgoing, communicative people who need to be amongst themselves and share in each other's joys and sorrows. Sometimes it was more important for them to live near another family than it was to keep a job or house.

Within three months of starting their lives in the provinces, two of the families in the first group came back to Madrid, one with the intention of emigrating to France and the other because they did not want to be alone in a province in which, they said, they had not been well accepted, even although this meant giving up an established job and the promise of a flat.

This was only the beginning. Afterwards, many families in the first and the second groups came back to Madrid complaining that they had been unable to integrate, that their salaries were too low, or that their working conditions were bad. They were lodged in hostels at the programme's expense until arrangements could be made to send them to other provinces where conditions were presumed to be better. The Red Cross looked after 14 of these families until new jobs could be found for them and the Ministry of Labour took responsibility for another three.

Between June 1980 and February 1981, when the Ministry of Labour completed a full report on the settlement of refugees in Spain, 23 families left Spain without notice, all of them presumably to France.

It is difficult to understand why they behaved in this way, why they should have abandoned their work and accommodation (as if in a kind of chain reaction of sympathy for one another) only a few months into their settlement, without considering the possibilities of starting a new life or giving new friendships a proper chance to develop.

Perhaps the Spanish population expected them to behave too much like Spaniards or Latin Americans, but there is no evidence that they were in fact rejected. On the contrary, the Spaniards were on the whole exceedingly helpful, affectionate and sympathetic. Perhaps the refugees felt insecure because they were unemployed or isolated. Some had complained about being ignored by the authorities and in several instances the children had not gone to school.

The families that fled to France without any previous notification or warning were possibly motivated by the desire to settle in a country where some of their relatives and friends were already well established, rather than because the French government was doing anything particularly special or different for its refugees. It is probable that because other refugees were already settled in France and organisations existed there to give them support and advice, new refugees could take more advantage of what opportunities were available and, consequently, it became easier to find a job. Although objectively conditions may have been easier in Spain (where at least they did not have to share a flat with another family), subjectively they probably felt more at home in France with their fellow countrymen showing them the ropes.

Also, a number of families may have all along intended merely to use Spain as a bridge to another European country. In some cases, however, the departure from Spain was legal because of a family reunion and several single people left to join their parents or brothers in the USA, Canada, Germany or Holland. They were always driven by the same underlying need to regroup with their own people and to live as if they were in their own country.

In any case, the fact that so many families left the provinces in which programmes had been organised to facilitate their integration, presented the authorities responsible for them with a difficult problem. After working for a whole year, they began to feel as if they were starting all over again, but this time with the added disadvantage of having to deal with obviously frustrated families destined for a difficult integration.

Since there were no shelter centres available, the returning families had to be lodged in hostels, in some cases for quite a long time, and this too had certain negative effects. Some became depressed and inert, merely waiting for the government to feed and house them without making any attempt to change their situation. Others adopted a more aggressively negative attitude and refused to accept any job that was not exactly what they wanted.

Several Chinese restaurants offered them jobs, but even when these were accepted, they never lasted for long, despite many of the Vietnamese refugees having claimed to have been chefs. There were also offers of domestic work, both for childless couples and single women, but they too were usually a failure, as were the jobs in farming and the agricultural sector in general. One of the problems was that they just did not have the qualifications required for the kinds of jobs they wanted to do, especially at a time when the labour market in any case had very few jobs to offer.

During their period in Madrid, the refugees should really have been doing more to become integrated and to acquire further skills. Some of the younger people and a few of the adults did attend various courses to train as mechanics, plumbers, or even hotel managers, but these courses were not specifically designed for them, so only those with a good grasp of Spanish were able to derive any benefit from them at all.

As time passed, the families began to realise that, despite their isolation, they were in fact better off living in smaller places, where it was easier to find work and where the local committees were in a better position to give them personal help. Moreover, in that the local authorities and voluntary agencies favoured provincial distribution and had committed themselves to supplying each family with a house and monthly grant until they found work, as well as financial help to those who wished to start their own businesses, there were strong incentives attached to the provincial option.

Some People and Institutions behind the Programme

Boys' City

Boys' City is the name of an institution founded by a priest, in which boys and girls of different ages and nationalities work and study in a community in which everyone is assigned special duties and responsibilities. It is mostly financed by a wellknown travelling circus. Children working in the circus are also educated in Boys' City, where regular classes are organised to fit in with their circus training and performances. Daily work is democratically shared.

Father Silva, the institution's director, suggested that Boys' City take in four ten-year old refugee boys, with of course the consent of their parents or guardians and the programme's approval. The children's families were already settled in the Balearic Islands. The children were very happy in Boys' City and their Spanish improved enormously. But, at the beginning of the new term after having spent the summer holidays with their families, although they had the opportunity to do so, they did not come back.

The Mercedarian Brothers in Madrid

When the Mercedarian Brothers heard through the media about the refugees's impending arrival in Spain, they contacted the Ministry of Labour with an offer to accept two or three single boys into their community, where they would be given board and lodging and an education.

After an interview, three of the boys accepted the Mercedarian Brothers' hospitality. The experience was successful and the boys remained in the community until each had found his own way. The Mercedarian Brothers gave one of the boys, Phonexay, enough money to bring his parents out of Laos. The parents spent a while in a refugee camp in Spain before joining a daughter in the USA. Phonexay himself eventually joined them in California in 1986 and still writes to the Mercedarian Brothers, whom he refers to as his 'Spanish Papas'.

Navalcarnero (Madrid)

Navalcarnero is a little village near Madrid where four families were settled. The Ministry of Housing provided them with rented houses and their children attended the village school. Since Navalcarnero is near Madrid, the people in charge of the programme in the Ministry of Labour could visit them often. The parish priest in the village treated them as if they were his own parishioners.

It was a real pleasure to see how quickly the children were integrated into the community and played unproblematically with their Spanish friends. The families, however, did have problems over these years, but no more so than their Spanish neighbours, who, like themselves, were living during difficult times, with loss of work and high levels of unemployment, but none the less in the hopes of a better future.

There had been changes in the families, with new babies, a wedding and two deaths, but the Chinese were now part of the neighbourhood, with their good and bad days, like everybody else. The children were growing up and in the spring of 1986 a great feast was held in Navalcarnero. The parish priest was celebrating the 25th anniversary of his priesthood and everyone was in the church for the event. The real event, however, was that seven people were going to be christened and, apart from a baby girl of 6 months whose father was a Catholic, the others, aged 7 to 18, were all doing it because they really wanted to.

It was touching on this occasion to see the whole village participating in the ceremony and congratulating the newly christened, to see their happy, joyful faces. Now that some years have elapsed and brought many more happy memories, the earlier moments of loneliness, misunderstanding and insecurity are generally things of the past.

Communication and Coordination

When the settlement programme was being implemented, a close relationship was maintained between the programme's coordinators in the Ministry of Labour and the Red Cross, CARITAS and various other departments, local authorities, voluntary agencies and private people who offered their help.

Social workers from the Red Cross and CARITAS helped in areas such as child care, the distribution of clothing, activities related to maintaining cleanliness and hygiene, and the organising of vaccinations and various other clinical tests.

The permanent staff in the Ministry of Labour found out what jobs were available, interviewed prospective employers and organised the refugees' work permits. They also kept in touch with the local authorities which, with help wherever possible from the voluntary agencies, were carrying out the same activities at a provincial level. They were also in charge of regrouping the families, the children's schooling, any legal proceedings that might have to be dealt with in public offices, the organisation of training courses for adults, as well as various other helpful activities, such as visiting the families in their homes or accompanying them to the doctor.

The Spanish Red Cross and CARITAS helped mostly in the cases of the displaced families which had left the provinces of initial settlement and were provisionally being housed in hostels in Madrid. These agencies also covered all the expenses of travelling and lodging when the families were eventually resettled in other provinces. The Red Cross also provided medical assistance, where necessary, extra money for babies and help in claiming various statutory rights, such as old age pensions.

The Ministry of Justice provided a great deal of help to the programme through the work of its Children's Protection Council, which included all refugee children under the age of 16 in its own programmes. The non-governmental agency, CEAR, made its contribution towards settling the families by providing financial aid to those wanting to start up their own business. And, in addition to paying the travelling expenses from the transit centres to Spain, the UNHCR supplied the translators cum social workers who stayed in the residences with the refugees and other members of the programme and who also later visited the families in the provinces to make an assessment of how they were settling down.

On 12 December 1980, the Spanish government passed a resolution to establish an inter–ministerial commission, which would be responsible for organising the settlement of refugees from south–east Asia. This commission took over the duties and responsibilities of the committee within the Ministry of Foreign Affairs, which until then had informally been in charge. The commission was made up of representatives from the Ministries of Education, Culture, Justice, and Public Works, from the municipalities, and from the Red Cross and CARITAS.

By October 1981, all the refugees had already been distributed in the provinces and were generally adapting to their new lives, although they still needed help from time to time, especially with employment or housing problems. At this point, the Secretary of State for Foreign Affairs, the director of the Red Cross and personnel from the Ministry of Health & Social Security and the Ministry of Labour, realising that the full integration of the refugees would take a long time, decided between themselves that the Red Cross and other voluntary agencies should take over complete responsibility for the refugees, for they already had the appropriate infrastructure with which to do so. An agreement was then drafted whereby the organisation and direction of the settlement of those families not yet fully integrated was transfered to the voluntary agencies.

The previous committee ended its activities and transferred all the relevant documents to the Red Cross, but its members continued to help until all pending matters had been solved.

Conclusion

At present (1988) the Asian refugees have been living in Spain for eight years. No doubt there are still families with problems, but many of these problems would be the same as those faced by any other Spanish family. The Red Cross continues to help in exceptional circumstances, as, for example, when a woman with small children becomes widowed. Some of the families are running small business, others are fully integrated into their jobs and several have left Spain to regroup with relatives in other countries. The children, as always, have fitted in without any problems.

The introduction of a new asylum law has brought the refugees better protection, new centres and offices, and some additional programmes.

As I mentioned earlier, many of the problems were probably due to the small number of Asian refugees in Spain which made it difficult for them to develop any group consciousness. The refugees had to get ahead by their own efforts without the support of their own people.

5 REFUGEES AND NATIONAL POLICIES: THE NORWEGIAN CASE

Ragnar Naess

The Norwegian Setting

With its four and a half million inhabitants, Norway today enjoys a more favourable economic position than most other European countries in terms of its standard of living and low levels of debt and unemployment. This is mainly due to the development of the oil industry since 1974, cheap energy even before the oil boom through hydro-electricity and, in the post-war years until 1970, one of the largest merchant navies in the world. The merchant navy is, however, now being restructured after the crisis of the early 1980s – through international registering and the use of cheap third-world crews.

Until the late 1970s, unemployment was well below 1 per cent. It only increased to an average of 2 per cent, although with considerable regional variations, in the years between 1982 and 1984.

Norway is a young country in that it regained its independence, lost since the 1300s, relatively recently. Although it achieved independence from Denmark after the Napoleonic wars, it was shortly thereafter forced into a union with Sweden which lasted until 1905. It was ruled by social democratic governments from 1935 until 1963 and, after a few brief interludes of right-wing government, is still so governed today. It continues to rely on roughly the same type of state welfare policies, which emphasise central economic planning more than most other West European countries.

Immigration

Because of Norway's late industrial development and heavy reliance on imported labour in the years 1900–1920, there was very little immigration until the late 1960s. Even this, however, was low in relation to the population at large (from less than 1 per cent to 2.5 per cent of the population in the years 1970–85) and in terms of actual numbers.

In the years prior to the First World War, Norway received approximately 2,000 Jewish refugees, after the war some 500–600 refugees and displaced persons and, after 1956, approximately 2,000 Hungarian refugees.

Immigration from the third world rose sharply after 1970, especially from Pakistan, Turkey, Morocco and India. In 1975, following Britain's 1971 immigration legislation and the 1973 closure of Germany's borders (as well as those of other countries), Pakistani immigrants arrived in Norway. Not long after, Norway also closed its doors to most new immigrants other than family members of those already in the country and workers with skills that were particularly scarce in Norway. Intra-Scandinavian immigration (from Sweden, Denmark, Finland and Iceland) has, however, been free since 1953 and continues to be so.

From 1974 onwards, Norway received a number of Chilean refugees and, from 1976 onwards, a number of Vietnamese boat-people who were being picked up at sea by Norwegian vessels. There were enough of this last group to make the Vietnamese the second largest group of Asians in Norway (5,500 in July 1986).

Until 1986, Norway operated with an annual quota of 600 refugees received through the UNHCR. After that date the quota was raised to 1,000, although in actual practice the number is usually somewhat less. The annual number of asylum-seekers rose from a little more than 100 in the early 1980s, to 895 in 1985, 2,700 in 1986 and just under 9,000 in 1987.

Resettlement Programmes

In the early post-war years the resettlement of refugees admitted by the Aliens Office was entrusted to the Council for Refugees (*Flyktningerådet*), which had wide (although vaguely specified) authority to deal with all matters relating to the resettlement of refugees. The legal basis of its authority was derived from Norway's social security legislation.

After a significant increase in the numbers of refugees in the late 1970s, most of the work of the then inadequately-staffed and insufficiently backed Council for Refugees was taken over (in 1982) by whatever particular municipality received the refugees. This takeover followed what some observers regarded as the Council's virtual collapse. A newly-established Refugee Secretariat, operating as a branch of the Ministry of Health & Social Security, was to assume responsibility for the first six months of the refugees' stay in the country, after which the municipal authorities were supposed to take over.

This new system is destined to be replaced by yet another from 1988 onwards, when everything relating to refugees and immigrants will be dealt with by the Directorate of Aliens located in the Ministry of Labour & Local Administration (*Kommunal – og Arbeidsdepartementet*).

The main reason for the change is the recognition that it is virtually impossible to implement national policies with respect to immigrants and refugees when the responsibility is shared by several different government offices and there is no strong central executive authority. Under the new arrangement, refugees will be resettled by five regional offices operating under the Directorate of Aliens, whose local offices will negotiate with the various municipalities about the reception of refugees.

Interplay of Organisations & Professions

The reception and resettlement of refugees is a complex institutional process involving a number of central and local organisations and several different professions. But beyond this level of analysis, the reception of refugees raises deeper questions of human values, questions that are subject to peculiarities and contradictions of their own.

At the institutional level, the increase in the number of refugees and asylum-seekers in the 1980s created two fairly serious problems - the relationship between central government and the local authorities, and the relationship between the state and the Norwegian Red Cross.

First, the state and local authorities. Under the 1982 reorganisation of resettlement schemes, local municipalities were supposed to assume responsibility for the refugees after six months, but by 1984 it had become clear that the system was not working as it should. At this time, a debate emerged about the performances of both the Refugee Secretariat and the municipalities. Initially, complaints came from the refugees themselves, who insisted that, among other grievances, they were being inadequately informed about how their cases were going and that they had to wait for excessively long periods of time before their resettlement procedures were implemented.

In 1987, the Refugee Secretariat itself accused the municipalities of refusing to accept refugees in sufficient numbers to assure a regular flow. The Norwegian Association of Local Authorities responded by publishing the various contracts it had made with the state since 1982, in which the state had agreed to take on a number of responsibilities concerning the provision of interpreters and other resettlement issues, but which it had never in fact carried out. Despite this controversy, by late 1987 more than 4,000 asylum-seekers had been placed in municipalities, which indicates a greater level of cooperation than might at first have been anticipated.

Cooperation for settlement has, however, raised questions about the position of refugees in the labour market. For a number of years it has been agreed policy to disperse refugees by resettling them in small groups in the smaller municipalities, despite the research evidence that refugees tend to recluster in the big cities to create viable communities. This tendency could be offset if there were genuine success in creating jobs outside the major growth areas. The arrival of refugees in the smaller municipalities has in fact provided a major test of the feasibility of Norway's regional policies, a test that so far has not been positively assessed.

The State Apparatus & the Red Cross

A second institutional conflict arose in respect of the role of the Red Cross. In 1984 or 1985, the President of the Norwegian Red Cross approached the Refugee Secretariat asking for help in dealing with the increasing number of refugees.

As early as 1982, clear warnings had been given to the Secretariat that their apparatus needed strengthening. By 1986 it was apparent that the

Secretariat was incapable of processing all the asylum-seekers itself. In August of that year, the Red Cross was approached and asked to find lodging for some 20 asylum-seekers. This was the beginning of an operation that has led to the establishment of an Asylum-seeker Department within the Red Cross with a budget of some 500 million Norwegian Kroner, 400 employees and close to 50 units of accommodation. The Department has a current workload of 2,500-3000 asylum-seekers. By April 1988, the Red Cross had received 5,500 asylum-seekers, over half the total arriving in Norway since the organisation's involvement two years earlier.

The role of the Red Cross can best be described as providing a buffer, which conceals the inability of the state apparatus to deal with the issue of asylum-seekers itself. The relationship has not, however, proved a happy one. The Red Cross emphasises that it consented to the job because of its humanitarian goals, but complains that the State never respected the independent status of the organisation, and proceeded to treat the Red Cross as any subordinate office.

Moreover, since the autumn of 1987, the Red Cross has pressed for precise plans as to the future of the organisation in a refugee reception apparatus run by the state. As a signal that its cooperation could not be taken for granted, the Red Cross closed down its biggest accommodation facility, the ship 'Friedtjof Nansen'. New state-run regional units for the reception of asylum-seekers are slowly being put into operation during 1988 as is the building of 3000 houses. However, it is estimated that the Red Cross's involvement will have to continue for at least another two years, until these facilities come on stream.

The Principles of Acceptance and Rejection

Beneath the level of institutional conflict is a more fundamental area of controversy over the actual criteria for receiving refugees and asylum-seekers. Following the rise in the numbers of asylum-seekers from 1986 onwards, border police and the Aliens Office increasingly adopted a policy of returning incoming asylum-seekers to their places of departure, with only the most cursory of investigations into their cases, instead of the thorough examination of each individual case as stipulated by the law.

In 1985, a number of Iranian asylum-seekers were returned to Turkey without due consideration. Indignant reports in the press led to a concession by the Aliens Office, who contacted the asylum-seekers in Turkey and allowed their admission to Norway. Two years later, a number of asylum-seekers went on hunger strike demanding that each of their cases be treated adequately. The Norwegian church intervened and talks took place between the authorities, the church and the hunger strikers. These resulted in certain concessions being made to the church and to hunger strikers' demands.

A similar controversy arose over the issue of refugees having their applications turned down but being admitted on humanitarian grounds. In March 1987, the government decided to tighten up on the reception of asylum-seekers, with the explanation that only 25 per cent of those who arrived as asylum-seekers qualified as 'real' refugees. In May 1988 the Ministry of Justice repeated a claim that a high proportion of asylum-seekers were not 'real refugees'. Of the 1988 applications for asylum, the number of 'real refugees' is said to be below 10 per cent.

Such statements by officials do not properly take account of the difficulties faced by applicants like the Iranians leaving because of the Iran-Iraq war. Though this is a 'non-economic reason' it is still not covered by the 1951 Convention, at least as it is interpreted in Norway today. The official statements thus function to label all asylum-seekers as people who pose as something very definite - 'real refugees' - while in fact being 'not real refugees'. While undertaking research project for the Norwegian Alliance of Local Municipalities, I had ample opportunity to witness the damage being done by this type of statement.

The issue was taken up in the election for municipal offices and the right-wing Progressive Party's increased share of the vote (from 5.5 per cent to 11 per cent) is attributed to its vehement attack on the government for admitting too many so-called 'labour migrants' and its underhand use of xenophobic slogans in the pre-election campaign. In a poll conducted in May 1988, the Progressive Party notched up support of 21 per cent of the respondents. While not using the same type of language as its Danish sister party, who openly present 'Muslim immigrants' as a threat to the Danish people, the Progressive Party has been using roundabout xenophobic slogans in their campaigns for some years.

It is almost certain that the Norwegian authorities will introduce policies to stop the influx of asylum-seekers and there is little likelihood of the quotas for refugees being raised. It remains to be seen whether or not the newly-organised resettlement policies will work more effectively than the former procedures.

Institutional Racism

The issue of institutional racism has been a subject of debate in Norway since the beginning of the 1980s. The Norwegian Research Fund for the Humanities (NAVF) has launched a research programme to ascertain whether the authorities' methods of control and immigration policies are biased against people from the third world.

The first immigration documents, which date back to the early 1970s, show a complete acceptance of Scandinavian immigrants because of their close cultural ties and geographical proximity.

The findings (Bo 1986) indicate that the 1975 immigration clampdown discriminates against third world immigration in so far as immigrants from third world countries are only allowed to enter as family members, whereas a steady stream of Europeans can continue to come into the country under the rules exempting skilled personnel.

Content analyses of policy documents from the 1970s indicate the presence of an underlying philosophy that it is undesirable to mix people from different cultural backgrounds. This is expressed in the syllogism that because Norwegians tend to react to the more 'foreign looking' immigrants, the state has a particular responsibility to control this type of immigration. What is not explicitly said is that the popular mood – actually the mood of that part of the population that is less informed and less liberally–inclined is given precedence over the interests of people looking for a better future in Norway. The consequent policy is not well–defined, but none the less operates with an all–embracing central idea that Norwegian animosity should not be pitched against third world immigration.

This policy is in line with what, in Britain, has been referred to as the 'new racism' (Barker 1981). In this work, Barker argues that a fundamental redefinition of the concept of racism as a social phenomenon is required since the discrediting of 'old racism' after the Second World War. The new racism does not argue that people belonging to different *races* are *inferior* (such is the language of old racism), but that people belonging to *different cultures* should be kept apart. Central to the new racism is a normative implication about people's 'feelings' about foreigners – this results in a form of philosophical naturalism.

In Norway restrictions on immigration were defended in at least four ways: (i) one had to close the borders in order to make an effort to improve the lot of the immigrants (an effort that never materialised); (ii) that to be able to migrate to a given country was not a human right; (iii) that the third world immigrants admitted to Norway would enjoy rights on par with the host populations; and (iv) that some rough parity had been established between the number of third world immigrants admitted compared to the number of Western 'experts' in third world countries.

To insist that immigration of a certain category of people poses a threat, and that this threat is lessened in proportion to the numbers admitted, has direct implications for the various types of discrimination found within the country. For example, in my fieldwork, covering five firms employing third world immigrants, one of the firms had a maximum quota of 10 per cent in this category. The management defended this quota with reference to official immigration policies, policies that also seemed to be enunciated by the trade union.

Other indirect effects of the state's immigration policy include cases of firms, local communities or apartment associations (*borettslag*) refusing to take in or admit more black immigrants on the grounds that it causes 'problems' or that one must not take in 'too many'. Complaints of racial discrimination are answered by the argument that if Norway cannot tolerate more that 5 per cent of black immigrants, why should a firm, a neighbourhood or any other 'Norwegian space' be expected to tolerate more (Naess 1986).

'Racism' as a Label

It can be argued that the policies and practices described above are 'racist' because, directly or indirectly, they aim to prevent non–Europeans from entering Norway and that their negative effects on the lives of black immigrants in Norway are considerable. However, conventional wisdom and official statements often argue that racist doctrines and racial discrimination are manifestations only of particular views about biology and heredity. This view prevails, despite common definitions given in encyclopedias, which quite often define the concepts more broadly to include discrimination on the basis of ethnicity and nationality.

This preoccupation with narrowing down the use of the word 'race' to its literal meaning is a characteristic feature of the Norwegian debate. Apart from its semantic interest, which is of little intrinsic importance as such, the narrow usage is probably mainly an attempt to minimise the chances of finding any obvious similarities in attitudes, societal processes or government policies with South Africa, Nazi Germany or the American South before 1964, when discussing 'racial discrimination' in Norway.

It is further said that the term 'racism' tends to halt serious debate. People who feel targeted by this expression get offended and angry. Many commentators have responded by avoiding the term 'racist' – a decision that testifies to a form of loyalty between Europeans. More specifically, it is a form of loyalty that insists that any debate presupposes rational and moral actors. To talk about 'racism' is not only bad manners, it excludes your opponent from rational discourse by implying that he or she is outside the common moral community.

Conclusion

As the Norwegian style of avoidance may be part of the problem rather than part of a solution, it may be useful, by way of a conclusion, to try to establish whether the emerging European policies towards third world refugees and immigrants can be deemed 'racist' or not. An analysis that defines aspects of post-war Norwegian (and European) immigration policies as expressions of racial discrimination and that perceives European countries as 'racial orders', in the sense that Greenberg (1981) does, must accept as its starting point the idea that comparisons can be made between so-called 'racial orders'. That there will be important differences, for example, in the degree to which basic human rights are violated, is hardly surprising, but there may also be fruitful possibilities of comparison, especially of the processes leading to the interdependence of popular reactions and government policies.

A generalised model of the institutionalisation of racism involves at least five features: (i) ethnically distinct groups with the capacity to maintain their social boundaries; (ii) 'migration', both physically and socially, so that groups have a partly shared and partly separate life space, culturally economically and socially; (iii) formal laws or less formal rules deployed to foster exclusionary practices; (iv) the dominant group excluding the subordinate group(s) from better-paid positions in the labour market; (v) the initial spheres of exclusion widening to encompass other areas of social behaviour and human encounter.

This last feature may take the form, in popular parlance, of 'blocking the loopholes'. Two examples from Norwegian immigration practice can be cited. The suspicion that immigrants were entering Norway through arranged marriages, led to the formation of a special police squad for the control of such marriages. Residence permits could be revoked if a couple divorced within two years. Other 'loopholes' have been stricter control of students, tourists and refugees, who are depicted as labour migrants in disguise. In respect of asylum-seekers, the Norwegian authorities propose following British legislation in making travel firms and airline companies responsible for checking travel documents. The White Paper announcing such legislation made it clear that the purpose of selective visas and the use of travel agencies is to *prevent* people reaching the Norwegian borders, so that the strength of their asylum applications need not be judged.

Whether or not the claims of the refugees are genuine is irrelevant to the argument I am advancing here. The point I wish to emphasise is that policies have operated to progressively poison the bridges of common values between the Norwegian population on the one hand, and third world peoples on the other, as these bridges are one after another made the object of official suspicion. The link between immigration policy and refugee policy is that the former prepared the way for the latter, by defining third world immigrants as a problem.

Norway's own position is somewhat paradoxical in that it vehemently defends human rights on international platforms and ranks among the world's largest per capita donors of development aid, yet adopts such stringent measures to curb immigration and to prevent asylum-seekers from entering the country, that it has been criticised by the UNHCR. Norway admits relatively fewer immigrants, asylum-seeker and refugees than most other countries despite its better economic circumstances and a labour shortage almost as severe as that of the late 1960s.

Political moves, particularly from the left, but notably also from the church, are being made to rectify this situation. A difficult problem is one of how to separate the issue of the moral obligation to receive refugees, which not even Norway's small neo-Nazi groups have challenged, from the question, which is inevitably raised alongside it, of how many refugees (in actual numbers) should be accepted into the country.

It has been pointed out that no moral theory can be justified without a set of presuppositions about what is socially viable. The prospect of a small nation drowning in refugees may partly explain the Norwegian public's willingness to swallow the Progressive Party's campaign, the like of which Norway has not experienced since the ultra-right movements of the 1930s. All Norwegians agree that they have a moral obligation, but also seem to feel that in their case definite restrictions are necessary.

The alternative to this blinkered view is to retheorise the role of the European nation-state in the wake of the post-war patterns of migration. Even if abolition is not called for, the implicit idea of the state as a culturally-defined group of people must necessarily go. To insist that the binding force that makes up a society is a common culture and not the rule of law, irrespective of race, religion, sex, and nationality, spells racism in today's context, and must go. An alternative view of the state, is to see it simply as a geographically-defined institution for the production and allocation of policies, not as a natural space for culturally–defined groups. Eventually, border controls must be tied to neutral criteria, in order to reverse the process of defining the majority of the world's people as a problem.

6 RESETTLING REFUGEES FROM VIETNAM IN BIRMINGHAM

Danièle Joly

Introduction

Until 1979, only a relatively small number of refugees from Vietnam[1] had been admitted to Britain. In 1975, 99 children were airlifted from Saigon to Britain. By 1978 Britain had admitted 300 Vietnamese refugees mostly rescued by British ships, to which the 345 boat refugees rescued by the ship, Well Park, were added. In 1979 numbers changed dramatically since, following appeals by the UNHCR and a United Nations conference in Geneva (July 1979), Britain announced its intention to take 10,000 refugees from Hong Kong. Later more people were allowed in because of an extended definition of family reunion. Today there are altogether between 18,000 and 20,000 Vietnamese refugees in Britain.

The work of reception and resettlement was not carried out by the British government. Voluntary agencies have had this responsibility. Initially these agencies were Ockenden Venture[2] and the British Council for Aid to Refugees (BCAR). The BCAR thereafter merged with the Standing Conference for Aid to Refugee to form the British Refugee Council (BRC) in 1981. Save the Children Fund (SCF) and Refugee Action (from the time of its creation in 1981) also undertook resettlement work.

As regards the first arrivals, reception and resettlement were in no way planned or coordinated but happened on an ad hoc basis according to the resources and initiatives of the voluntary agencies. However, in October 1979, at the initiative of the Home Office, the Joint Committee for Refugees from Vietnam (JCRV) was set up consisting of representatives of each agency with a secretariat of Home Office staff, which operated until 1981. Within this structure each voluntary agency retained its operational independence. The JCRV had the responsibility of coordinating the programme, and providing a forum for policy discussion. In practice it seems that coordination and exchange of experience were minimal. Nevertheless some rationalisation of the work took place on the basis of territorial division. There was still no division of labour between the agencies along the line of tasks to be accomplished: all the agencies were involved in selection, reception and settlement, but they agreed to divide the country geographically among themselves.

Today the BRC plays a central coordinating role replacing the JCRV. Refugee Action looks after resettlement in Scotland, Yorkshire, the South and East Midlands; Ockenden Venture takes care of the West Midlands, Manchester, Merseyside, the North East of England and the North West, including North Wales. Each agency resettles the people who come to the reception centres for which it is responsible. They all receive funding from the Home Office and the extension of the 'Vietnamese programme' led to the awarding of £280,000 to cover the years 1984-1987 – later prolonged until 1988. The current programme is due to be terminated in 1988 and an evaluation is at present taking place with a view to putting forward a new proposal.

The British government has failed to come up with any well-defined policy on the resettlement of refugees from Vietnam. The only aspect of resettlement which partly resulted from a clear government preference has been the dispersal policy of the early 1980s. Altogether the British government has simply handed over the tasks of resettlement to refugee agencies.

There is a dearth of research on Vietnamese refugees in Britain.[3] The little that does exist tends to concentrate on the background of people from Vietnam (Dalglish 1980; Pearson 1982) on the reception centres which initially hosted them (Brand 1981; Mougne 1985) and on health questions (Lam 1980; Phillips and Pearson 1981).

A few reports and articles look at aspects of resettlement (Edholm et al. 1983) and the work of refugee agencies (Levin 1981). Most of the documents written on these two themes consist of unpublished reports from refugee agencies themselves. No publication is available as yet on the community from Vietnam in Britain and the response of local authorities to refugees from Vietnam has been little researched (Finlay and Reynolds 1985).

This study focuses on a particular area, Birmingham, which displays several interesting features. It is now the headquarters of Ockenden Venture (UK). It has a substantial population from Vietnam, the second largest after London, but the largest within a single local authority. Birmingham City Council has begun to show some interest in refugee issues, and a regional refugee council is being set up. The data have been gathered through interviews with voluntary agency workers, local authority officers, health workers and refugee organisation representatives; and the study of relevant archives.

Ockenden Venture in Birmingham: History

'The story of Birmingham is really the start of the story' said Barrie Denton about Ockenden Venture's involvement in the resettlement of people from Vietnam.

Ockenden Venture's work in the refugee field had begun as early as 1951, with the care, resettlement and education of refugee children coming from post-war displaced persons camps in Europe. Ockenden Venture was registered as a charity in 1955 and raised funds from private donations, continuing its work with refugees in Britain and abroad. In 1971 it opened an orphanage in Saigon and when the 'Daily Mail airlift' brought over the children from Saigon, in 1975, it took care of them. Ockenden Venture's ethic has promoted the notion of voluntary help and support and this is illustrated by its early resettlement operations in the Midlands.

When the first boat rescues took place in 1976, the BCAR agreed to help if the Home office paid its costs; as a consequence, it opened a reception centre in Parsons Green in London. Joyce Pearce, chairperson of Ockenden Venture, agreed to organise the resettlement from the BCAR reception centre. Barrie Denton, then assistant chief probation officer in Birmingham, took on the responsibility of resettling the families from Vietnam. Through contacts with housing associations, he obtained houses for these families; other aspects of resettlement were catered for by personal contacts and community volunteers. Barrie Denton describes it as follows:

> I called our friends to a supper party and I said 'we have got a problem'. ... One said, 'I used to be a teacher, I will deal with education', another one said 'my firm has a wagon, we can move furniture', another one said 'I'll make some curtains'. There was no planning in that activity but later, that became very much a pattern of how we operated and they began to be called support groups.

At that stage, all the resettlement work was done by volunteers. The first three families moved into housing association accommodation on 6 July 1977. The process continued, more families arriving, two or three at a time. Until 1978, the work was done in Birmingham by Ockenden Venture alone and on the same basis of low key personal contacts. Ockenden Venture opened its first reception centre in Barmouth, from then on doing both reception and resettlement work.

The media dramatised the issue of the 'boat people' with the arrival of the Well Park, a British registered ship, carrying 345 refugees from Vietnam. The scale and style of the operation were thus altered. The SCF was brought into resettlement work. The publicity and the lack of coordination between agencies led to competition as all the agencies operated throughout Britain, performing similar tasks. All over the country different people were contacting local authorities. Birmingham for a while was not exclusively served by Ockenden Venture as the SCF had opened a reception centre in Solihull and had resettled some of the occupants in Birmingham, having obtained accommodation from the housing department. The actual territorial demarcation between agencies was finalised in 1982. Barrie Denton continued to do the work on his own but became a full-time Ockenden Venture worker, with a secretary, based in Birmingham from May 1978; from October 1979, the Home Office refunded the cost of his salary.

The first Vietnamese programme awarding substantial Home Office funding to voluntary agencies began in 1979 because of the dramatic increase in the numbers of refugees from Vietnam. The JCRV was also formed at this time. Ockenden Venture appointed its first additional worker. It is worth noting that the title of this post was 'support group liaison officer', rather than 'social worker', thus serving to further the community support outlook which had been previously established. In the following months and years Ockenden Venture became a massive organisation with 26 reception centres and over 200 staff, including housing and resettlement officers. Its operational headquarters were situated in Birmingham.

Four main features provided the guidelines for the resettlement work.

(1) Local community support. The idea of a volunteer support group is more characteristic of Ockenden Venture than of any other agency and guided many decisions; for instance, in his first six months of paid employment with Ockenden Venture, Barrie Denton had as one of his responsibilities to investigate whether there was a need to set up a housing association for Vietnamese refugees. The report on this issue concluded that a housing association was undesirable; Denton's opinion was that the refugees should not be separated from the community but be made part of it. It was therefore deemed better to appeal to housing associations and local authorities. This decision tied in well with the concept of a support group, for relying on support groups also meant calling upon the help of a variety of voluntary agencies, including churches and the Rotary Club, as well as gaining the interest of individuals, both in the community and in organisations, such as housing associations or the housing departments of local authorities. The publicity given to the 'boat people' stimulated the volunteer spirit in that it prompted a lot of spontaneous offers for help. By 1983 there were 18 support groups in Birmingham; these had initially been recruited from organisations such as the Rotary Club, the Round Table and the churches.

(2) The concept of dispersal. It was both Ockenden Venture and government policy to encourage dispersal. Ockenden Venture's approach was to avoid sudden saturation of an area to prevent what has come to be called 'compassion fatigue' (a phrase coined in the United States). As the provision of housing was in no way mandatory, but depended on the goodwill of housing associations or local authorities', and as welfare care relied on the local support of volunteers, Ockenden Venture wanted to ensure that the local community could cope with the numbers settled in one single area. 'Not less than four, not more than ten'; those were the magic numbers of families cited by Barrie Denton for any single town. The idea was to aim for dispersed clusters, thus also ensuring that a family would not be resettled in complete isolation.

(3) Family reunion. From early on family connections were taken into account in the geographical distribution of accommodation. This also entailed the attempt to arrange for relatives arriving later to be housed near their family.

(4) A centralised and regional structure. Ockenden Venture resettlement officers were based outside the reception centres and operated on a regional basis, a patch system; they were directly accountable to the Birmingham office, unlike the SCF whose resettlement work was done from each reception centre. Ockenden Venture's formula offered the advantage of providing support in the area of resettlement after people had left the reception camp. Ockenden Venture's usual practice was to provide support for between 15 and 18 months after the families were resettled, at which time a formal letter was sent to them informing them that this period was over. It was presumed that they should by then be able to seek advice from citizens advice bureaux or social services with the help of local contacts they should have made.

The government wanted all the reception centres vacated by the end of 1982. However, when the JCRV was disbanded in 1982 it was clear that the resettlement of Vietnamese families was not over. The agencies succeeded in obtaining funding for a further two years to take care of the early stages of the actual resettlement. This leads us onto the present era.

Current Situation: Staffing and Main Characteristics

The Ockenden Venture office in Birmingham employs workers from the West Midlands to look after resettlement in this region, but in while Birmingham is the headquarters of Ockenden Venture (UK), the Birmingham office also employs national workers. The office occupies two terraced houses in Lozells, which is an area with a fairly substantial Vietnamese population. Its staff consists of the director of Ockenden Venture (UK), the team leader of Ockenden Venture's regional workers, two regional workers, one part-time housing officer (who has held the post for seven years, thus providing continuity and experience), one family reunion administrator, one supervisor of the community programme workers, two resettlement officers for the West Midlands, eight clerical and administrative workers and one cleaner.

Although Ockenden Venture has retained most of its main features, it is worth noting that there have been some modifications and changes in its style of work and staffing.

- Whereas Ockenden Venture had initially refused the BRC's offer of MSC (Manpower Services Commission) posts, since 1985 it has been employing eight MSC community programme workers. It was felt on reflection that the increased workforce would be useful and that it would provide an opportunity for Vietnamese people to gain experience and training. Unfortunately, funding for training was seriously delayed and only eventually materialised after repeated complaints. MSC workers are employed for one year, at £3.50 an hour for 18 hours a week. Only one out of the six workers, the supervisor, is full time and she has twice obtained a six-month extension of her contract. One of the main drawbacks of these posts is that they never last for longer than a year, which means that it is impossible for the workers to gain any real accumulation of experience.

– Ockenden Venture has increased its staff of Vietnamese workers (there are now six) of different backgrounds, from North and South Vietnam, Chinese and Vietnamese, men as well as women. This allows for translating and interpreting work to be done whenever necessary.

– The end of the dispersal policy. The dispersal policy was abandoned because it was a failure, which the government and all the agencies now acknowledge. Families settled in small towns or villages moved out of their own accord to London or Birmingham, even if this meant living in overcrowded accommodation or paying exorbitant rents to a private landlord. It became increasingly obvious to Ockenden Venture's housing officers that there was no point in dispersing the families, for they would simply leave their first place of settlement and need further help being rehoused in a place of their own choice. Although the JCRV was critical of the dispersal policy as far back as 1982, it was only eventually abandoned in 1984. Since then the housing officer, who interviews people in the reception centres, has been giving the Vietnamese far more choice in the decision about where they will eventually settle. If they know anything about Britain, their first choice is generally London and their second choice Birmingham. If they do not know Britain at all, they ask for a big town with a large Vietnamese community, which again points to London, Birmingham or Manchester. The trend is thus for the grouping of Vietnamese populations in a few large centres.

– The emphasis on support groups has given way to a new approach to 'community development'. The position of 'support group liaison officer' has been replaced by that of a 'regional worker', for whom addressing statutory agencies is considered one of the more important of their responsibilities.

– The trend towards greater professionalism, developing nationally and previously seen in other agencies, has now been extended to Ockenden Venture. Its regional workers are being appointed from the ranks of qualified community workers and their team leader has had 15 years of experience working with the Danish Refugee Council. In addition, the programme incorporates additional training for regional workers. Although the low salaries and underqualified or undertrained staff (the negative aspects of working with volunteers) still present problems, discussions are now taking place between the employees and the executive committee to see if salary levels can be raised and pension schemes, which do not exist for Ockenden Venture's workers, introduced.

- The regional structure has become generalised; already firmly established in Ockenden Venture previously, it now obtains in other agencies.

The 'Post-Settlement Programme'

The last three of the above-mentioned features came from a programme financed by the Home Office between 1984 and 1987 and were developed as a result of the initiative shown by new Ockenden Venture workers.

The new programme was based on a joint proposal put forward by the BRC, Refugee Action and Ockenden Venture, to each of which it had become evident that the task of satisfactorily settling the Vietnamese populations would be far from complete in 1984. The agencies met in September 1983 to discuss the issue and to put forward a proposal. There were various aspects to this proposal,[4] which extended the notion of 'community development', but basically it set out 'to identify and mobilise the appropriate resources at a local and regional level which, with guidance and support from a national resource network in specialised subject areas, will be able to provide the services most needed by the Vietnamese to enable them to stand on their own feet'.[5] The £580,000 budget in the original bid was reduced by more than half and a sum of £280,000 granted. This funded the new posts created to implement the proposed plan. For Ockenden Venture it has meant the appointment of eight regional workers (two in Birmingham, two in Manchester, two in Merseyside and two in the North East) and one team leader. Refugee action has its own regional workers. The BRC staff for this programme includes a host community development officer and an education and training officer.

According to this proposal, the regional workers' responsibilities are to assess the needs of the Vietnamese population and to identify a 'community action network', which is somewhat vaguely defined in the proposal as to be able to 'mobilise assistance within the local statutory and voluntary system'. Their other tasks include setting up a regional refugee council, an interpreting service and a 'crisis intervention service', with a view that the latter will eventually be taken over by the statutory services. Furthermore, regional workers are supposed to ensure that 'influential' local people become involved in the areas of housing, education, health and employment, while at the same time encouraging the refugees to form their own community organisations. On the one hand, therefore, 'community development' means sensitising and mobilising the host community (including its statutory services), whereas on the other hand it also means helping the refugee community to organise itself.

In the West Midlands, the regional organisers divide the work between themselves on a mainly geographical basis, but also according to spheres of interest. For example, one of the regional workers is responsible for Birmingham as a whole, whereas the other pays special attention to health and social security problems throughout the Midlands. Regional workers are not supposed to do resettlement work as such and, at least in

Birmingham and the West Midlands, they do not need to because the Birmingham office already employs two settlement officers. While the settlement officers check housing conditions, ensure that the various facilities are installed when the families move in, introduce the families to their neighbours, register them with a doctor, enrol their children in a school, help with DHSS and welfare benefits, give advice on language classes and help to solve a myriad of immediate problems, the regional workers in Birmingham can at least concentrate on the tasks set out in the programme. As one regional worker put it, 'If Birmingham didn't have case workers, I would never do community development work, judging by the people who come through this door'.

Ockenden Venture, voluntary and statutory agencies and the Vietnamese Community

The nature of Ockenden Venture's work is such that it fosters a natural relationship with the Vietnamese population. In addition to its initial resettlement work, it offers an advice service to which clients regularly come for help with different kinds of problems. These may range from guidance in filling in forms they do not understand to counselling in the event of marital breakdown or intergenerational conflicts. Some of the links Ockenden Venture has developed with other voluntary and statutory agencies have grown from its resettlement tasks, from, for example, Ockenden Venture's housing officer having to communicate on a regular basis with the Birmingham city housing department or other housing associations. Others arise from the frequent contacts the resettlement workers have to make with schools, doctors and social security.

In the early stages of the Vietnamese arrivals, Ockenden Venture launched an appeal to several voluntary bodies, churches and charities for financial help and towards the setting up of support groups. Statutory bodies themselves call upon Ockenden Venture when they have to deal with Vietnamese people who often cannot speak English; such bodies include the DHSS, hospitals, doctors, schools, the social services, the police and the housing department.

In addition, a number of students (often psychiatric student nurses) have come to Ockenden Venture for information in connection with their work; several social work students from Westhill College have expressed an interest in doing their placement there. These contacts are, however, usually made on an individual basis.

It was only really with the introduction of the most recent programme that initiatives have been directed specifically towards statutory bodies and some voluntary organisations. The list of such bodies contacted by regional workers is impressive. Most were approached as part of a systematic exercise to raise awareness of the existence and needs of the Vietnamese population in Birmingham and to try to persuade these organisations to adopt measures to meet these needs. Regional workers' reports contain repeated comments on the agencies' continuing ignorance about refugees and their corresponding lack of resources, for example, an absence of any translating or interpreting facilities and no multilingual workers.[6]

One report stressed what the regional worker saw as an important goal: 'We still need to push for positive employment practice by statutory departments in order that Vietnamese workers can be strategically placed within local authorities to provide an effective service to the community.'[7] All the main Birmingham City Council departments were approached, as were several educational establishments and community and youth centres. Some of the departments were contacted with a view to solving a specific and immediate problem. The Recreation & Community Services Department, for instance, was asked to help with an international Vietnamese scout encounter, an event which attracted a certain amount of publicity and drew attention to these young people's needs.

A great number of voluntary bodies were also contacted, the main ones being the Community Relations Council (which until then had shown no interest in the refugee groups), the YMCA Chinese association and Christian Aid.

The most notable achievements so far are fourfold:

First, some communication has been established with the Midlands Vietnamese Community Association (MVCA); at first through cooperation with the employment officer and, later, in meetings with the association's chairman. Although these contacts are limited, they do represent some kind of breakthrough, for, until then, the MVCA had refused to acknowledge Ockenden Venture's existence.

Second, the support given to the scout group resulted in a highly successful event attended by 50 Vietnamese scouts from Berlin. The assistant director of youth and community development in Birmingham's Recreation & Community Services Department, the Birmingham Association of Youth Clubs, an area youth officer and an area community development officer all participated. The Race Relations Unit offered to help, the assistance of various councillors was sought and even local scout groups began to show an interest. All this activity resulted in a gift of £300 from the Race Relations Unit, the loan of equipment and the use of Sheldon Country Park for an international scout camp in August 1986. Even the more senior scout authorities, the scout secretary and the scouting district commissioner, showed signs of moving away from their rather unhelpful initial response, which had been hostile to the idea of a Vietnamese scout group carrying out its activities in the Vietnamese language.

Third, an article on the work of Ockenden Venture and on the objectives of its latest programme was placed in the Birmingham Voluntary Service Council's journal of January/February 1986. The article proved fruitful, for it led to closer cooperation between Ockenden Venture and the Midlands Area Housing Association, which, incidentally, subsequently employed a Vietnamese housing officer and set up a special meeting with its Vietnamese tenants. It would seem that this kind of publicity could fruitfully be extended to a number of other organisations and individuals.

Fourth, in addition to the initiatives mentioned above, there has been a major breakthrough as far as Birmingham city is concerned, particularly with its social services and housing departments and the Race Relations Unit. Moreover, a regional refugee council is in the process of being organised. Collaboration between the BRC's host community development officer, Ockenden Venture's regional workers and the Race Relations Unit has played a determining role in this development.

Room for Improvement

More problematic areas have been the DHSS, the educational authorities and the Manpower Services Commission, where, despite constant efforts on the part of Ockenden Venture workers, results have been either disappointing or non-existent. The difficulty in relating to the MVCA is a definite drawback, as is Ockenden Venture's lack of involvement with groups such as the Catholic Pastoral Centre and the Buddhist Association.

In the voluntary sector, Ockenden Venture has failed to make any impact on the law centres, the action centres and the citizens advice bureaux.[8]

People from Vietnam in Birmingham: Overview

Birmingham, which after London has the second largest Vietnamese population in Britain and the largest of any single local authority, has seen a steady increase in the number of Vietnamese residents since 1980. The figure rose from 716 in 1982, to 1,157 in 1984 and now, according to Ockenden Venture's latest figures, stands at 1,620 (see Table 6.1 below), although a number of agencies estimate a higher figure of between 1,800 and 2,000. Over half this population is concentrated in two adjacent areas of Birmingham (Handsworth and Lozells) in which the few associations that do exist are also based. Of the 390 families living in Birmingham, 200 are in either Handsworth, Lozells, Hockley, Newtown or Winson Green, all of which are in the inner city and frequently regarded as a single, large, deprived and disadvantaged area. There are slightly more men than women (124.5 men for every 100 women), with about a third of the population being under the age of 19 and about 5 per cent (82 people) over 60.[9] The population from Vietnam is by no means a homogeneous one with a clear distinction existing between the Vietnamese group and those of Chinese origin (between approximately 40 and 60 per cent). There are also differences between people from the North of Vietnam and people from the South, as well as a range of religions, socio-economic backgrounds and levels of education.

Table 6.1: Vietnamese in Birmingham

Area	*Number*	*House-holds*	*Men*	*Women*	*Dependents under 19*	*Dependents over 60*
Aston	109	32	63	46	42	6
Alum Rock	19	4	12	7	9	–
Balsall Heath	15	5	5	10	5	2
City Centre	16	5	11	5	4	1
Edgbaston	59	13	29	30	16	3
Erdington	45	8	23	22	13	4
Handsworth	766	192	420	346	356	40
Lozells	82	20	47	35	42	3
Lozells	31	7	18	13	14	1
Moseley	38	12	28	10	9	1
Ladywood	54	14	32	22	16	3
Northfield	36	7	18	18	16	–
Hockley	14	4	7	7	3	1
Harborne	23	5	12	11	7	2
Nechells	74	17	44	30	40	3
Newtown/ Perry Barr	30	7	16	14	10	3
Quinton/ Selly Oak	35	8	17	18	13	2
Sheldon/Sparkhill/ Sparkbrook	58	11	30	28	16	4
Stechford/Washwood Heath/ Tyseley	50	7	28	22	20	2
Winson Green/ Yardley	66	19	38	28	21	5
Total	**1620**	**397**	**898**	**722**	**672**	**82**

Source: Ockenden Venture Figures

Because people from Vietnam seem to find Birmingham a relatively attractive city (it is said to have better housing and educational facilities than other places and to offer a certain amount of job outlets), the Vietnamese population there is stable and possibly even growing. Because of Birmingham's multicultural population, a number of language classes are provided and there is also a substantial network of public transport. Newcomers are also attracted to Birmingham's 'China-town', which offers a wide range of exotic products, especially foodstuffs. There are two Chinese supermarkets in the city centre, which seem to have been responsive to the needs of their Vietnamese customers in that they have extended their range of ingredients to cover specifically Vietnamese tastes, including fish sauce imported from France. The Vietnamese tend to wear European clothes in Britain, for they find the flimsy long tunic and trousers traditionally worn in Vietnam unsuitable for the English climate.

There are, however, a number of problems. Less than a quarter of the adults speak English and even fewer (20 per cent) have jobs. Domestic difficulties arise when the man of the house receives welfare benefits, thereby losing the status and respect traditionally accorded to a breadwinner (Lam 1980: 254–5). Agency workers have noted how frequently quite serious intergenerational conflicts occur in Vietnamese families within the first decade of their resettlement in Birmingham.

Having looked at some of the characteristics of the Vietnamese population in Birmingham, I would now like to turn to the role and character of some of their associations and their relationship with statutory and voluntary bodies.

The MVCA

The MVCA, which is now a well-established advice centre in Birmingham, was first set up in 1982 and turned into an advice centre in 1983. It received some assistance from the Church of England Children's Society which allowed it the use of a room in a house in Handsworth. When it obtained some funding of its own, it rented two rooms and a kitchen on the same premises for £1,500 per year. The MVCA has received continuous funding since 1983, first with a £2,500 grant from the Cadbury Trust, then, in 1984, with £3,500 from the West Midlands County Council and again, in 1985, with a £12,000 grant from the same source, but this time specifically earmarked for an employment development project. Thereafter the responsibility for funding was taken over by the Birmingham City Council. The MVCA was initially run by volunteers, but, since June 1985, has received a number of posts from the MSC community programme.

Its current staff comprises one employment development officer, as well as six part-time and three full-time workers (of which there is one coordinator, two advice leaders, four advice assistants, one visiting leader and two visiting assistants), all of whom are working on the community programme. The MVCA is administered by a steering committee of six members assisted by a board of advisers and 20 area representatives.

According to the chairman, the MVCA's main objectives are 'to bring the Vietnamese together to preserve our national culture' and, as he puts it, 'to help those who have difficulties in arriving here'. In this way the centre helps about 10 clients per day. Many of these require assistance with sorting out their DHSS or housing benefits, others need help with family reunions and some merely come for general advice. Between 17 November 1986 and March 1987, 429 people used the centre and, according to its records, it managed to obtain £1,000 in benefit grants and £1,500 in insurance claims on behalf of its clients during this period.[10]

The MVCA is also called upon whenever a translator or interpreter is needed in the Vietnamese language. (None of the members of staff are, however, fluent in Chinese.) The employment development officer is consulted mostly by young people about training and employment.

Besides giving advice, the MVCA also organises a number of other activities, including children's Vietnamese language classes (on Saturdays), a Vietnamese pop group, which was formed in 1984 and which has performed for other Vietnamese communities in the UK, as well as at the MVCA's annual general meeting and at Tet festivals, a Vietnamese classical music band (which plays Vietnamese traditional music) and a summer play scheme held in August and attended by about 100 children (mostly between five and ten years of age) who are taught to read and write in Vietnamese and taken on day trips. In 1985 and 1986, the play scheme was given a £500 grant by the Recreation & Community Services Department. The MVCA's youth group, however, has been rather ineffective and its scouts are now operating independently of the association.

The MVCA's chairman has also arranged to hold Vietnamese language classes (at the Brass House language centre) and lectures on Vietnam's history and culture, which are attended by policemen, English service providers and any other interested individuals. Three of the MVCA's leaders are examiners in Vietnamese for the London Chamber of Commerce & Industry.

Relationship with Other Bodies

The MCVA's relationship with Ockenden Venture is practically non-existent, or at best strained, which causes a certain amount of discomfort to institutions, groups or organisations wishing to work with both. The MCVA has links with several of the departments of the Birmingham City Council, which sometimes uses its interpreting services. Its information sheet claims that it liaises with 'the police force, schools, the social services, health centres, doctors, dentists and other agencies'. It has also, as I mentioned above, cooperated with Brass House and participated in the first seminar on the Vietnamese organised by the Race Relations Unit on 1 May 1986. Since then its relationship with the Race Relations Unit has become more distant, partly because of the Race Relations Unit's collaboration with Ockenden Venture. The MVCA is a member of the BRC and, on 9 October 1986, was elected on to its executive council, where it serves along with three other refugee organisations.

Although its cultural functions are limited, the MCVA (which claims to be the first Vietnamese advice centre in the UK) obviously has a useful role to play in organising summer programmes and language classes, as the demand and attendance testify. It is also used as a referral point by the providers of various services, although this aspect of its work has not yet been fully exploited.

The MCVA has had particularly effective and well organised relationships with funding bodies, with the Birmingham County Council, the Birmingham City Council and the MSC all presenting convincing proposals and annual reports. When additional support was needed on one occasion to further a grant application, it successfully turned to the MP, Jeff Rooker.

There are, however, certain problems which impair the service provided and restrict the range of the association's clients. One such problem, which is exacerbated by an MSC ruling which stipulates that new workers have to be employed every 12 months, is that MSC workers are poorly trained and inexperienced. A second is that the MVCA's members are predominantly South Vietnamese (rather than a balanced mix of Vietnamese, Chinese, Southerners and Northerners), which in turn creates a similar distortion in the advice centre's clientele. There are very few Northern or Chinese Vietnamese coming for advice, in the case of the North Vietnamese possibly because they find the MVCA's staunch anti-communism offensive. The MVCA's leadership is actively engaged in trying to bring about the political 'liberation' of Vietnam and has links with like-minded political organisations in the United States and Canada. It also holds an annual commemoration of the fall of Saigon (on 30 April 1975). The Chinese Vietnamese are also reluctant to come forward because there is nobody on the staff who is of Chinese origin and/or who speaks Cantonese.

Finally, young people feel they have insufficient say in how the association is run and that it fails to serve their needs. The traditional respect due to elders in Vietnam is standing in the way of any changes being made in the leadership and in the association's orientation.

The Catholic Pastoral Centre

The Catholic Pastoral Centre is an extremely important focus of attention for the Vietnamese population. A Vietnamese priest, Father Peter Diem, played a central role in establishing this centre and is himself very influential among the Vietnamese Catholic community. He came to England in 1980 and, finding it difficult to establish himself in London, where he had spent eight months among members of the Catholic establishment, he decided to come to Birmingham, where he had been well received and where two priests (one of whom was based in St Francis's Church in Handsworth) had offered him accommodation and financial help. He chose the Handsworth option because of the large number of Vietnamese families living nearby. Since then Father Peter has been actively and effectively bringing together the Catholic community. This has involved visiting at least 20 reception centres (the parish paid for some of his travelling expenses) and assisting new settlers by accompanying them on visits to doctors or the DHSS offices and helping them to find houses.

In the early years between 1980 and 1982, Father Peter, who was trying to encourage Vietnamese Catholics to come to Birmingham, ran into some difficulties with Ockenden Venture, which was trying to implement a dispersal policy. These differences have since been resolved and Birmingham now boasts a large and close-knit Catholic community of 650 people. This has been increased not only by arrivals from the reception camps, but also by conversions from Buddhism. Between 1981 and 1987 Father Peter baptised over 100 people. His readiness to extend his practical help to the non-Catholic Vietnamese population has undoubtedly contributed to this process. The Catholic Pastoral Centre consists of two houses, of which one is used as a home for large families. Two more Vietnamese priests have been ordained (in 1985 and 1986) and the three of them now also service other Catholic communities in the UK.

Father Peter and the Catholic Pastoral Centre not only seek to maintain and extend the religious character and social cohesion of this community, but they also try to preserve its Vietnamese identity. Father Peter emphasised this point when he said, 'I encourage children to speak Vietnamese at home and English outside. They should become English by nationality but remain Vietnamese by culture'. A mass in Vietnamese is held in St Francis's Church each Sunday which has a regular attendance of between 300 and 400 people. Every Thursday and Saturday, about 100 children aged between eight and fifteen come to study the catechism in Vietnamese (along with other elements of the Vietnamese language and culture) and a Vietnamese choir of 40 children has been practising regularly since 1981. There are also other cultural activities based at the Catholic Pastoral Centre, including two Vietnamese dance groups (for children over 10 and under 10 years old).

In actively trying to preserve the Catholic faith among his parishioners, Father Peter encourages parents to send their children to Catholic schools. So far, there are about 45 Vietnamese children at St Francis's primary school in Handsworth, about 20 at St Claire's primary school and 40 at St John Wall's secondary school. Father Peter keeps in close contact with these schools, thereby providing a point of reference in the event of any queries or possible problems.

Another feature about the Catholic community from Vietnam is that it is largely composed of Vietnamese, for very few Chinese Vietnamese are Catholics and, as Father Peter put it, 'Chinese Buddhists are much more difficult to convert'. Almost all the Catholics are also from South Vietnam.

The Catholic Pastoral Centre in general and Father Peter in particular maintain regular contact with a number of British institutions. Apart from Catholic and other churches, these include the various schools, Handsworth Technical College, the Steward Centre, some hospitals (especially the Dudley Road and All Saints hospitals), various social services departments and the Birmingham City Council's Race Relations Unit. The priests appear to have a reasonable relationship with the MVCA, to whom they refer people in need of practical advice.

The Catholic Pastoral Centre is definitely an important focus for a large section of people from Vietnam and could be used to greater effect to introduce the Vietnamese population to the appropriate British statutory and voluntary bodies.

The Buddhist Association

The Buddhists also have a gathering place but they are far less organised than the Catholics. Although there are between 200 and 300 Buddhists in Birmingham altogether, the city has neither a Vietnamese Buddhist temple nor a resident monk. There is a Buddhist temple in Birmingham, but Buddhists from Vietnam rarely use it, preferring rather to get together in a family house (called a pagoda)[11] in Handsworth for collective meditation and worship. A monk is invited from London for the celebrations of the main Buddhist festivals and usually addresses between 15 and 20 faithful. Parts of the ceremonies are in the Vietnamese language. Occasionally a monk is invited from France or the United States to teach the Buddhist doctrine and to talk about other topics, such as life overseas. All the families tend to know one another in this essentially Vietnamese community and some may even travel abroad for particular festivals. One family, for instance, has been twice to Bordeaux (in France) for the annual international children's celebration, the full moon festival. It is unusual, however, for the Buddhist Chinese from Vietnam to take part in these gatherings, for they usually prefer to worship at home.

There appears to be no antagonism at all between Buddhists and Catholics. This is confirmed both by Father Peter (who lived with a Buddhist family when he arrived in London) and by devout Buddhists.

The Lamson Guides & Scouts Troop

The Lamson Guides & Scouts Troop was formed in Birmingham in 1985 by experienced scout leaders, who had been involved in the scouting movement in Vietnam since 1968 and who regarded this as the best way of bringing Vietnamese children together to teach them Vietnamese customs and their mother tongue. The members of the troop, which includes boys and girls, Christians and Buddhists, are all from South Vietnam. The Lamson Guides & Scouts Troop comprises a guide company of 15 girls (aged between 7 and 24) and a group of 25 boy scouts. Since 1986, it has been producing a quarterly magazine in Vietnamese, the *Huong-Dao Vietnam*, which is circulated to Vietnamese scouts in Germany, France and other European countries. All its activities are conducted in the Vietnamese language, with traditional Vietnamese folk and camping songs being sung around the camp fire.

To start with, there were some serious practical problems for they had no sponsors to help finance the operation and no premises in which to hold their activities. Moreover, their members were unfamiliar with the British system and did not know how to gain permission to use the parks and other public facilities, for in Vietnam such applications are unnecessary. So far they have been using the MVCA yard and a meeting room in St Francis's Church, but they wish to be independent of the MCVA and Catholic Pastoral Centre and are trying to find other meeting places.

The Lamson Guides & Scouts Troop, which is registered with the scout movement in Britain and takes part in its activities, also participates in international events along with other Vietnamese scout and guide groups in Europe, Canada, the United States and Australia.

From this brief study of Birmingham's Vietnamese community, it has become apparent that the sections of the population most in need of assistance are the old, the young and some of the women. The MVCA had at one time tried to launch a women's association, but was unsuccessful. Ockenden Venture and the social services have together set up a women's group and a luncheon club for the elderly, but these groups have only recently been set up and are still unable to stand on their own feet. A few young people have approached Ockenden Venture for assistance in obtaining premises for a youth club. A Vietnamese take-away restaurant, the Saigon Garden, has been opened in Lozells; a Vietnamese disco was also opened, but with rather short-lived success.

An impressive number of magazines is published in Vietnamese, mostly in London. These include *Noi San*, published by the Vietnamese Cultural Society, *Bantin Newsletter*, by the London-based Vietnam Refugee National Council, *Viet-Bao*, by the London Vietnamese Association, a women's magazine, a Buddhist magazine and a young people's magazine. From Birmingham, the Lamson Guides & Scouts Troop publishes a magazine and the Catholic Pastoral Centre publishes a monthly, entitled *Song*.

These associations only, however, serve some sections of the Vietnamese population in Britain. These do not include people from North Vietnam or those of Chinese origin.

The Race Relations Unit

The Race Relations Unit (or to be more specific, the Race Relations & Equal Opportunities Unit) is a local authority department which has taken a considerable interest in refugees in general and in people from Vietnam in particular. It has played an important part in raising issues connected with refugees and in obtaining responses from other departments. When, for example, the Association of Metropolitan Authorities (AMA) wrote to the chief executive about hosting a West Midlands seminar on the Vietnamese, the request was passed on to the Race Relations Unit. People working in refugee agencies have noticed that local authorities tend to relegate refugee matters to bodies dealing with race and ethnic relations, even if the ethnic or race relations officers concerned are not particularly interested in refugees as such and prefer to concentrate on the problems of the larger Asian or Afro-Caribbean minorities.

The Race Relations Unit in Birmingham, however, has been different in this respect and has responded to approaches from the AMA, the BRC and Ockenden Venture by attending to refugee issues along with its other responsibilities. It believes that refugees, as a disadvantaged group, also suffer from discrimination, especially since most of them come from the third world and in any case are frequently black. The Race Relations Unit had already sponsored a report on the Chinese and Vietnamese in Birmingham and was given permission by the Race Relations Committee to organise a seminar on the Vietnamese in the West Midlands (in cooperation with the BRC and Ockenden Venture). This meeting, which took place on 1 May 1986, was attended by approximately 100 people, including representatives from all the local authority departments in Birmingham and from other authorities in the West Midlands, as well as representatives from various voluntary organisations, refugee agencies and Vietnamese groups. The MVCA's chairman was one of the speakers and afterwards the Race Relations Unit circulated the meeting's report and recommendations to the other departments. The Race Relations Unit then scheduled a meeting with department representatives for a year later (it was held on 20 May 1987) so that the departments' reactions could be reported and evaluated.

Most of the departments, particularly social services and housing, have been responsive to the recommendations that were made. The department of education, however, despite the interest taken by some of its staff, has been noticeably elusive and unresponsive at the managerial and administrative levels. According to Rose Austen, who has taken on the responsibility for this area of work, the difficulty is to obtain the attendance and cooperation of officers who are both interested in the issue and high enough in the management structure to be able to do something about it. The invitation to the meeting of 20 May 1987 was an attempt to elicit this kind of cooperation. All the chief officers were asked to send a representative to contribute to the meeting in two ways. First, to report on the measures the department was taking to address the needs of Vietnamese refugees in Birmingham and, second, to participate in discussions with Vietnamese representatives at the meeting to identify strategies which could be pursued by the department in conjunction with voluntary agencies and with the Vietnamese themselves.

Through its interest in the Vietnamese residents, the Race Relations Unit decided to broaden its scope of action and, in conjunction with Ockenden Venture, to organise a conference entitled 'Towards the Setting up of a Regional Refugee Council'. This was held on 25 February 1987 and was attended by about 85 people, including local authority and voluntary organisation representatives. In all ten refugee groups were represented. Among the issues discussed were the status of refugees, the policy of return, resettlement, employment and training, education, social welfare, health and culture. A representative from the Scottish Refugee Council and from a Newcastle citizens advice bureau, both of whom were doing work for refugees, were called upon and recommendations from the standing conference of local and regional authorities of Europe were consulted. A provisional steering group composed of 14 refugee representatives was made responsible for drafting a proposed constitution, to be discussed and ratified at a subsequent conference for which the Race Relations Unit had already been promised the funding. The Midland Refugee Council was formally constituted at this conference, which took place on 11 December 1987.

It is not so much that refugees are a contentious issue in the Birmingham City Council, but rather that they are a non-issue and that there is no council policy for them. The strategy for action, as the officer in charge explained, is (1) to raise the profile of the issue; (2) to encourage and assist the setting up of a refugee pressure group. A single group bringing together refugees from all origins is seen as the best solution, for it would be representative of a substantial number of people as opposed to separate national refugee groups; and (3) to obtain responses from local authority departments. One member of the Race Relations Unit added that such initiatives might produce a climate in which a policy on refugee issues could actually be developed, or at least should be worked towards, but thought that it would be difficult to achieve unless the ground had been laid for it, as nothing ever happens quickly in local government.

The Race Relations Unit did make a number of recommendations but, although these developments appeared promising, they have been thrown into jeopardy by the abolition of the Race Relations Unit, as a separate entity, in May 1987.

Conclusion

Now that a decade has passed since the first group from Vietnam arrived in Britain, it is possible to assess the process of settlement with sufficient hindsight to be of benefit to present and future groups of refugees.

The Vietnamese experience has shown that the dispersal policy is a failure and that front-end loading funding is unsatisfactory. It has also shown that it is unfair to place the entire onus of the resettlement work on voluntary agencies. The burden is too great and these agencies are now trying to involve the statutory bodies in refugee issues. The positive commitment of the Race Relations Unit to the issue of refugees (before its dismantlement in May 1987) resulted from such an effort.

We have seen that community associations do have a useful role to play for particular sections of the Vietnamese population. It is worth noting that all these associations actively promote Vietnamese culture and identity in addition to fulfilling their specific function as advice centre, religious gathering, youth group or whatever. We have also seen, however, that large sections of this population, namely the Vietnamese of Chinese origin, the Northerners, women and most young people, do not participate in the activities of the existing associations. It remains to be seen whether or not the Midlands Refugee Council, which is meant to include all groups of refugees, will be more successful in this respect.

Notes

1. Refugees from Vietnam are frequently called Vietnamese refugees. In reality a substantial number of these refugees are of Chinese origin and do not refer to themselves as Vietnamese.
2. Discussed in further detail below.
3. For details on the literature pertaining to refugees in Britain, see D Joly, Refugees in Britain: an annotated bibliography. Centre for Research in Ethnic Relations, Bibliography No.9, 1988.

4. According to the Ockenden Venture representative the proposal comprised very different things because it was the result of a compromise between the three agencies.
5. Joint Operation Committee, Vietnamese programme (1984–87), Proposal to the Home Office.
6. Vietnamese programme evaluation, Regional officer's report forms, David Crisfield, 1 July – 30 September 1986, West Midlands.
7. Vietnamese programme evaluation, Regional officer's report forms, David Crisfield, 1 April 1986 – 30 June 1986, West Midlands.
8. In Newcastle, a citizens' advice bureau is collaborating with a refugee association to provide specialised advice to refugees.
9. Figures gathered by Ockenden Venture.
10. Report from the employment development officer, 17 November, 31 March 1987.
11. A pagoda is a place of worship in a private family house, as distinct from a temple dedicated to worship only and occupied by a monk.

7 REFUGEES & TURKISH MIGRANTS IN WEST BERLIN

Jochen Blaschke

Community Formation

As Fredrik Barth (1969) points out, ethnic boundaries are both an expression and a mechanism of social interaction. Nevertheless, a distinction still needs to be drawn between social interaction *per se* and the processes of ethnic ascription. This distinction should be emphasised for both methodological and theoretical reasons. On the one hand, in the process of social interaction, the culturally specific symbolic complexes with which particular populations are ascribed crystalise to establish ethnic milieux, the individual elements (but not intrinsic unities) of which can be subjected to social analysis (Blaschke 1965). On the other hand, established social science methodologies are well attuned to studying the social structures and ideas that arise through interactions, both within bounded social groups and among them.

The data on refugees in the Turkish migrant community of Berlin are a peripheral outcome of a research project on political aspects of immigrant community formations in Great Britain and the Federal Republic of Germany. This project, which started in 1982, has been particularly concerned with a comparison between the Pakistani and Kashmiri communities in Birmingham and the Turkish and Kurdish communities in Berlin. The methodological approach, which involved continuous field visits, concentrated on interviewing political activists in the communities and experts on both the immigrant and autochthonous populations. The content of these rather loosely-structured interviews related to the institutionalisation of religious and political organisations and world views.

In this chapter I concentrate on the formation of social organisations and their interactions, a phenomenon I shall call the 'formation of the ethnic community'. I am not concerned here with the universality of ethnic community formation processes in so far as these apply to all immigrant communities. Such a question would require comparative studies of various immigrant groups, especially those that appear assimilated. Instead, this chapter specifically discusses one particular type of migrant (refugees) in the formation of a particular ethnic community (the Turkish community) in West Berlin (Blaschke 1988)

Community Development

The Turkish community in West Berlin developed in three phases. In the first phase, which lasted from 1961 until labour immigration was stopped in 1973, contract labourers, the so-called *Gastarbeiter*, arrived in the city. They found some 500 Turks already there, who had come to Berlin as students or businessmen, or who were the descendants of an earlier wave of refugees to Germany following the breakdown of the Ottoman Empire. Only occasionally did the 'older' group assist the new immigrants. Members of an Islamic sect who had been forced to leave Turkey began to build a religious network, some of the students attempted to politicise the Turkish workers and a few businessmen recruited some of the new workers for their activities.

The Turkish workers in Berlin were housed in barracks in compounds built by their employers, with the constant reminder that when their contracts ended they would be forced to return to their homeland. All of them considered the situation temporary. The *Arbeiterwohlfahrt*, one of the three largest German welfare institutions, looked after their interests. Otherwise they experienced no local orientation beyond some union concerns (Thränhardt 1984).

Political discussions were mostly confined to the students, but the workers did occasionally discuss problems in the homeland and, in exceptional cases, employment policies.

Refugees from Turkey had begun to arrive in West Germany by the early 1960s. A military coup d'état was a decisive factor, even in this early flight, which came mainly from Kurdish national and religious circles. These individuals tended to enrol in a study programme or find employment as contract workers. Despite their actual political status, very few gained formal recognition as 'refugees' (Blaschke & Ammann 1988).

Only with the second wave of immigration, which started around 1970 and ended in the early 1980s, when much greater numbers of refugees entered West Germany, did the situation change. This phase was characterised by the reuniting of nuclear and extended families and by the refugees' dissatisfaction with their status as contract workers. Although this second wave of immigration is strongly correlated with the coup d'état of 12 March 1971, it should be understood as part of a chain of migration which was interrupted only when the employment of foreigners was stopped in 1973. Since then only the rights of family members and official recognition as a refugee offer immigration opportunities. In addition, a few functionaries (such as the occasional imam, teacher, or artist) received special entry permits.

Most of the refugees who fled from the 1971 coup did so because they were suspected of socialist or separatist activities. In 1973, Turkey experienced limited democratisation and the numbers of refugees fell, but two years before the military coup of 12 September 1980, there was yet another wave, this time even larger, which reached its highpoint in the winter of 1980 (Kardam 1988).

In the early 1970s Turkish refugees and students, with their various social democratic, communist, separatist or Turkish nationalist ideologies, began to establish a network of workers' groups, many of which also served as meeting places for Muslim sects banned in Turkey. In this new setting the refugees were particularly active, both as propagandists for their various ideologies and as middlemen in the new organisations. The year 1980 marks the beginning of the third phase in the formation of a Turkish community in Berlin.

This third phase was characterised by the maturation of Turkish organisations and ideologies. The groundwork had been laid in the 1970s when, with the help of an articulate elite (which emerged from the second wave of immigration), most of the organisations were founded. The now established community began to organise and act in the political sphere and to develop internal differentiation.

During the course of 1980, new kinds of Turkish associations were formed in Berlin, among which were two political organisations especially set up to present the interests of a united Turkish 'community' to the German public and to German institutions. Although it was rather stretching a point to present themselves as a united community, this did signal the beginnings of a new ideology. Turkish politicians in the community ceased to imitate the political discourses of politicians in the Republic of Turkey and, instead, began to formulate their own interests as representatives of an immigrant community. Moreover, the Islamic associations began to struggle for recognition as acknowledged religious bodies in Germany. Until then, they (especially the Muslim societies) had directed all their political energies towards Turkey itself. This was for them an important struggle because West Germany only recognises Christian and Jewish congregations as religious bodies and only recognised bodies can receive public money (Blaschke 1984).

Since 1980, local Turkish politicians have tended to promote their causes through specifically German channels, such as parliament, councils and committees. Also in 1980, the various Turkish associations came together for the first time to demonstrate against the newly introduced immigration and ethnic relations legislation. At the same time, Turkish journals in Germany started to turn their attentions to Turkish events in Germany rather than to concentrate exclusively on developments in Turkey, as they had done in the past. From 1980 onwards, German politicians were more and more having to accept that the political aspirations of the German Turks had a place in the federal and especially the local political arena.

Since the late 1970s, the Turkish community has established a number of associations which, until then, had either been subsumed in the Turkey-oriented club culture or monopolised by the large charity organisation, *Arbeiterwohlfahrt*, which is officially in charge of Turkish immigrants. The new organisational network includes workers' associations, youth groups, sports clubs, religious organisations attached to various Muslim movements, small business federations and unions.

Almost all the applications for asylum from Turkish citizens arriving in West Germany after 1970 were either based on the applicant's ethnic identity or referred to the Turkish penal code, in which Article 141 states that it is a punishable offence to establish the domination of one social class over others, to eliminate a social class or to disturb the existing social and economic order.

Under Article 142 it is forbidden even to campaign for these goals. These articles had been taken over from the penal code of fascist Italy in 1936 and extended (in 1938) to include even peaceful attempts to reach the named goals. During two separate periods, from 1961 to 1971 and from 1974 to 1980, when government in Turkey was more or less legitimate, these articles were modified to apply only to the use of violence (Kardam 1988).

After 1980, these laws mainly affected Kurdish nationalists, fundamentalist or orthodox Muslims and socialist union or party activists, although individual members of opposition parties, or of the various political movements the government either tolerated or terrorised, were also affected and fled. As a result there are a considerable number of Turks in West Germany who were persecuted on the basis of simple party membership. It is the refugees from this group who have been principally responsible for the political agitation (mainly confined to the student body) and for the left's political fragmentation within the Turkish community in Berlin. They have also played an important part in founding the Turkish press organisations in West Germany and have set up most of the Turkish bookstores.

They have become union spokesmen, writers, publishers and cultural leaders. Others, especially the second generation who have successfully integrated themselves through the German educational system, express their social commitment through supporting the activities of women's groups and other grassroots organisations.

Kurdish Refugees

Refugees from the Turkish part of Kurdistan are also affected by Articles 141 and 142 of the Turkish penal code (Schneider 1988). In addition, the accusation of separatism (and in Turkey anyone openly expressing Kurdish individuality is guilty of separatism) is sufficient ground for arrest and persecution. In certain circumstances even the use of the Kurdish language is enough. Nevertheless, like the members of Turkey's left-wing movements, the Kurds found a sympathic refuge in various organisations in West Germany.

Although exact statistics are unavailable, from rough approximations based on regional participation in the emigration movements to Germany between 1961 and 1973, it seems as if between 20 and 40 per cent of all the Turkish immigrants in West Germany are Kurdish, or, in other words, approximately 40,000 of the estimated 120,000 Turks living in Berlin. Kurds from Iraq, Iran and Syria, although insignificant in terms of numbers, also play an important part in the various Kurdish associations (Blaschke & Amann 1988).

Given the large numbers involved, it is hardly surprising that nearly all refugees from Kurdistan have friends or relatives eager to integrate them into their network of social relations. Kurdish refugees occupy a whole range of positions in the various Kurdish parties and associations that have sprung up since the days when the old nationalist guard formed the

European Kurdish Student Union and a few functionaries immigrated to Germany as workers.

Even the students in the first Kurdish association (the Association of Kurdish Students in Europe) arrived as refugees. Most of them, however, were the children of the landed gentry who studied socialism at European universities and, through this experience, developed a nationalist ideology; the Kurdish nationalist movement in Turkey has direct roots in this student group. The most important association, though, was the Kurdish Students' Society of Europe (KSSE), from which many leaders of the Kurdish national movement arose.

This close link between socialist and nationalist ideological elements was also manifest in the organisational zeal of Kurdish migrant labour, especially in the newer associations which came into being in the late 1960s and early 1970s as Kurdish unionists and socialists separated themselves from their Turkish counterparts and agitated among their fellow Kurdish/Turkish immigrants. In confidential interviews the middlemen of leftist Kurdish groups regularly admit to having once been student activists and refugees. Nevertheless, it is important to differentiate here between the various 'refugee' statuses; many migrant labourers from eastern Turkey had political motives for immigrating but, until 1973, the methods of achieving foreign employment made a formal application for political asylum unnecessary.

The successive waves of refugees fleeing from Turkey's political crises after 1978 radically altered the character of Kurdish associations in the Turkish community. A number of previously active organisations now no longer existed. The socio-political front of Kurdish nationalism had moved to the homeland, with Kurdish associations in Germany being oriented specifically to that region. This reorientation, which began in the early 1970s when Mustaffa Barzani became leader of the Kurdish war of independence in the Near East, was soon reinforced by the removal of Kurds from Iraq, by the Islamic revolution in Iran and by the Gulf War.

Kurds who are active in West Germany (and most of them, as I noted earlier, are refugees) have recently, besides lending their support to Kurdish national aspirations in the homeland, been trying to help Kurds within West Germany as well. As a result, a large number of social and community facilities have been organised, including women's groups, youth clubs, language classes, small printing facilities and neighbourhood cafes. These stand in stark contrast to the limited support the state agencies (comprising the Red Cross, the *Arbeiterwohlfahrt* and, to a lesser degree, the Evangelical Church) have been prepared to offer. Here again the new wave of independent associations demonstrates the continuing potential of activist refugees and students.

The Kurdish community in West Germany, particularly in Berlin, has its roots in the kind of Kurdish nationalism of exile represented and promoted by students and refugees. This has changed over time as different groups of refugees and Turkish migrant labourers jostle for positions in exile and as political events unfold in the Middle East.

Yezidi Refugees

The Yezidi are a small religious minority from the Kurdish-speaking parts of Turkey who first came to West Germany as migrant labourers. Since the end of the 1970s, however, they have been coming as political refugees and struggling for recognition as a politically-persecuted group (Blaschke & Hasso 1988).

Most Yezidis arriving in Germany come from Turkey. A few come from Iraq or Syria and generally receive asylum as members of Kurdish resistance movements. At present there are between 5,000 and 7,000 Yezidis, representing about 600 families, living in West Germany and West Berlin. Most live in the west of the country, especially around Emmerich am Rhein and in the area from Celle to Hanover, where they came as migrant labourers in the 1970s. Between 10 and 15 per cent have official refugee status, an additional 30 per cent have applied for such status and the rest have residence permits as migrant workers. Many of those applying for refugee status live in special barracks and are virtually cut off from their fellow Yezidi in surrounding residential areas.

As the victims of direct or indirect persecution in their homeland, few Yezidi had any alternative but to emigrate. Even before 1971, they were proportionally over-represented among Turkish migrant labourers and were more likely to be 'political refugees' than *gastarbeiter*. As the first link in a chain, they established a social network which made immigration possible even after the employment clampdown of 1973.

Not only did this network try to bring all Yezidis together in a single association so that they were better placed to argue for asylum as a group, but it also attempted to revive religious traditions that had either disappeared or developed differentially in isolated villages. In other words, it could be argued that exile in Germany has given the Yezidi an opportunity, not only to reconstitute themselves as a distinct social and cultural group, but also to conserve and develop their own social traits and traditions.

Unfortunately the German state is still rather unsympathetic to this Yezidi quest for identity and shows no sign of altering its restrictive asylum policies. A few social workers have, however, attempted to support the Yezidi network and there are some lawyers, who benefit professionally from the Yezidi self-help associations, who have shown an interest in helping them establish grounds for legal action.

The introduction of a more repressive immigration policy in West Germany has been decisive in the case of the Yezidi. The employment clampdown in 1973 kept out many Yezidi who would otherwise have easily been able to emigrate to West Germany and would have kept them out altogether had it not been for the efforts of various political organisations, especially the Yezidi self-help associations. With West Germany's borders becoming increasingly difficult (and since 1986 virtually impossible) for foreigners to penetrate, the Yezidi have now lost any further chance of immigrating to Germany. Yezidi already living in the country are mainly concerned about improving their social conditions and ensuring that their applications for asylum are successfully presented before the courts. Since

German courts have in the past handed down conflicting decisions on the asylum applications of individual Yezidi, it is difficult to guess how these will be legally handled in the future. By 1983, however, the administrative courts (and later several of the higher courts) recognised the Yezidi as a persecuted group, with one administrative court in the town of Stade, for example, deciding that the:

> Jeziden are now and for the forseeable future will be subject to political persecution in Turkey. ... The religious groups of the Jeziden in their home villages in the south east of Anatolia are persecuted by Muslims – at the moment continuously – without receiving state protection either individually or as a group. ... The Jeziden are *de facto* without rights.

Putting political pressure on officials to allow families and fellow villagers to be reunited and to visit each other more easily is one way of improving the current plight of Yezidi refugees. Local initiatives to improve the living conditions of Yezidis housed in barracks and compounds are also helpful. Large families, often without any social assistance, are having to do without even simple comsumer goods, such as toys for their children. Moreover, these refugees have come directly from East Anatolia and require social and legal counselling. There is a particularly large amount of work to be done in this area.

The Yezidi often run into difficulties with the courts. This is because, rather than presenting their defence in the Western rationalist tradition, they try to deal with the authorities in an East Anatolian manner, in which success is achieved through submission and corruption. Counselling the Yezidi on their political rights and obligations would appear to be crucial.

Until the end of the 1970s, the Yezidi population in Germany operated through a real or imaginary kinship network, to which most Yezidi exiles were bound by family ties and religious duties. Religious life was kept alive by the occasional visit of a religious official from the Middle East. These religious and social ties were, however, difficult to sustain, especially since many of the religious traditions were unknown or lost and very few people in the community had any theological knowledge. This was because most of the educated Yezidi lived in Syria and Iraq (their religious centre) rather than in Turkey and undertaking a pilgrimship to Iraq was as difficult from exile as it was from Turkey.

Through the development of a Yezidi self–help organisation, set up with support from the immigrant political community, Yezidi refugees were given an opportunity to revive even their religious traditions. The new Yezidi organisation was able to integrate the community and to develop ideas of a self–determined future for its members. Refugees and refugee policy provided the vital pivot for this tiny community's survival.

Conclusion

Because political persecution is one of the few remaining grounds for legal immigration, public attention is drawn to the conditions giving rise to emigration, especially to the political repression in the refugees' home countries. In a great number of individual cases before the German courts and in the media at large, the socio-political conditions leading to immigration are increasingly being brought to the public's attention.

Refugee movements are not simply legitimated forms of economic migration, as the expression 'economic refugee' (a contradiction in terms) suggests. The fact that the refugee must, by definition, have had a confrontation with individual or collective repression in itself shows that such a purely economic analysis is inadequate to encompass the phenomenon. Neither the mass return of Spanish workers to their homeland when Spain became a democracy nor the exodus from Turkey by workers following the military takeover could possibly be explained as economic phenomena.

Chain factors also, however, affect the migration of refugees, for established ethnic communities are important in offering an infrastructure for assimilation. Political refugees have, from the very beginning, played an enormously important role in the political, economic and cultural activities of Turkish ethnic communities. This is partly because these communities have an above average percentage of intellectuals and politically-committed members, representing a small but important elite among the immigrants. In the 1960s many of these were religious leaders; there were even more in the 1970s. The growth in political organisations was principally due to the influence of party cadres forced to flee Turkey. The refugee movement, which began in the 1970s and became very much stronger after the military coup in 1980, included most of the artists and scientists who, together with the students, today represent the main articulating agents in the Turkish community.

Quantitatively, however, most of the immigrants participating in the process of chain migration were members of ethnic minorities. These groups were able to push through their demands for asylum because of the political situation in Turkey. Their immigration led to strong ethnic differentiation within the Turkish community.

Relations are ambivalent between political refugees and migrant labourers within the migrant communities. Although the refugees are important as intellectual representatives for their communities, the rest of the community tends to accept them, not as refugees, but simply as other migrants. The more the refugees seek support within their community, the more difficult their position becomes both individually and in relation to the wider German society, for they have to legitimise their special right to asylum yet behave as if that right did not exist.

8 THE POLITICS OF GENDER IN EXILE: CHILEANS IN GLASGOW

Diana Kay

Introduction

This chapter examines the situation of migration arising from political exile. It forms part of a more extended study of the experiences of Chilean men and women exiled in Britain since the military overthrow of the Allende government in September 1973 (Kay 1987). The data for this study were gathered in a series of in-depth interviews with 36 Chilean men and women (mainly married couples) exiled in Scotland.[1] An underlying theme of the research is the importance of differentiating the exile experience by gender as well as social class. Women's experiences both before and after migration differed from men's in significant ways. However, these differences are submerged when the theoretical framework adopted locates migrants or exiles solely with reference to the public domain of employment and formal political organisation and neglects their location in the private domain of family and kin relations.[2]

Gender and Migration

Since the mid-1970s a growing body of work has emerged stressing the need to differentiate the migration process and experience by gender (International Migration Review 1984). This literature focuses on economic migrations and, in particular, on the movement from the periphery of southern Europe or north Africa to the more advanced industrialised societies of western Europe. As part of this trend there has been a shift away from treating women solely as dependants of male migrants to a focus on women as subjects whose migration is socially and economically significant in its own right. One of the issues singled out for attention has been the impact of migration on the position of women in society. Researchers have addressed the question of whether migration liberates women and, if so, what factors lie behind the change, and how it can be measured. The early literature on women migrants, reviewed by Morokvasic (1983), suffers from a number of weaknesses: women are treated as an undifferentiated category, and their pre-migratory experiences are either ignored or treated in a static and stereotypical fashion – the 'typical' woman migrant is seen as someone from a backward peasant society, outside market relations. Accordingly, the migratory process is conceptualised as a movement from 'traditional' to 'modern'

The literature on exile, while sparser in quantity, does not differ substantially in emphasis. The focus on an undifferentiated political subject and on formal political organisation underpins an often unacknowledged bias towards the experiences of male political refugees. Exiles have commonly been differentiated in terms of social class and/or generation, but much less frequently by gender. The specific experiences of women in exile have only recently begun to be addressed (Oliveira da Costa et al. 1980; Silva-Labarca 1981; Vasquez 1982; Neves-Xavier de Brito 1986). This chapter aims to contribute to filling this gap and to remedying some of the shortcomings of the earlier work on women migrants noted above.

The Chilean Exile

The background to most exile experiences is a society in crisis. In 1973, Chile faced a political crisis of major proportions where contradictions had passed the point of accommodation and where class struggle had escalated into class war. Three years earlier Chile had made world headlines with the first democratically elected marxist president, Salvador Allende. Through a programme of radical structural reforms, the Popular Unity government aimed to transfer power from the foreign and national bourgeoisie to the working class, peasantry and middle classes and to lay the foundations of a future socialist society. Half-way through Allende's elected term of office, the armed forces seized power and initiated widespread repression, leading to the imprisonment, torture and exile of thousands of Popular Unity militants, supporters and their families.

Although it is difficult to put an exact figure on the numbers who left Chile following the coup, there is no doubt that the Chilean exile represents a mass exodus from the country.[3] The scale of the Chilean exile is a reflection both of the popular and potentially revolutionary challenge presented by the Popular Unity movement and of the depth and severity of the repression unleashed by the military junta to contain it. This has resulted in a much wider scattering of exiles than the previous pattern where exile in South America had largely been contained within the continent.[4] It also means that the Chilean exile community extends beyond the political elite to include many rank-and-file socialist sympathisers and supporters.

Clearly any attempt to analyse the exile experience needs to incorporate a class perspective. The Chilean exile community includes former government ministers, high-ranking civil servants, intellectuals and professionals, as well as many routine white collar and manual workers. My sample comprised seven men and four women in professional occupations (high-ranking government officials, university professors), six men and five women who had been engaged in more routine white collar work (generally lower levels of the public administration, education, health and social services), and six male manual workers drawn mainly from those industries newly nationalised or intervened during the Popular Unity government. The experiences of these groups with their widely differing educational levels and location in the social structure differed substantially both before and after exile. Intellectuals and manual workers in my sample pitched their accounts at different levels of theoretical sophistication, of generality and abstraction. The careers of these two groups had also diverged in Chile. Manual workers tended to have primary or incomplete secondary education, early entry into the labour force and involvement with the marxist political parties through trade union struggles at the workplace. The intellectuals, meanwhile, had several years' university education, an involvement with socialist politics as part of a theoretical critique of society and more sporadic involvement with the labour movement and working-class fronts outside the university.

More striking, but less publicly acknowledged within the exile group, were the differences by gender. The widest gender gap in my sample emerged between some highly 'politicised' class-conscious men with a strong sense of collective biography and a group of eight 'privatised' women whose biographies focus on their roles as wives and mothers in a family setting – a difference which becomes all the more remarkable when it is borne in mind that these same men and women are marriage partners. These differences were not just at the level of historical detail but concerned the characterisation of whole epochs, so that what some men identified as the peak experience in their lives (Popular Unity) some women related as a negative and distressing event in theirs. Whilst the men had a socially constructed perspective involving a critique of class society, a vision of an alternative socialist society and a political project to transform one into the other, the privatised women's project was oriented around the well-being of individual family members and public events were judged by their impact on the family group. Whereas the men defined themselves as 'participants' or 'agents' in the revolutionary process, some women had remained aloof from the social struggles taking place outside the home. Any problems they experienced had been articulated as private troubles to be solved individually or to be borne with resignation.

These gender differences in accounting can be related to men's and women's different involvement in public and private domains. Whilst the men's accounts were heavily weighted towards their roles as political militants and wage earners, the women's accounts centred around the family and kinship group. However, the distinction between a male public world and a female private world needs to be refined, for 9 of the 17 women in my sample had worked outside the home in Chile and had participated in political organisations in the public sphere. However, their economic and political participation in Chile before the coup had still differed significantly from men's. Rather than being randomly distributed across the public sphere, certain parts of the economy and polity – often those carrying less prestige – had been mapped out as 'women's work' or 'women's politics', forming a distinct female public sphere. Five Chilean women in my sample had been employed as secretaries, school-teachers, nurses. The exception to this patterning was a group of four highly-qualified professional women (employed, for example, as a physicist, an engineer, an economist and a senior civil servant) where labour shortages had often outweighed gender considerations in recruitment. Even in these cases, however, the women's continuing responsibility for family and home inhibited them from defining themselves, or being defined by others, solely in terms of their public roles. These nine women, who straddle both the public and private spheres, form a distinct category of social actor in this study as 'public–private' women.

Involvement in wage labour in Chile followed a class-related pattern amongst my sample, being confined to women in professional and non-manual occupations. This patterning can be related to wider changes in the structure of demand for female wage labour in Chile (Safa 1977). The expansion of the service sector of the economy and the burgeoning state bureaucracy created jobs for women with a degree of education in clerical work, public administration and the social services. Women from the middle sectors, then, had had jobs to go to, unlike many working class women as the sluggish performance of industry and the capital-intensive pattern of industrialisation had reduced the size of the female proletariat. The economic opportunities for women with few formal qualifications were such as to deter some from seeking work outside the home unless compelled by economic circumstances. Larger families and the articulation of a stronger and cruder version of machismo amongst working-class men reinforced this pattern. This meant that the significance of being female diverged considerably between women from different social classes. Whilst some professional women had been directing teams of men at the workplace during Popular Unity, some housewives had been expressly forbidden from working outside the home by their husbands.

Gender Divisions and Popular Unity

These gender divisions, which are of interest in themselves, take on heightened significance when the socialist beliefs underpinning the Chilean exile community are borne in mind. This brings into focus the wider question of gender inequalities within a socialist movement, and within the Popular Unity movement in particular. Although the Popular Unity programme envisaged widespread changes in class relations in the public sphere, gender relations had not been given equal attention. Compared to the fundamental critique of the public sphere, Popular Unity's proposals for the private sphere were ad hoc and partial: references to women in the programme were few and far between. Together they did not add up to a radically new version of private life.[5] Indeed, it is plausible to argue that bourgeois definitions of the private sphere remained dominant during the Popular Unity period (Chaney 1973).

This marginalisation of gender divisions can partly be explained by the pervasiveness in Latin America of an overt ideology of male superiority known as machismo, but it was also built into the strategy and tactics of the Chilean left. The predominance of a particular form of marxist economic determinism, which assigned priority to the contradiction between capital and labour at the point of production, reduced the question of the family and women's position within it to the status of an ideological effect whose transformation depended upon changes in the economic base. The emphasis given to transforming relations of production in the public sphere had been reinforced by the absence of an autonomous women's movement. Those who argued for the need to broaden the struggle to include issues such as the family, sexuality and personal life were a few lonely voices (Bambirra 1971; 1972).

The downgrading of gender divisions can be further explained by electoral considerations. The left had been hesitant to introduce changes in the private sphere, given the ideological dominance of the right in this area. Popular Unity's one-sided focus on relations of production meant that it lacked a vocabulary for talking to women in the private sphere and that, consequently, the struggle was on far less favourable terms than in the public sphere where it enjoyed organised mass support. This was to have serious political repercussions. As the class struggle deepened in Chile, the bourgeoisie drew upon its privileged rapport with women in the private sphere to regain control of the public domain by turning the mobilisation of women into an important plank of their counter-revolutionary strategy (Mattelart 1976; de los Angeles Crummett 1977).

The absence of a gender critique meant that male-female relations were carried into exile largely unexamined. Exile, by laying bare aspects of gender relations which had been obscured in Chile, disturbed some taken-for-granted notions about men's and women's places and provided the impetus for new insights into gender subordination. Arguably, gender roles have been transformed more in exile than during a period of socialist experimentation, though not exclusively or primarily through contact with the host society.

Public and Private Domains

During periods of accelerated social change both public and private domains undergo quantitative and qualitative change. Within the space of little more than ten years, the Chileans have lived through a period of socialist experimentation and a military dictatorship in their own country and a period of exile abroad in a developed part of the capitalist world. Rather than a fixed and static distinction, the differentiation of public and private spheres needs to be conceptualised as a shifting terrain, whose contours are reshaped through changes in the distribution of power in society. In the Chilean case, the highly politicised and expanded public sphere of the Popular Unity period was very different from the controlled and contracted public sphere of the military junta, as well as from the miniaturised public world which emerged in exile. Likewise, the extended private domain which women had known in Chile was very different from its impoverished and restricted counterpart in exile.

Specific constructions of the public-private distinction reflect a set of power arrangements between social classes and between men and women. The ability to set, police and enforce the public-private boundary reflects the superior power capability of the dominant group in society. Where this group enjoys cultural hegemony, the dominant set of public–private classifications will largely set the horizon of thought and action of subordinate groups so that trespassing is infrequent. However, dominant definitions never go completely uncontested. The boundary between public and private spheres may be the subject of struggle between subordinate groups attempting to reclassify issues, activities or personnel and the dominant group attempting to defuse, co–opt or suppress the challenge. In this case there is a continual process of negotiation around the public–private boundary. In this process previously 'non–political' spheres may be politicised, with implications for the position and status of women in society. One of the underlying purposes of this chapter is to analyse how and when the private domain becomes the focus of political debate and to examine the obstacles to placing gender on the political agenda.

The Heightening of Contradictions in Exile

Exile brought dramatic changes for all categories of actor. For men the overwhelming sensation of exile was one of loss of power. The loss of a valued public role predates exile proper, beginning in Chile with the coup when they had been banished overnight from public life. Exile added a new dimension to this sense of powerlessness. The acquisition of refugee status entails the loss of citizenship and, initially at least, the assumption of a number of dependency roles, such as that of claimant. The loss of power involved on becoming a refugee is often reinforced by the dominant image of refugees as poor helpless creatures, in a desperate plight and without the resources or capacity to fend for themselves, held by the public at large and built into the practices of many refugee assistance programmes.[6] The experience of powerlessness can also be differentiated by class amongst my sample. For many middle–class exiles, this involved the loss of a degree of personal influence and autonomy which they had known in their working lives in Chile. For manual workers, it was expressed in terms of the loss of collective power which had arisen from the political and organisational context of their labour in Chile. Furthermore, the attempt to reconstruct a Chilean public sphere in exile was fraught with difficulty. The exiles were cut off from the semi–clandestine political front in Chile and put into an unfamiliar British political context, so that political practice was necessarily restricted. Stripped of public position, the men were also stripped of the structural basis for their position as head of the family. The men, then, felt superfluous not only to what was going on in the public sphere but also to wives and children in the family.

Women's experiences of loss and deprivation differed from men's. Given the different social location of women before exile, there was no uniform experience in exile but two contrasting sets of experience. Both groups of women experienced a change for the worse in their situation. For the 'public–private' women, the main problem was how to accommodate their dual role in a situation where they were bereft of the kind of domestic help they had known in Chile. The exclusively private women's problems centred around the loss of their kinship networks, which had formed the foundation stones of their private domain.

The 'Public–Private' Women

For those 'public–private' women accustomed to working outside the home, exile brought the question of women's unequal access to public life sharply into focus. This group of women initially had to renounce many public activities, however reduced in scope, through the demands of child care. Many became full–time housewives for the first time in their married lives. Even after the coup, most 'public–private' women in my sample had continued in their jobs or found alternative employment. In this respect exile can be experienced as a retrogressive step by some women.

Being female in British society was experienced as much more oppressive by this group of women than what they had known in Chile, where gender subordination had been cushioned by class privilege. Chilean middle–class and professional women had experienced no significant opposition to, nor difficulty in finding, work outside the home in Chile. Their labour was often in demand and, given their material situation, they had been able to combine jobs with domestic responsibilities by engaging a maid. During the Popular Unity government this private solution had been supplemented by the increased level of collective child–care provision at the workplace. As a last resort many of these women had been able to count on female kin living in the vicinity. Thus, these women had constituted a privileged group of women whose class position and educational level had blunted the disadvantages of gender to the extent that many denied the relevance of sexual discrimination to their lives. Francisca, who had undergone five years of university training before qualifying and finding a professional post, remarked about her life in Chile, 'I never felt that my future had to be cut because I was a woman. I never felt any discrimination or was made to feel less able than a man.'

In recounting their lives under Popular Unity, the professional women in particular resisted differentiating their experiences from men's in any way. They perceived gender differentiation to be more marked in Britain than in Chile, contradicting the popular view that less–developed countries are more sexually stereotyped and restrictive for women than the developed world.

The 'public–private women' were initially unable to reconstruct their foothold in the public sphere and were forced back into the home by what had been, until exile, an unquestioned sexual division of labour in the family. In Chile the escape outlet of the maid had not only enabled these women to take up paid work without experiencing the full force of the 'double shift' but had also underpinned the pattern of male non–involvement in domestic life. In this way, the maid had kept the potential conflict between men and women in the family at bay.

Initially, many women accepted this re–ordering of their lives for the chance it gave of re–establishing family life on a firm footing. Many felt that mothering took on an added importance in the exile situation and that they owed it to their children to provide a focal point of stability at a time of maximum disruption in their lives. At the same time, however, these women realised that this renewed commitment to family life had a price – the renunciation of public activity, particularly paid work, in which many had invested an important part of their self-image. Paid work had not only meant a degree of economic independence but, in some cases, had also acquired a political connotation. Some women regarded the fact that they had continued working outside the home in Chile, when they had had the option of dropping into domesticity, as part and parcel of their political contribution to the Popular Unity process. Where paid work had carried this expanded meaning, housework carried the negative connotation of being privatised labour, associated with narrow and conservative views of the world.

In many cases these women's loss of a public role was initially shared with their men. As the men gradually regained a foothold in the public sphere (generally through taking up a World University Service (WUS) grant) the contrast between the men's activity and their own stagnation was hard to take, especially where the women considered themselves to be professional equals.[7] Until exile, these women had been able to compete, if not equally with men, much more equally than they could here, stripped of all support in the home. As time passed, more 'public–private' women expressed a growing awareness and resentment that the costs of exile were not being equally shouldered by men and women. In this way, exile exposed gaps in what had often been regarded as egalitarian relationships.

Regaining a public foothold, as all the 'public–private' women in my sample sooner or later achieved, did not put an end to their difficulties for it forced them to find new ways of accommodating their public and private commitments. In exile this group of women experienced the contradiction between their family and public roles in heightened form. Not only were they in a position to challenge the definition of domestic labour as 'women's work', but also to question its private status by raising it as a public issue. They were in a position to challenge the boundaries set by men to the political sphere by placing gender onto the political agenda. Before analysing how the 'public–private' women set about confronting or containing this contradiction, I shall first turn to the experiences of private women in the home.

The Private Women

Unlike the 'public–private' women, the private woman experienced being a housewife as unproblematic and part and parcel of her self-image. Managing the home and bringing up children were what legitimised her very existence as a woman and gave her a sense of purpose in life. Falling under her exclusive charge, these activities were the one area where men deferred to her judgement. In short, they were her domain.

While home-making and child-rearing continued in exile, they took place in a very different context from that which the women had known in Chile. Part of this transformed context was experienced as being for the better. Many private women felt that they had found tranquility in exile after the hard times in Chile since the coup: the material basis of the private domain was secure and their men were out of harm's way. Silvia described her contentment in exile in the following way: 'This is the first time I've felt calm since the coup. All my nervous tension has disappeared and I feel really well. The main relief is not having to worry where the next week's money is coming from.' The women also appreciated the higher degree of rationalisation of domestic labour in a developed country, with the greater accessibility of supermarkets, processed foods and labour-saving devices. However, if housework was experienced as less burdensome in exile, it was also more solitary. Housework in Chile had taken place within the context of wider family and community relations which had reduced the deprivations of their labour in the home. By comparison, housework in exile became an impersonal, isolated and solitary activity. Going into a supermarket was convenient and required the minimum of language skills but it also meant that the women went about their work silently and alone.

While housework was experienced as lighter in exile, child-rearing loomed much larger in the private women's lives. Many private women had depended heavily on female kin, especially their mothers, for child-care and child-rearing advice. What had been a shared female concern in Chile now became the responsibility of a single woman. The private women not only found mothering more burdensome in exile, but they also experienced a social devaluation of motherhood. In Chile '*señora con guagua*' (woman with baby) had been a passport to a seat on the overcrowded buses and, during Popular Unity, the surest way to jump the food queues. This veneration of women as mothers had given Chilean women a form of 'mother power' (Stevens 1973). In Britain, by contrast, the private women experienced motherhood as bringing few such privileges. Compared to the relatively powerful private domain which some had known in Chile, the private women experienced an erosion of their power base in exile and a fall in status for their traditional roles. They had lost the 'women's world' in which they had felt they were respected and valued members of society.

Stripped of their kinship networks, the private women could only look to their husbands for adult company and support.[8] However, this made for great instability in marriage, for it gave husband-wife relations a load they had been unaccustomed to carrying. In Chile the absence of marital dialogue had been obscured because husbands and wives each moved within their respective large and rewarding domains. In exile, by contrast, both domains shrank and men and women in these highly segregated marriages were brought face-to-face with the consequences of having inhabited different worlds, for they had little shared conversation and few joint activities. Laura, whose marriage broke down in exile, recalled how: 'We never acted as a couple in our marriage. We never did anything together. We never discussed anything. I feel as if I've been living with a person I've never known.'

Furthermore, the men's and women's goals increasingly collided in exile. While the women were desperately anxious to re-establish family life in exile, the men were equally anxious to rebuild their political lives. This tension between the men's political engagements and the private women's home-centred focus was not something new. During Popular Unity the men's intense political activity had meant that they had practically disapppeared from the home. Although the men's political activity was reduced in exile, its overall impact on the private women with no other kin to fall back on loomed disproportionately larger. Where the men's absence from the home was for the purposes of wage-earning, this was regarded as legitimate by the private women as the men could be seen to be playing a supportive family role. Where it was for the purposes of political activity, however, the private women were less content, for the men seemed to choose this over and above time spent with the family.

As with the 'public-private' women, exile made the private women acutely aware of male privilege. To many private women the men's political activities increasingly came to be linked to their own private subjection in the home. Men could go out because women stayed in. The women mentioned how they always had to hurry when they went out, compared to the freedom of men who could come and go as they pleased. Although the private women's notions of socialism were generally vague and confused, the one clear idea they had about it was that it entailed equality. Given the glaring inequalities they perceived between their own lives and the advantages men enjoyed, the women began asking questions. Mariana turned to her husband in my presence and remarked: 'There's something I don't understand. If we are fighting for a socialist society, why is the man like this with the woman. If it's socialism we're after, why does it have to be so *machista* (male chauvinist)? Doesn't socialism mean the equal participation of men and women? Why are the men like this with their wives then?' In this way the women exposed a contradiction in their marriages between the men's public radicalism and their private conservatism.

Renegotiating the Terms of the Gender Order

Both groups of women in my sample, therefore, experienced a change for the worse in their situation. By stripping women of their respective support structures, exile not only increased women's experiences of subordination in the home and marriage but also brought into focus men's privileged access to public activities. These initially high costs of exile for both groups of women shook taken-for-granted notions of men's and women's place and led to a power struggle between men and women to renegotiate the terms of the gender order. The strategies women pursued, however, and the goals they strove for differed.

In some respects the private women appeared the more verbally oppositional of the two. They were subject to a much cruder version of machismo from working class men, had less room for manoeuvre and fewer opportunities for letting off steam. However, although these women railed against machismo, few – if any – were arguing for a radical transformation of gender roles. Most merely wanted a little more freedom in their marriages to take up extra-domestic activities and a little more consideration and respect from men for their private roles.

Most continued to regard their power as lying in the private domain and did not want men to be too active in the home, regarding this as an unwelcome intrusion into their affairs. However, they did want men to upgrade the status of their domestic labour. As unpaid labourers working in the seclusion of the home, the private women received little social recognition of their work. They wanted the men to recognize, not only by their words but also by their deeds, that women were doing a worthwhile job in the home. To many private women the private, not the public, was the more important sphere. In this way they inverted the men's model by substituting the primacy of family life for the primacy of politics.

In their attempt to recuperate the privileged meaning of the private domain, many women turned to their men to reinforce the deference, honour and respect they felt they deserved as women. In some women's eyes, men were no longer paying women the respect they were due. They had forgotten their manners and language in the women's presence. Gloria complained: 'Women have lost respect in exile. The fact that men are now using bad language in front of women shows that they no longer consider what women think. Men no longer feel the need to apologize to women. There are very few gentlemen amongst the Chileans.' Many women did not want to come down from their pedestal, experiencing this as a form of moral equalling and thereby an erosion of part of their power base.

The private women were not, however, alone in experiencing a loss of power, for both the public and private domains were impoverished in exile. The balance between male power (located in the public domain) and female power (located in the private domain) became the focus of a gender struggle. While the private women wanted the men to attach more importance to their private domain and to respect female prerogatives, the men were equally eager to minimise time spent in the private domain (women's sphere) and to maximise time spent in the public domain (men's sphere). Each partner, then, attempted to prioritise their domain vis-à-vis the other's. To the men's 'politics first, then the family', the women countered with 'family first, politics second'. Each partner drew upon the other's vocabulary in an attempt to press their claims. The women drew upon the men's political vocabulary (socialism = equality) to press for the the equality of women and their domain. The men, meanwhile, drew upon the women's moral vocabulary (women's liberation = immorality) to restrain the private women's demands for more freedom in the marriage.

In this struggle to renegotiate the terms of the gender order, the women played an active role in setting some of the ground rules and laying down some of the limits. In this way they exercised power and influence in drawing up a new map of male-female relations. By speaking up and making claims on men, some private women underwent a change in self-image from the 'women who put up with their lot' or the 'little birds' which they described themselves as having been before the coup. Some private women felt they had been profoundly and irreversibly changed by exile.

Ana described how she had changed in the following way. 'In Chile I was extremely quiet. I let others decide everything for me. What I've learnt in exile is that I've also got the right to speak and give my opinion. I'm not going to go back to Chile and shut myself in. This exile experience is going to remain part of my life for ever.'

For these women, exile constituted a period of personal growth and development. By finding a voice in exile many private women moved in the opposite direction to many men who experienced exile as an overwhelming sense of having lost their voice.

A number of factors account for the abandonment of the private women's resignation. Some of these relate to the removal of control mechanisms over the women's lives in exile; others to their own experiences after the coup both in Chile and in exile. While men's control became more explicit in exile, the structural basis for that control was considerably weakened. At one and the same time the private women experienced male domination as more irksome yet less invincible than it might once have appeared. Many men – particularly manual workers, to whom most of the private women were married – spent long periods in exile being unemployed. The loss of the men's breadwinning role had implications for their authority over women in the family. Living off social security was not regarded by either men or women as giving the man the same claims over his wife and her labour as if he had earned the money directly himself. Furthermore, the fact that in cases of marital breakdown the women could support themselves economically in exile through the social security system loosened the economic dimension to the women's resignation.

A second factor behind the women's more outspoken stance involves the reduction in kinship controls in exile. Alongside the support and comfort proffered by the extended family there was also a perception of the control it exercised, particularly over women's lives. By removing the private women from the kinship fold exile caused great personal suffering, but also provided the chance for these women to develop in a more autonomous way.

A feeling that women could breathe a little more freely in exile was reinforced by their observations of women's lives in Britain. Unlike the professional women, many housewives experienced gender differentiation as being weaker in Britain and relations between men and women as looser than they had known in Chile, particularly where they came from the outlying provinces. Not all the private women's learning, however, stemmed from contact with British society, for some of these women's experiences in Chile after the coup had demonstrated new capabilities. Women who had been forced to take charge of the household and earn a living while their men were in prison had often surprised themselves by what they had been able to do. Although some private women, who had been thrust into the public arena in this way, were happy to return to the home in exile, others were unwilling to shut themselves in quite as tightly as they had done in the past. Some were eager to maintain their new found self-confidence and skills and seek out a degree of extra-domestic activity in exile.

While the private women had an alternative model to the men's dominant one, it was one which drew its very strength from gender difference. The women's private offensive was aimed at reasserting the status of their private domain vis-à-vis the men's public world. In its one-sided focus on the private sphere, this model remained as partial as the men's dominant one with its exclusive focus on the public domain.

Private Trouble or Public Issue?

Having one's own domain could be perceived by the private women as carrying certain advantages compared to the ambivalent position of those women who straddle both the public and private spheres. Partly for this reason, a new political model is more likely to emerge from the 'public-private' women, whose very lives straddle the public-private divide and who have access to public arenas where they can raise questions about the domestic division of labour as a public issue. However, placing gender on the formal political agenda presented special problems for this group as many were conceptually entangled with the men's political definitions and participated in the dominant male political model. As has been seen, the men had a particularly powerful model of social reality and one which had been potentially dominant at a societal level during the Popular Unity period in Chile. However, this model had largely bracketed the private domain from serious political consideration. Women party members had thereby acted out their political commitments within a framework which did not wholly fit their experience, for while they were exploited as wage workers like the men, they were also oppressed as women. Where women had participated in party political organisations alongside men, they had tended to do so in a context defined by men and marked by a masculine ethos.

The 'public-private' women's involvement in this predominantly male political framework had not been without its difficulties in Chile. Those women who were politically involved had been unable to invest as much of themselves in their political roles as the men, for their family responsibilities had pulled the other way. The kind of total commitment expected of the exemplary political militant, without a private life, on call 24 hours a day and ready to leave at the drop of a hat, had been unattainable for women with children. Few women, usually those without children, enjoyed what the men referred to as an 'organic tie' to the party, whereby a militant surrenders himself to party work and discipline. This had the effect of maintaining the higher echelons of party life as a predominantly masculine preserve.

Although the verbal ideal held by men in the sample had been for women to work '*hombro a hombro*' (shoulder to shoulder) alongside men, as equal partners in the class struggle, the way in which women's position in the family prevented this from being achieved in practice had been glossed over. It had been implicitly understood that women's domestic responsibilities would affect their level of political participation. Such high levels of political activism as befitted a man had not been expected from women. Similar allowances for family commitments had not extended to men. Not only would men absenting themselves from party work for family responsibilities have been seen as reflecting the persistence of 'petit bourgeois traits', but it would also have brought into question their masculinity. Gender assumptions about men's and women's roles in the family thus gave rise to a political sexual division of labour, whereby men had been the full-time activists and women the supporters who dropped in and out of party life as their family commitments permitted.

Although these women had been able to count on considerable support in the home in the form of domestic help, their finely-tuned arrangements for balancing their public and private commitments had been stretched almost to breaking point during the hyped-up pace of political life under Popular Unity. However, the boundary of the political sphere had been so taken-for-granted that it had never occurred to the women to raise the question of women's position in the family at a party meeting. Experience had taught them that this was not the kind of issue that got discussed there. Doris, a professional woman who worked mainly with men, recalled how 'the party never discussed the particular problems faced by women members. I never felt able to discuss the subject of women's liberation with the men. Not that I thought they wouldn't be sympathetic. I just felt that it was my responsibility to sort out my family commitments. It wasn't something I felt able to bother the men about.'

Rather than challenging the men's control of the political agenda, women party members in my sample had stifled their interests in order to fit in with the men's way of seeing things. They had maintained this lack of fit as a personal tension.

While the pressures on the 'public-private' women to break free from the dominant political model increased in exile, an examination of the role of women in the politics of the particular exile community studied reveals that they failed to challenge publicly those practices which reproduced their subordination. Some women continued to endorse openly the men's political definitions by joining with men in downgrading and demoting a set of issues which were of particular concern to them. Others kept alternative definitions to themselves. Yet others deflected any insights they had made into gender subordination by arguing that Chilean women are much 'more liberated' than British women and contrasting the raw deal women have in Britain with the better deal they have in Chile. The extent to which their 'freedom' in Chile had depended upon the exploitation of another woman, in the form of a maid, remained a blind spot in some women's accounts.

Rather than mounting a public challenge, the 'public-private' women made a number of individual bargains and arrangements with their men in the private sphere. Their skills and energies went into devising ways of minimising the impact of the contradiction through behind-the-scenes negotiations with their men. Asking men for help in the home had not formed part of these women's expectations before exile. The active involvement of men in the home had generally been regarded by both men and women as deviant and unmasculine. For women to challenge men's freedom from domestic duties was not only to go against established gender norms but – in the case of longer marriages in particular – to challenge a well-entrenched pattern of accommodation between husbands and wives. Changing this pattern meant renegotiating the terms of the marriage relationship.

A few women in my sample opted not to confront men but to shoulder the domestic load alone by simplifying and rationalising domestic labour. Others reduced the demands they made on men by deflecting requests for help onto older children. Those women with young children, however, could not exclude their husbands so readily from the domestic scene. The help that these women requested from men varied from a minimal to a more important share in the running of the home. It was where the gap between the women's requests and the help received from men was experienced as too wide by the woman that marital conflict erupted.

Although the degree of male involvement varied substantially, in all cases domestic labour and child-care remained the woman's overall responsibility. Instances of role reversal were seen by both partners as temporary arrangements and those cases of more sustained male participation were still clearly under female directives. These women, then, largely acted to maintain domestic labour and child-care as a female responsibility and to blame themselves for shortfalls in their domestic arrangements in exile. In reallocating domestic responsibilities, the 'public-private' women not only had to confront male opposition to domestic involvement in some cases, but also undo years of gender socialisation. Given these difficulties the process of redefining domestic labour as a joint responsibility of men and women remained partial and incomplete.

Revolution in the Revolution?

While the ensuing struggles between men and women were largely articulated at the level of the household, these upheavals in the home were not without public repercussions. There was a general awareness in the exile community that marital difficulties and breakdowns had gone beyond the level which passes by without comment to become the subject of widespread concern. There was what could be defined as a 'private crisis' which called for a degree of collective rethinking and action by men. As the women lacked an agenda, men were free to dictate the terms on which the private sphere entered public debate.

The dominant model of the family held by male party members stressed harmony and coincidence of interests between members. Drawing upon the male political vocabulary, Alejandro commented: 'It's understood that the family nucleus has no reason to have different interests, that theirs is a permanent alliance. There's no class struggle within the family but rather all are fighting for the same ideals.'

However, this model of the family as a harmonious unit was increasingly strained as both groups of women struggled in their marriages, at times to breaking point. Women had a new and different vocabulary for talking about the private sphere, in which words like 'raw deal', 'slaves', 'imprisonment' and 'machismo' figured prominently.

In effect, the men were faced with two types of grievances from the women. First, there was the private offensive mounted by those women who experienced the men's political activities as detrimental to their family-oriented goals. Secondly, there were those demands from the public-private women for men to play a more active role in the running of the home if they were to engage in public life in exile without working a double shift.

With respect to the first set of grievances, the private women's 'privatised' outlook and satisfaction at certain material improvements in exile caused their men considerable misgivings. At a time when the men were desperately trying to hold on to their political goals under adverse conditions, the private women were seen to be undoing their work in the home. Moreover, the damage went even further, for, given women's pivotal role in the socialisation of the young, the private women transmitted this personalised world view to their children. This factor was particularly significant given the dearth of alternative socialising agencies in exile. Under these circumstances the family took on critical importance in maintaining the political ideals of the exile community by forming a politically-conscious second generation in exile. Given this, the view that it was sufficient for the man alone to be politically committed in that he stood for the family group, came to be increasingly questioned. In Alejandro's words: 'Unilateral commitment is counter-productive because it means that the home stands for one thing and the man for another. It means that the man's offspring will not be so clearly formed in their ideas as when the whole family follows the same path.'

The existence of a group of privatised women was seen by the men as not only depriving the cause of part of the adult population but also of a new generation of coherently politicised recruits. In the men's eyes the women were a hindrance, an obstacle to the forward march of the revolution. However, there was no perception of women as having any rights or goals outside the men's political definitions or viewpoints. The men reformulated the women's troubles into political problems for men.

This was evident in the kind of remedies and solutions proposed. In the men's eyes the women had to come to see things like the men. Sheltered in the privacy and isolation of the home, the women were seen to be closed off from a set of experiences which had politicised the men. By bringing women out of the private sphere and into the public domain, the men hoped to break down the women's individualism and repeat the pattern of their own politicisation. Declarations put out by men began to register the need to involve women in the political life of the exile community. Tagged onto the bottom of one political circular appeared the following: 'It's equally important to hand over activities to our *compañeras* who, in many cases, have paid a higher cost in exile with scant or no political participation and with very little contact with the community in which they are living.'

Although the men were more verbally open to bringing women into exile politics, women were not being offered an equal and valid place in the public sphere. In all cases men decided what and how much to hand over. The political-sexual division of labour, with men as the 'professional militants' and women as 'supporters', continued unchanged. Even this limited and partial incorporation of women proved too much for some men, who continued to regard public life as their monopoly and resisted any measures that reduced their control over women.

While the men were more open to bringing women into the political sphere in exile, they also wanted to control and contain their entry. Women were clearly being 'brought' into the men's political framework and definitions. The men acted to close off and discredit alternative ideas which they felt were beginning to penetrate the home. In most men's eyes the separate organisation of women around gender inequalities merely helped to reproduce capitalist society by dividing the working class and fragmenting its political efficacy. The male activists not only regarded sexual politics as politically divisive but also as 'un-Chilean'. The dismissal of sexual politics as a set of western and foreign ideas carries particular force in the exile context, where there is already widespread concern about loss of national identity. Appeals for the defence of Chilean culture in exile, however, were generally made without any critical examination of what should or should not be preserved. Family and gender ideologies, which had been carried into exile unexamined, were uncritically defended in Britain as forming part of Chilean national identity. The men reacted to what they regarded as widespread sexual permissiveness and family disintegration in British society by counterposing an idealised version of Chilean family life. Through these political and moral controls, the male party members effectively closed off a set of meanings which could have given coherence to the women's grievances in the home.

Women's entry or re-entry into the public sphere revealed a second contradiction which the men had to confront in exile. 'Permitting' women to engage in a degree of political life brought into the open men's freedom from domestic work. As has been seen, this formed the core of the second set of grievances men had to address in exile. While some men resisted becoming more involved in the running of the home, others assumed a more active role and a few came to define their domestic involvements as part of their political stance. The 'responsible' militant was someone who lent a hand in the home, who fulfilled his commitments in the private as well as the public sphere, who was consistent in both his public and private behaviour. However, men's involvement with domestic labour and child-care did not lead to a fundamental revision of their political model. Men's helping in the home was condoned by local party organisations so long as it did not interfere with or displace their party political engagements. The political parties continued to demand top priority in a (male) militant's life, above family commitments, 'capitalist' work schedules, etc. When one man asked for a lightening of party duties in order to accommodate his enlarged domestic role, he was asked by the party leadership if both he and his wife needed to have jobs. The political parties, then, continued to reproduce the sexual division of labour in the family which left men free to assume the major political responsibilities while women shouldered most of the domestic load.

Conclusions

By disarticulating both the public and private spheres and bringing them into a new and more problematic relationship, exile opened up male–female relations to re–examination and shook the whole way of talking about gender relations in terms of coincidence or complementarity.

Yet, although exile gave rise to the conditions for an emerging gender consciousness, as this chapter shows, there were also difficulties of translating grievances into public policy demands. While Chilean women in this particular exile community were becoming gender conscious, their collective identity as women remained weak and any notions of shared female experience were clearly class–restricted. The two groups of women were drawn from different class sectors, had different objectives and different experiences. Each group, however, sought its objectives through a process of private negotiation with men in individual households rather than through the construction of female solidarity groups.

As has been seen, the 'public–private' women were conscious of having had a 'raw deal' in exile and took action to reclaim a public role. Any insights made were not, however, developed into a coherent alternative political model and admitted to the public sphere. Rather, these women largely respected the men's political boundaries and hierarchisation of political concerns. The problems experienced by these women in challenging the men's political agenda reaffirm the difficulties of mounting a full–blown gender challenge. Given the degree of male opposition to women organising separately, these women may have perceived the costs of such a challenge as too high.[9] The Chilean women's difficulties in breaking their silence in exile point to the need for a strong women's solidarity group to socialise insights, build up confidence and overcome the fear of public ridicule.[10] Where women's solidarity is weak or absent, men can show concern for women without fundamentally transforming their secondary public status. Differentiation can, of course, mean the opening up of a separate path for women and one which legitimises their secondary status in society. Given this many women may prefer to remain 'up front' with men in the mainstream of political and economic life. Differentiation, however, can also mean the recognition of women's distinctive experiences and of the need for women to struggle separately to ensure that the public sphere is a place where both women and men can feel equally at home.

At the same time as facilitating the emergence of new models, the transitory definition of exile may act as a brake on the reworking of personal identity. Indeed some 'public–private' women envisaged a solution to their domestic problems as following from their longed–for return to Latin America. Many may have been hoping to resume their former strategies on their return to Chile, where there was seen to be less need for feminist vocabularies. Finally, the decision not to press their grievances in public and to confine their struggle to a process of private renegotiation with men has not been without its benefits for many women. Some have been able to reach a new accommodation with their men in the private sphere which dispensed with the search for collective strategies. In some cases, then, individual strategies did pay off and in a few cases renegotiation has been quite far-reaching.

With respect to the private women, their model drew its strength from gender differences. Alternative definitions of the private domain, especially those that questioned women's central role as mothers, were experienced as profoundly threatening by many private women. In reproducing their role in the private domain, women may not be merely victims of false consciousness but may perceive certain benefits of gender role differentiation. Several authors have commented on Latin American women's stake in the family as a powerful institution in which they exercise power (Jaquette 1973; Stevens 1973). Yet other authors paint a different picture of women's dependent and subordinate position in the family (Garrett 1978). In effect, these conflicting pictures may be two faces of the same reality: women are both superior and inferior, both 'power and pawn' (Pescatello 1976). Indeed it is in this very ambivalence that the resilience of gender roles to change may lie. In this respect attempts to redraw the boundary between public and private spheres by socialising some previously 'private' activities or by expanding men's role in the family may be experienced as undermining women's power in the private domain.

The absence of a coherent and public challenge by women meant that the men were able to manage the 'private crisis' within the confines of their own political model. This does not mean that male–female relations went unchanged in exile. On the contrary, they were shaken up a great deal. Women's struggles in the home successfully changed day–to–day relations between men and women. Chauvinism was muted and machismo disguised, while more overt public demonstrations of male power were avoided. However, these changes were ad hoc responses and adjustments to a largely private and uncoordinated challenge from women. The theoretical core of the men's political model remained untouched.

The renegotiated gender order which emerged in the particular exile community studied remains highly precarious and fluid. Neither set of public–private contradictions has been fundamentally resolved. Nor are these contradictions likely to be resolved on return to Chile, at least under the present regime. Women will be returning to the more overt and rigid differentiation of gender roles at present enforced by the military junta (Change 1981; Bravo and Todaro 1985). Those 'public–private' women who suspended insights in exile in the hope of eventually regaining their privileges in Chilean society are likely to be frustrated.[11] The return to Chile, with its present rigid endorsement of the public–private distinction, is likely to bring yet another period of dislocation and upheaval. While all exiles are likely to experience serious problems of readaptation to their own country, gender grievances are likely to be acute (FASIC 1981).

Notes

1. The fieldwork for this study was carried out over a 14-month period during 1979 and 1980. An average of four lengthy visits was made to each exile's home. Interviews were conducted in Spanish and husbands and wives were interviewed both jointly and separately using an open-ended question format which asked respondents to reflect back over their lives from Popular Unity, the coup and exile. In any process of biographical reconstruction, the past is reshaped in accordance with the subject's present ideas of what is or is not important. Furthermore, in giving an account, respondents are subject to varying degrees and types of control. While many men interviewed were subject to party political controls, many women's accounts fell under the private control of their husbands. In both cases the accounts I received represent the respondents' version of events as they saw fit to present it within the specific context of an interview and to myself in particular.
2. In drawing up the interview sample my main concern was to explore the variety of public and private experience over time. The interview group is not a random sample of the Chilean exile community, but rather a group which has been selected through a degree of quota sampling with a specific purpose in mind: the differentiation of historical experience according to the social location of the actor.
3. A 1984 study carried out by the Chilean Centro de Investigación y Desarrollo de la Educación (CIDE), gives a total of 200,000 to 250,000 exiles. Quoted in Angell and Carstairs 1987.
4. For a spread of the Chilean refugee population see Joint Working Group for Refugees from Chile (1975) and Joint Working Group for Refugees from Latin America (1979: 34). For an account of British policy towards Chilean refugees, see Browne 1979.
5. Popular Unity hoped to benefit women from the popular classes generally through such measures as higher wages, lower inflation, improved housing and social services. More specifically Popular Unity envisaged improving women's status within the family by granting married women full civil status, by equalising the situation of children born in and out of wedlock and, in a Catholic country, by introducing divorce legislation. Popular Unity aimed to facilitate women's incorporation into the paid labour force by extending the provision of nurseries and creches at the workplace and by introducing school meals. In addition, they aimed to encourage women's participation in public affairs through the creation of a Ministry of the Family. Many of these measures had not been implemented at the time of the coup, having been blocked by the opposition-dominated Congress. Others, such as extending women's economic role, were difficult to achieve in the short term.
6. The Joint Working Group for Refugees from Chile, set up in July 1974 to resettle Chilean exiles in Britain, consciously struggled against the paternalistic assumptions underlying the work of many refugee bodies and actively encouraged the Chileans to participate in the resettlement programme.
7. Initially the WUS scholarship programme for Chilean refugees unintentionally underpinned gender roles by restricting grants to one per family, which largely went to men. Even when easing up on this restriction, 75 per cent of the holders of WUS awards are men, increasing to 88 per cent at the doctoral level (WUS 1979: 15).

8. Given the loss of kinship networks, it is surprising to note that those Chilean women within visiting distance did not see more of each other. However, this is just another indication of the way in which the extended family had formed a self-sufficient world for some private women, who were unaccustomed to visiting or discussing personal matters outside family circles.
9. This does not mean to say that the costs may not be reassessed in the future or that Chilean women in other exile communities had reached the same conclusion. Silva-Labarca, writing about Chilean women exiled in France, found more evidence of women taking their struggles in the home into the formal political arena and challenging sexist practices within the party structure. However, she also notes that they remained wary of autonomous feminist organisations and clearly differentiated themselves as '*políticas*' (political women) from '*feministas*' (feminists) (Silva-Labarca 1981).
10. Neves-Xavier de Brito's study of Brazilian women exiled in France, where women exiles had formed an autonomous feminist group, argues that contact with and participation in the French feminist movement was crucial in providing them with a positive model to counter the anti-feminist prejudice of the Brazilian community and political groups (Neves-Xavier de Brito 1986: 77).
11. Nor have women in Chile stood still since the coup. There has been a growth of women's organisations, most centred around solidarity work but some more directly raising gender divisions as a political issue (Palma 1984; Bravo and Todaro 1985).

9 THE PROCESS OF TRANSCULTURATION: EXILES AND INSTITUTIONS IN FRANCE

Ana Vasquez

Introduction

People who have to live abroad for long periods of time have their own specific ways of relating to the institutions of their country of residence, but, at the same time, unconsciously or deliberately, they organise their own institutions. In this chapter I shall analyse, from a psychological perspective, how a group of exiles from the southern cone of Latin America related to the French institutions as well as towards the institutions they themselves created. This is of particular interest to us because it is through studying what confers upon each exiled community its very own characteristics that it is possible to deduce with precision and certitude the common traits shared by all exiles: the condition called exile.

The Exiled Population Studied

When the first wave of exiles started to leave the southern cone during the 1970s, it was possible to define an exile as a person compelled to abandon his or her country for reasons of personal safety and for whom return was forbidden. In cases of *prolonged exile*, however, people begin their exiles at different times, joining successive waves of exiles which correspond to the specific historical circumstances prevailing in their countries of origin. As a result, the people exiled between 1973 (the year of the *coups d'etat* in Chile and Uruguay and a year in which many Argentinians had to leave) and the late 1980s, do not present the same characteristics.

The first wave of exiles to arrive in France was composed mainly of intellectuals, professionals and left-wing political leaders, with only a small proportion of the trade union and political leaders being of working class or peasant origin. Most of these exiles therefore enjoyed a certain amount of social power, which clearly distinguished them from the population of immigrant workers residing in France: a population composed of rural workers, the unemployed and the underemployed, who had few or no qualifications. Immigrants were people who had never experienced any social power in their countries of origin. Finally, there was a definite difference in the way in which the exiles and the immigrants viewed themselves and their futures. Despite having been pushed by economic pressures, the immigrants regarded themselves as responsible for their departures and saw their settlement in France as the realisation of a plan, a promotion. If or when they returned was a decision they alone would make.

The exiles, by contrast, felt that their departures were forced, that exile represented the failure of a collective project in which their own lives were enmeshed; moreover that return was forbidden and did not depend on a personal decision. Unlike the immigrants, who conceived of their stay away from their country as a period of learning or of acquiring money, the exiles had no project other than to return, their lives in exile were in parentheses, transient and without great significance, a period of waiting for the chance to return to their country (where, they imagined, real life would be resumed).

But among the exiles themselves there were also changes as they came to realise that the Latin American dictatorships would remain in power for some time. This explains why successive waves of exiles tended to manifest such different characteristics. Although militants, resistance fighters and people who had suffered imprisonment and torture continued to arrive, their numbers began to dwindle against those who, although opposed to the regime in exile, had not been directly persecuted by it. In addition, large numbers of young people began to leave the southern cone simply because they felt stifled by dictatorship and wanted to seek new horizons. These people, however, retained their right to return and this began to introduce some important changes into the exile community's self-image.

In the 1980s, the repercussions of the economic crisis have caused more and more people, especially Chileans (since democracy has been restored in Argentina and Uruguay), to migrate and it has become increasingly difficult to differentiate between the economic migrant and the political exile. With a few notable exceptions, those leaving now, in the late 1980s, are coming from the more impoverished social groups which are being hardest hit by the military regime's economic policies. Also, these most recent exiles tend to locate on the outskirts of the cities rather than in the cities themselves, as their predecessors had done.

The first wave of exiles established distinctive behaviour patterns, various collective projects and institutions, a particular self-image and a number of myths about itself and France. The second wave aligned itself to this model of exile. Recently-arrived groups, however, are unlikely to establish contact with the exile community and their patterns of behaviour more closely resembles those of other immigrant communities residing in France. This chapter will therefore focus predominantly on the earlier groups of exiles.

Exile in a Historical Context

The existence of these differences means that exile must be looked at in its historical context. From the point of view of the individuals and groups concerned, there is a vast difference between becoming an exile and having lived abroad for 10 or 14 years. How people perceive their environment is obviously influenced by the socio-political context in which they experience it, but in the case of exiles they are influenced by two contexts – the one 'back there' (which becomes increasingly unreal as the enforced stay away from it lengthens) and the one in the host country (which is also liable to change over time as attitudes towards foreigners, especially exiles, become modified). With respect to the exile population under consideration here, three stages can be distinguished:

- The *first stage* is marked by the trauma of departure (often surrounded by violence) and by the person, as well as the group, establishing a set of defense mechanisms to cope with the sense of loss. As with a bereavement, the experience creates deep psychological wounds and there is also a strong feeling of guilt. The intensity of their interest in the situation 'back home' has a powerful influence on how they place and project themselves abroad. For a long time they continue to live with their hearts and minds in their country of origin: metaphorically speaking, they are unable to land in France.
- When the sense of bereavement and guilt is partially overcome, exiles are ready to initiate the process of transculturation, which characterises the *second stage*. At this point, they can psychologically open their suitcases, place themselves in France and start to live in the real present.
- As the period of exile lengthens, there is a *third stage* during which exiles review the myths and values that structured their lives and begin to forge individual projects.

French Institutions and Behaviour Rituals

Every society sets up institutions to structure the lives of its members. Apart from the norms which explicitly state how these institutions and their personnel should function, a number of codes (which are often implicit) also operate to ensure that individuals conform to the institution's demands. For example, if caught committing a parking offence, people are faced with several options – they can pay a fine, try to bribe or threaten the officer, or argue it out in court – the appropriateness of each being determined by the context in which the situation occurs.

Civil society in Latin America is less structured than it is in Europe and, as such, offers far more opportunities for adaptive behaviour. But in that the army is the most structured institution in most Latin American countries and, under a dictatorship, takes over institutions individuals have to confront on a day-to-day basis, exiles inevitably perceive of it as repressive, restrictive and intolerant. The net result is that, *because exiles base their relationships with institutions in the host country on their experiences of similar institutions in their country of origin*, in Europe they tend to regard any highly-structured organisation as an agency of persecution. It is unfortunate that their first introduction to institutional life in exile is to the police who have to regularise their documentation. During the first stage, when countless institutions are offering help, exiles are psychologically unable to see and take advantage of these openings; to do so would involve being accepting of an institution they perceive of as repressive; it would also involve envisaging exile as more than transitory which, at that stage, is emotionally unacceptable, wholly inconceivable.

In France, various institutions (such as schools, local government, the national health service and government ministries) offer a wide range of services, but those wishing to avail themselves of them must first go through a series of precise codified procedures, commonly referred to as 'institutional rituals'. For example, documents have to be presented in a particular way, various formalities associated with appointments and interviews have to be observed, and certain personal details have to be divulged. Latin Americans interpret all these rituals as 'police control', or 'intrusions into their private lives', or 'manias', or 'obsessions', or they simply fail to perceive them at all.

French and Latin American codes of behaviour vary considerably over such things as politeness and time-keeping, especially in an urban setting. In Latin America, for example, it would be considered impolite to arrive on time for a dinner invitation; a woman will keep people waiting (even for work appointments), but will not tolerate being forced to wait herself; and a director will keep people waiting merely to demonstrate the importance of his position. While the French regard punctuality (with respect to both date and time) as an essential prerequisite in any dealings with an institution, the Latin Americans adopt very different rituals relating to institutional time-keeping. During the first stage of exile, when Latin Americans unwittingly and frequently transgress French norms, they interpret the official's reaction to their behaviour as obsessional, rejecting or ill-willed and often end up abandoning the process merely because they have failed to understand the nature of the problem.

Further difficulties confront the Latin American exiles when they attempt to negotiate the French postal services. Because such services in Latin America are invariably scant and irregular, exiles have had little experience of French postal courtesies when they arrive in the country. Several years usually pass before they consider using the post to communicate with people in the same city. They are unaware that that 'every letter must be replied to', which is an important implicit norm in France. Parents overreact to communications from their children's schools, automatically assuming that either they or their child must have misbehaved. If they receive a note indicating that their child has been late or absent from school, they attach considerable significance to it, not realising at first that it is merely a routine bureaucratic measure designed to safeguard schoolchildren. They tremble whenever an envelope arrives marked *Préfecture de Paris* (the agency responsible for France's municipalities and school correspondence), because in their countries there is no préfecture other than the police. To digress a little, until 1987, all letters to social security (the body responsible for medical matters) were delivered free of charge. When told about this, many exiles simply did not believe it – they were convinced it was a joke. Even some university professors refused to believe it was true and over many years continued to send stamped envelopes.

But in what ways, one might ask, does the disorientation of exiles differ from that of other foreigners who remain in France for long periods? It is important to remember that most of the exiles in France were middle class and were used to exercising a certain amount of social power. They 'knew how' to address themselves to institutions and, like most people, tended to assume that their old approaches would be equally effective in the new context. Failing vis-à-vis the new institutions became their first experience of a loss of power, of an intolerable 'lack of know how'. This they deflected into their personal defense mechanisms by developing a certain 'rejection-idealisation', manifested by feeling that they were 'only passing'. After a few more clumsy episodes - for which they blamed the institutions concerned - many exiles gave up their attempts to deal with institutions, but nonetheless continued to compare them unfavourably with those they had left behind and with how they themselves would have dealt with the situation.

Only during the second stage were the exiles, through a slow and contradictory process, able to establish regular relations with the French institutions. These relations, which emerged and intensified as the process of transculturation developed, accommodated both the personal characteristics of the exiles and the points of view of the institutions. In the first stage, group characteristics defined the individual; in the second stage, the transculturation process was grafted onto each individual's past. Experiences of former travels had a particularly positive influence, whereas the direct effects of repression seemed to distort their integration.

In other words, the exiles had begun to understand what they could gain from specific institutions if and when they enacted the proper proceedings. For example, subsidised or free meals are available for schoolchildren in cases of unemployment or low wages. Many exiles qualify for this benefit, but it does require filling in forms and producing documents at precise dates. At first the procedure appears too complicated, but because the benefit is considerable, they start to help each other to apply. Enjoying the benefits then leads them to make comparisons with their country of origin and, little by little, their interest in finding out about the benefits and requirements of the different institutions (social security, maternity allowances, language courses, training in skilled jobs) widens. The extent to which the exiles have changed becomes apparent when they meet newly-arrived compatriots who behave as they had done years before.

Paradoxically it was during this stage, rather than shortly after arrival, that the exiles began to recognise the need to learn the language of the host country. In the first stage, most exiles considered it unnecessary to learn the language well, partly because they believed they were only passing through, but also because a feeling of guilt (shared and sustained by the rest of the group) made it inconceivable for them to try to carve out a position for themselves. Before they were ready to learn the language, most exiles had first to overcome their grief and come to terms with the magnitude of the disaster. Some exiles were less inclined than others to overcome their communication barriers. Those who invested the least in language learning were usually those most committed to their past in Latin

America, those who still had political commitments there, or those who had simply never developed the habit of systematic study. Here the relationship between cause and effect metaphorically 'bites its tail' because frequently those who fail to integrate are those who idealise the 'homeland' and try to return even under disadvantageous conditions.

Certain processes are initiated when the exiles come to recognise that they have no choice other than to settle into a protracted exile. This realisation is both painful and slow. It not only involves acceptance of the failure of the global project 'back home', but also an understanding that life in France is as important as it is in their country of origin and that they have allowed certain opportunities for learning and development to pass them by. But once the exiles accept responsibility for the 'here and now', it awakens in them a renewed interest in integrating with French institutions, not only to receive benefits, but also to participate in and contribute to them.

It is important to bear in mind, however, that the institutions involved with the reception of exiles usually see their own role as helping during the first stage (with the newly-arrived) and perhaps extending this to the beginnings of the second stage when transculturation commences. Yet it is only at the end of the second stage and during the course of the third stage that exiles are psychologicallly ready to integrate socially (at work and with local friends and neighbours) and to start seriously learning the language. It is unfortunate, therefore, that programmes of integration and support are rarely available during the third stage, when they would be most fruitful.

The Institutions of the Diaspora

On arrival, exiles feel very much like the survivors of a shipwreck. Between daily life in France and the recent past back home, the abyss is so deep that it forces them to question obsessively the catastrophe in which they had been both victim and protagonist. As I mentioned earlier, the beginnings of exile are scarred by the traumas of the *coup d'état*, the departure and the sense of bereavement. Those who arrive are survivors, but to continue to survive they have to create spaces in which they can reproduce their lost world. I also mentioned that every community creates its own institutions. Those of the exiled community, especially during the first stage, characteristically lack official backing (from embassies, ministries etc.) and, in that their objectives are disconnected from the concrete reality of their members' lives, tend to be thought of as provisional, they are centred 'back home' and their aim is to support the resistance.

The exiles of the southern cone reproduce their institutions within the framework of their former political organisations. According to Igonet-Fastinger (1983), politics constitutes the most important symbolic reference for exiles, and is an essential premise in their self-definition. But thc influence of the political parties over these institutions means that the parties' ideological behaviour and modes of action are also reproduced:

as a result, the fate of exile is division, internal squabbles and ideological dismemberment of the community.

Although, in the beginning, the exiled community provides a space in which each of its members can overcome their anonymity and 'be somebody', it does not take long before this is transformed from a space of protection of identity into one of control and culpability.

As time passes and opportunities for a social life in the community are restrained by the political crisis of exile and, as political reference groups in the country of origin begin to fragment, the objectives of the institutions also change. While continuing to explain and justify their existence in terms of what support they are giving to the resistance, some time during the second stage the institutions begin to function primarily as a means of sustaining the social lives of the exiles. *Peñas*, the social clubs attached to the various political organisations, start to function primarily as places of entertainment, where new musicians and singers are promoted and where friends meet one another. Some *peñas* have even been organised commercially, which would have been unthinkable a few years earlier; there is also a renewed interest in exile art (theatre, painting, writing). Saturday schools are set up to help children retain their language and to learn about their own cultural traditions; funds are made available (as usual, without official support) to create lending libraries and to set up various kinds of workshops; women organise other forums. This is the period when politico-cultural activities flourish, but because consensus within the community is sought, these new institutions tend to empty themselves of their party-political content. As with other immigrant groups, exiles reincorporate their legends, their songs and their rituals around food. Conceptually imprecise and ambiguous though it may have become, the exiles nonetheless attach considerable importance to maintaining their cultural identity.

Finally, during the third stage, when exile seems to be lasting for ever, old class divisions start to reassert themselves, but, being contrary to the ideology of the group, are denied and carefully concealed. Those exiles who have proletarian origins will tend to organise themselves into social and sports clubs, whereas those from intellectual backgrounds are far more likely to organise themselves around their own specialisms (as researchers, teachers, artists, etc.). They are also more likely to enter into dialogues with their colleagues working in similar fields in their country of origin and to prepare themselves for the post-dictatorship period when they would hope to be able to return. Gallisot (1985–6) sees this tendency to integrate without breaking ties with the country of origin as an important characteristic of 'functioning in the diaspora'. In other words, *they integrate as exiles and because they are exiles*, but at the same time assume the role of an interlocutor, becoming a sort of ambassador.

Conclusion

From the evidence of the new institutions 'born in exile', it would seem that intellectuals are the most likely to invent strategies for protecting their individual and collective identities. They are invariably the first to come up with the magic formula of integrating as exiles (and because they are exiles) and yet building rather than burning bridges between their own country and France.

In this chapter, I have attempted to look at institutions in the diaspora because I believe they constitute as important an aspect of reality as the host country's own institutions. The exiled community creates its own institutions, but only with the help of the receiving country and, with the passing of time, both types of institution modify their roles, their perceptions of exile, and their relationships with exiles.

10 EMPLOYMENT AS A KEY TO SETTLEMENT

Alan Phillips

Introduction

This chapter, which is based on the experiences of many voluntary agencies working with refugees in Europe, as well as on my own personal experiences over the past 14 years of directing education and training programmes for refugees in the UK, focuses primarily on refugee employment in Europe. I examine some recent work which could be useful in designing future settlement programmes and make a case for giving priority to research into refugee employment. I show what moves are being made by many of the EEC governments to resist the flow of asylum-seekers into Europe. While some governments characterise asylum-seekers as economic migrants, voluntary agencies believe that economic considerations in Europe, including high levels of domestic unemployment, dominate asylum policies.

The employment of refugees is central to refugee settlement, but is none the less a controversial subject. Unemployed refugees can be seen as a burden on the state and employed refugees as taking jobs away from the host community. Alternatively, it can be argued that settlement programmes should give employment the highest priority, even if this means redirecting limited resources away from welfare support.

This is a neglected and under-researched area, in part because of the difficulty of obtaining accurate data and in part because refugee employment in Europe has often been low on the agenda of bodies concerned with refugees. Asylum and welfare issues have traditionally dominated policy issues. The reasons for this are various, but include the legal or welfare emphasis in many support agencies (such as the UNHCR), the inexperience of many voluntary agency and government officials in the broader employment field, structures and staffing that reflect the settlement needs of the 1960s and 1970s, when unemployment was low, defeatism due to the complexity of the task and silence to avoid harsher asylum policies.

In this chapter I seek to demonstrate that there is a need for research into the employment situation of refugees, as well as careful investigation of the ingredients being identified as leading to the successful employment and settlement of refugees.

Europe as a Sanctuary

In October 1987, Amnesty International expressed its concern about the behaviour of governments in 129 countries. The number of countries that persecute some of their citizens is growing, yet human rights issues are being accorded less importance in international diplomacy. The human rights concern expressed by President Carter and the award of the Nobel Peace Prize to Amnesty International happened a decade ago. Amnesty International (1987) notes that the 'world wide concern about the growing number of refugees has all too often been used to justify new restrictions on entry for asylum-seekers, rather than translated into pressure on governments to end the human rights violations that have forced so many into exile'.

Many European governments are much more concerned about the numbers of refugees they may be required to settle, so they restrict the possibilities of asylum-seekers reaching Europe by suggesting that they are only seeking a more prosperous lifestyle. There was an example of this in March 1987 when the British government introduced legislation entitled the Carriers Liability Act, which sought to fine airlines or ships bringing people to the UK without appropriate visas. This was in response to Tamils from Sri Lanka seeking asylum at British ports of entry. The UK Immigration Advisory Service regarded the law as a deliberate attempt to stop asylum-seekers having their cases considered by the British government.

The European Consultation on Refugees & Exiles (ECRE), a network of voluntary agencies, despairs over recent developments throughout Europe (ECRE 1987). In a recently-published policy statement, published in full in the **Documents** section of this book, it observes:

> Voluntary agencies in Europe concerned with refugees have become increasingly alarmed by the progress of these governmental discussions. They appear to be motivated by the intention to restrict access to the asylum procedures of European countries. Many of the meetings are taking place in secret and policies are being developed which do not result from consultation with concerned agencies. Parliamentary scrutiny of the process has been minimal... Considerations relating to the needs of individual refugees and to the need for a global approach to the world refugee problem do not appear to be taken into account.

There is concern that the lowest common denominator will be found when there is a harmonisation of asylum procedures in the EEC, due by 1992. An inter-governmental European committee already associates the entry of refugees into Europe with terrorism and drug abuse.

Asylum-Seekers and Economic Migrants

In 1986, the European Programme to Combat Poverty (EPCP) held a seminar involving participants from government and voluntary agencies from a majority of the countries of the EEC. Concern was voiced that various restrictive measures introduced so far will tend to affect adversely the social, economic and legal situation of those aliens already living and permanently settled in the European community. Stringent visa requirements and frontier controls, reduction of social assistance, compulsory housing facilities, limited rights to work and to freedom of movement are frequently applied to prevent and discourage further entries.

The participants considered that the restrictive measures to avert new flows of immigrants, asylum-seekers, refugees, ethnic minorities and aliens taken by member states of the EEC are based on economic considerations. They noted that 'these measure may incite the public to xenophobic reactions to aliens of any kind and that these may escalate to uncontrollable dimensions when the rate of unemployment and economic crisis are brought into causality with the increasing number of migrants, refugees and ethnic minorities' (EPCP 1986).

There is little evidence to support the argument that most asylum-seekers are economic migrants. Indeed the high level of unemployment among refugees in most EEC countries argues to the contrary. The country with probably the most restrictive policies on refugee employment (West Germany) but with the easiest access (through Berlin) had by far the highest number of asylum-seekers in Europe between 1984 and 1987.

In contrast, the Home Office (UK) does not prevent asylum-seekers who have been admitted into the UK from looking for employment once their application for asylum has been under consideration for six months. It is not, at present, prepared to allow such people to take training courses available to 'Convention refugees' and other members of the host community.

Nettleton (in Nettleton and Simcock 1987) has shown that since 1980, 79.5 per cent of asylum-seekers in the UK have come from seven countries - Iran, Iraq, Sri Lanka, Poland, Ghana, Ethiopia and Uganda. It is evident, both from a cursory examination of the international press and from Amnesty International's annnual reports, that certain groups in these countries have been in great danger. There is a clear *prima facie* case that these asylum-seekers have fled danger. Indeed, of the 18,000 cases determined in the UK between 1980 and 1987, over 70 per cent were accepted as genuine refugees. Unlike other immigrants, the movement of asylum-seekers has been forced upon them and is unplanned. It is not undertaken with the prospect of social and economic advancement and rarely is a part of a family reunion programme. Consequently it comes as no surprise that the EPCP (1986) stated that:

> The degree of impoverishment and social disintegration is likely to be visibly higher in the refugee population of Europe than in that of labour migrants. Poverty might be regarded in a more conventional sense as an indicator of the degree of social and economic integration or disintegration of refugees... The participants noted that impoverished families of refugees, migrants and ethnic minorities are often living in urban suburbs in inadequate housing conditions next to underprivileged indigenous communities. Many of these impoverished aliens are reportedly unemployed, only have rudimentary education, a rudimentary knowledge of the language and live on social security or unemployment benefits.

These broad generalisations grouping refugees, migrants and ethnic minorities together always need to be handled with care. Many refugees in the UK, for example, are well educated and others obtain earnings through the informal sector.

It would be naive to believe that the economic integration of refugees automatically leads to their social integration in the host community or to liberal asylum policies. Additionally, lawyers will argue powerfully that under the 1951 Convention on Refugees, economic considerations must not affect the determination of refugee status for someone with a well-founded fear of persecution. However, there is much more room for debate and for harsh policies by administrations when it comes to considering those wishing to resettle from third countries or coming from areas of conflict. It is apparent that effective settlement does play an important part in these policies and that, as the director of the US Committee for Immigration & Nationality points out, if it is ignored by private voluntary agencies it will lead to harsher refugee resettlement policies by government (European Seminar 1987). Public support for refugee settlement programmes is much easier to obtain if it is shown that refugees have found jobs in their new country.

Employment as Settlement

A crucial ingredient in the successful settlement of refugees is that they should become self reliant and self sufficient.

Asylum-seekers may arrive in Europe in a state of trauma and under great stress. They may feel rejected by their home country and guilty or anxious about those who have been left behind. Often they may feel alienated linguistically, culturally and socially, be isolated and experience racism. There are deep feelings of disempowerment and the nature of many settlement programmes are welfare led, creating a substantial dependency.

Settlement programmes for larger groups in the UK (and some other parts of Europe) are often unplanned, rapidly established in response to a crisis and dominated by the availability of accommodation. This leads to a *de facto* scatter policy. Usually accommodation is available in areas out of which the host community has moved to avoid high unemployment or unacceptable social conditions.

Governments and voluntary agencies offer welfare services for refugees with varying degrees of success, but the failure to look constructively at the strengths of refugees, their mobility, flexibility, determination, age, skills, education and experience. The emphasis on welfare problems greatly inhibits the development of refugees and prospects of self sufficiency and employment.

Ashby (1977) turned this approach on its head when he gave a broadcast on BBC Radio 3 entitled 'Einstein was a Refugee'. He showed that of recent refugees coming to the UK, 15 had become Nobel Prize winners, 53 fellows of the Royal Society and 28 fellows of the British Academy.

Field (1985) observes that for many adult refugees obtaining a job is central to the experience of resettlement. For a refugee who has been powerlessly dependent on the benevolence of the receiving country, the psychological value of obtaining a job will be greater even than for an unemployed indigenous worker.

A European seminar was convened in September 1987 on 'Refugee Training and Employment'. Representatives from nine European countries attended – Denmark, Finland, France, Germany, the Netherlands, Norway, Spain, Sweden and the UK. Perhaps the most remarkable aspect of it was that it was the first seminar of its kind in Europe.

At the seminar there was a consensus on the importance of employment, not only for settlement but also as part of the process of settlement. Delegates from the Scandinavian countries and the UK emphasised the value of work experience and spoke of how work, even of a temporary nature, can improve language, give an understanding of real work conditions, provide relevant on-the-job training, rebuild confidence, establish contacts and often leads to other better jobs.

Asylum legislation has been interpreted more harshly in recent years. Unless the subject of employment is tackled seriously and refugees valued for the contributions they make to European societies, the situation may continue to deteriorate. Furthermore, it is of no help to refugees to remain disempowered and dependent on the state if they can develop through work and become self-sufficient.

Research Priorities in the Employment Field

Having established the reasons for giving priority to employment in the settlement process, the next step is to identify what leads to fruitful employment of refugees and whether researchers have a constructive role to play.

This does not mean that a common position can be taken in countries as different as Finland and Portugal or that generalisations can be made about groups as diverse as Poles and Vietnamese. Each refugee's situation differs according to his or her own experience, skills and ambitions and according to the local environment in which he or she lives.

It would be a mistake, however, to overlook the parallels that do exist between various European countries and not learn from the survival and development strategies refugees have adopted. Much of what is written below is drawn from a seminar convened by the British Refugee Council (BRC) in September 1987, at which many similarities were observed across Europe, particularly between Sweden, Norway and Finland with their low levels of unemployment (1–2 per cent) and substantial social welfare provision, as against other northern European countries with comparatively high levels of unemployment (8–18 per cent).

A better understanding is needed of what enables refugees to find satisfactory employment. For the UK, Phillips and Hartley (1977) stress the value of language training and education. More comprehensively, Stein (1980), argues that the first phase of settlement (up to six months) should involve general orientation, as well as language and vocational training, with a view to getting the refugees 'job ready' as soon as possible. Thereafter the refugee is expected to obtain a job, which will often be menial, and combine this with part-time English language training. The job will provide work experience and improve language skills.

Field (1985), looking at the lessons of research, states that 'Stein's recommendations for a resettlement programme are presented plausibly and forcefully, and the principles behind them command adherence, but the details and time scales are supported by only very meagre evidence'.

There is now a variety of programmes and evidence in a range of European countries which can be used to test hypotheses. Comparative studies and carefully detailed models of good experience would be valuable to practitioners and important to policy makers. The discussions at the European seminar in September gave some clear indications of where these might be most useful and a precis of some of the issues that emerged follow.

Employment Information

It is startling how few reliable data there are on the employment of refugees in Europe. On certain carefully managed programmes, or in countries where the numbers are very low (Finland), there may be good data. In the UK it is not even known how many refugeees there are in the various regions, while in West Germany non-governmental organisations have heavily criticised the government's estimates of the numbers of asylum-seekers. What limited studies have been undertaken are unreliable, with the sampling rarely random and no independent verification of the respondents' answers. Verbal estimates of the level of refugee unemployment provided at the European seminar varied greatly, ranging from 20 per cent to over 80 per cent three years after arrival. (The one exception was Finland, where only 100 refugees are taken in for resettlement each year.) Unless ways of measuring refugee employment are found and new systems implemented, it will be impossible to mobilise resources effectively to tackle unemployment.

The BRC training staff are constantly frustrated by the lack of reliable data on the likely demand for training schemes in particular localities. Unless there is good information available which can lead to feasibility studies on what courses are relevant for whom, when and with what form of language support, it is impossible for them to formulate appropriate programmes or to persuade donors to contribute.

A basic survey of where refugees are, what education and training they have received and what they are currently doing is important in every locality in which there are significant numbers of refugees. It would then be possible to identify the sectors in which research was a priority or where programmes could be immediately developed.

Some consider refugees who fail to obtain work as a liability on the state and those who do obtain work as doing so at the expense of the host community workforce. These arguments carry weight when policies of sustained reductions in public expenditure are being implemented and when there are high levels of unemployment. Moral arguments about the need to spend state funds on refugees are ineffective when other social groups are also competing for funds from hard-nosed finance ministers.

Voluntary agencies seek to show that refugees enrich societies culturally and that settlement programmes offer practical ways of implementing agreed humanitarian principles. Governments are more likely to accept arguments presented as enlightened self-interest. For example, as the BRC (1987) maintained:

- Refugees often bring with them considerable talents and skills obtained through training and experience, which would be costly to develop.

- Refugees can create jobs for themselves and others in society, partly through their cultural and linguistic strengths. They will often take jobs that are not wanted by the local workforce or are difficult to fill in certain localities, or bring in highly demanded skills - for example, through settlement training in new technologies.

- Refugees are likely to be significant contributors to the economy if there is a modest investment in a well- planned settlement programme.

Though further evidence is needed to support the first two propositions, it is certain that the cost of providing long-term welfare support to refugee families is enormous if household heads and other family members fail to obtain employment. Language and vocational training programmes, as well as other types of employment initiatives, are bound to be cost effective for the receiving society if they have a reasonable chance of leading to jobs for refugees.

These arguments, produced by Field (1985) and contained in the BRC's policy statement, can, however, be double edged; what is needed are much closer cost-benefit analyses of investments in training and employment strategies.

The EPCP is one of many programmes in which ethnic minorities born in a European country, immigrants and refugees are all grouped together. In that there are similarities and differences in the employment situations of these groups, it is a mistake both to make sweeping generalisations and to fail to learn from other similar groups. Careful studies are needed to contrast and compare these groups' employment situations and to evaluate the results of particular employment strategies.

Value of Qualifications and Past Experience

It is often difficult to ensure that the employment skills and experiences of refugees are properly considered. Too often the failure to recognise qualifications obtained in another country, or a lack of practical experience in Europe become obstacles to obtaining employment. Unless employers are helped to undertand the value and equivalence of the refugees' former activities, they will be reluctant to risk employing them. The Norwegian Introductory Programme for Foreigners records that:

> Norway tends to disregard this intellectual wealth [of refugees], however, and refugees find it extremely difficult to use their education in their new home lands. Acceptances and recognition of foreign certificates/diplomas and degrees as equivalent to Norwegian degrees is very difficult to obtain. In addition refugees meet with a pronounced and general resistance to employ foreigners in qualified jobs.

The French refugee agencies, the Danish Refugee Council (DRC) and the BRC reported similar experiences. Action research is required into how to overcome these obstacles and to make the most of refugees' skills.

Individual Development Plans

Even refugees fleeing from the same country at the same time can come from a wide variety of backgrounds; it is consequently important to hold discussions with each individual, or his or her family, before embarking on plans for future training and employment opportunities.

Individual development plans set up in Finland and Norway were found to be very important, for they highlighted the need for cultural sensitivity, especially towards the major changes that may be experienced in the roles and positions of women. It is then possible to provide relevant language, vocational-training and job-searching skills appropriate to the individual, rather than simply accepting schemes designed by institutions for large numbers.

The value of an integrated programme, constructed at an early stage after arrival in the host country, was emphasised, in particular, by experienced workers from Sweden, Norway and Denmark, who noted that 'refugees find it a lot easier to learn Danish if the teaching is closely related to practical work, which is an important part of the work introduction courses'. Conversely, an enquiry conducted in 1984 in the Netherlands was critical of reception and introduction programmes which gave hardly any information on work. In a 1982 study of the UK's Vietnamese settlement programme, Jones (1982) noted that, 'At the outset of the programme it was clear that unemployment was to be a major problem for the refugees... For the large majority of refugees, however, attempts to get employment began after resettlement'.

It was noted at the seminar that employment is often given far too little attention in accommodation-led settlement programmes, although housing is usually easier to find than jobs. It was generally agreed that although a settlement plan should take account of the whole environment and place an important emphasis on housing and community contacts, employment opportunities should be regarded as the most crucial factor.

There are many examples of good-quality vocational-training or language-training programmes failing to lead to employment. The French *Fonds pour l'installation locale des Refugiés* (FILOR) has been able to provide training in information skills, secretarial work, accountancy, security work and taxi driving. It does note, however, that although the refugees generally feel that they have acquired a qualification and have been made competitive on the job market, few of them actually move directly into work. It is now continuing its training schemes, but targeting its activities more towards access to employment. As Jones (1982) diplomatically puts it, 'Not all the job training courses lead to permanent employment for the refugees and at the time of the survey only 35 of the 96 on a job course were recorded as having employment'.

Five years later the Vietnamese were still reluctant to take up training courses as they were unconvinced that this would improve their position.

In its successful Introductory Programme for Foreigners Norway emphasises the need for an integrated scheme involving early planning, language and vocational training in realistic environments, work and social-skills training, work experience, close links to employers, and post-placement support to both refugees and employers.

Case studies of successful development plans could provide invaluable insights into settlement problems. Comparing the benefits of individual or group approaches and finding out whether settlement plans should emphasise specialist rather than mainstream training would be particularly useful.

Local Initiatives

If the approach is to be thorough and professional, the data provided on local labour markets must project trends in patterns of employment. These can play an important part in matching new careers or job opportunities with the skills, experiences and ambitions of individual refugees.

In Denmark and Norway, where courses are geared to the needs of the refugees and designed to match local labour demands, there have been some significant successes. In Sweden, where refugees have been encouraged to accept short-term posts in areas where long-term employment is unlikely, there are fears that the kind of secondary resettlement that has occurred with Vietnamese refugees in the UK will take place. Refugees need to find effective ways of building bridges between themselves and specific employers through family, friends, agencies and other networks.

The DRC is placing considerable emphasis on a new initiative to work through local employment officers based in its premises. Both the Dutch Refugee Council and Ockenden Venture (UK) are experiencing some success in getting refugees into employment by building up strong ties between vocational training schemes and local employers.

The French agency, FILOR, has found that its considerable efforts to train refugees and to make them competitive on the job market have not led to the positive results it would have liked to have seen. Consequently, it too is paying more attention to local initiatives to co-fund the placing of refugees through job creation schemes.

It is essential to establish new ways of ensuring that employers and other employees do not see refugees as a potential problem, or as a problem after they have been appointed. The Norwegians, Swedes, Danes and Dutch now recognise the need to build a bridge between the local manager (the employer) and individual refugees. This has to be maintained and links with local trade-union representatives fostered.

Research into these models of good and bad practice, identifying the key data that are necessary for refugees to plan their future in a locality, would support the new emphasis on local initiatives and solutions.

Confidence Building

The strengths, talents and motivations of newly-arrived refugees are often not deployed to the greatest effect. These qualities should be made use of by giving refugees enough confidence, information and understanding to plan their own futures.

There is consequently a strong argument in favour of early and intensive programmes to introduce refugees to the host community and its language, to provide additional training and to adapt skills for settlement. Poor planning at the outset and the creation of dependency could bring heavy costs both personally and to the state.

All the Scandinavian delegates stressed the dangers of the welfare (as opposed to development) basis of many settlement programmes. Although often offered with the best of intentions, these programmes led to 'social clients and not self-reliance'. Several speakers spoke of how a refugee who did not obtain a job within a year or so of arrival could be 'disabled for life'. Remarkably, some refugees do manage to obtain jobs after long periods of unemployment, but it is difficult to remain independent and confident as time goes on.

The director of the City of Stockholm Immigrants & Refugee Board believes that the passivity enforced on refugees while they wait for permits, makes it difficult for them to enter the labour market. Job centres are finding it increasingly difficult to persuade refugees who have acquired their work permits to accept jobs when they have been forced to be idle for a couple of years.

Links with networks in both the host and refugee communities can build confidence and contacts. Meeting and making friends among the employed and unemployed alike can help refugees settle in without having to renounce their past. Many jobs are obtained through having good contacts, by knowing when they are available and by seeing how others succeed.

A refugee's own self confidence and ability to instill confidence in a potential employer is crucial. To make the most of their opportunities, refugees must understand the environment and present themselves well at interviews and in job applications.

The French participants at the seminar emphasised the need to give refugees sufficient information to find their way around the institutional maze. Very little has been written on how refugees can best develop, or have already developed, their confidence and capabilities in tackling European systems on their own; neither have there been many studies on the kinds of training provided for finding a job.

Work Experience

In most industrialised countries you have a much better chance of obtaining a job if you are currently employed. Ironically, for refugees it may be said that you need to have a job to get a good job. Since refugees, unlike immigrants, arrive without a job to go to, there is the danger of a vicious circle of continuing unemployment with employers not prepared to take risks with older employees in responsible positions if they have no directly relevant experience.

This may be overcome if vocational or language training is strongly linked to work opportunities and practical experience is obtained in the work place. One participant at the seminar pointed out that a language lesson with a picture of a saw was no substitute for using and talking about it in a carpentry workshop.

The benefit of experience of the real work environment was stressed and it was seen that temporary or subsidised employment schemes could be of particular value to refugees. Wage subsidy schemes were being developed in the Netherlands, Germany and Norway and, though expensive initially, were apparently successful.

To cope with the placement, however, the refugee must have a basic level of understanding of the language and at least one skill that is of real benefit to the employer.

When such jobs (and indeed subsequent jobs) are seen as stepping stones to settlement, rather than conclusions to a process, when continued language and vocational training is given in a sympathetic environment, and when counselling and support is also available to employers and employees, highly successful results have emerged. It was seen that where this had occured in Finland and in the UK the outcomes had been very worthwhile.

The BRC has supplemented its temporary work experience programme with substantial training opportunities and this has brought remarkably good employment results. Interestingly, the results for refugees are almost as good as for non-refugees. A close examination of this experience would be of great value and some good data are available. In view of the high priority being given to work experience and the growth of new initiatives, agencies are offering openings for action research in which innovative job placement schemes are being designed with a major monitoring and evaluation element.

Self Employment

It was noted at the seminar that, for some individuals, self employment was the way forward; it had the advantage of allowing the refugees' talents and motivations to come to the fore, but, for the majority, this did not in any way provide a panacea. It was difficult for refugees to understand the complexities of European economic systems, company law and taxation, not to mention the added difficulties of building up contacts, understanding the market and attaining capital. The enterprise training schemes being developed in Spain and the UK should provide valuable information on this and lead the way in establishing models on how significant numbers of refugees may best settle.

Though most small entrepreneurs receive no formal training, but learn informally on the job, there is a value in courses both to build the confidence of some refugees and to provide the necessary understanding of how to cope in an unfamiliar economic system. The new schemes in Spain, France and the UK require evaluation and comparision.

Traditionally, one way in which poorer groups have survived is through the informal economy, working long hours under poor conditions at home or (unofficially) in small factories. Though it is notoriously difficult to undertake research in this field, significant numbers of unemployed unskilled refugees are likely to have adopted this strategy. A deeper understanding of what is happening here and of how refugees can move from this informal sector, where they are often exploited, into the conventional employment market is needed. However, in that this is one of the few surviving stategies enabling the poorest to break out of the poverty trap, such research should be tackled with understanding.

Because participation in the informal economy is illegal, it is sometimes seen as an indictment of the refugees involved. It may also, however, be viewed as an indictment of refugee settlement programmes and evidence of the need for a radical change in favour of new employment strategies.

Note on Terminology: The nomenclature 'refugee' has been used in this chapter to describe those people who have been able to satisfy a government that they, personally, have a well-founded fear of persecution (often referred to as 'Convention' or 'A status' refugees). It also describes those who have sought asylum and applied for refugee status which was not given, but who were allowed to remain for a limited period with certain restrictions (often referred to as 'B status' refugees who, in the UK, have been given 'exceptional leave to remain'). The word 'settlement' has been broadly used to cover those whose first country of asylum is where they are in Europe and those who have arrived from a third country: the latter should more accurately be described as resettlement.

11 THE DETENTION OF ASYLUM–SEEKERS IN THE UK

Robin Cohen

Introduction

This chapter focuses on the detention of asylum–seekers, a phenomenon that may seem to some to be almost a contradiction in terms. Social convention in many societies has frequently dictated that a guest or a stranger with no hostile intent, or in a condition of distress, should be met with hospitality rather than the prospect of incarceration. In a number of societies (those of the Arabian peninsula being the best known), even sworn enemies are granted protection and treated with respect and courtesy once under a host's protection. Yet, in March 1987, an official reply to a question in the House of Commons revealed that there were some 130 asylum–seekers in detention in the UK. Outside the immigration agencies and the Home Office, few people were aware of these detainees until public attention was aroused by the scenes of 64 Tamil asylum–seekers demonstrating at Heathrow airport against being summarily removed in February 1987, and by the lease of a car ferry, anchored off Harwich, to accommodate asylum–seekers whose fate had yet to be determined by the Home Office.

Voluntary agencies dealing with immigration and refugee issues, such as the United Kingdom Immigration Advisory Service (UKIAS), the Joint Council for the Welfare of Immigrants (JCWI), the British Refugee Council (BRC) and the local office of the United Nations High Commission for Refugees (UNHCR), had all expressed their concern to the British government about the increasing numbers of asylum–seekers being detained, the longer periods involved and the conditions under which the detainees were held. In June 1967, the Medical Foundation, a voluntary organisation set up 'for the care of victims of torture', called for the right of asylum–seekers to seek legal and medical advice of their own choice.

While it is possible to regard such representations as the unduly alarmist special pleadings of over–concerned lobbyists, the agencies were given startling official support when a coroner's jury found that the suicide of a Ugandan asylum–seeker, Ahmed Katangole, in Pentonville Prison on 22 March 1987, showed 'official indifference and lack of care'. While the coroner said that this was the first time he had ever given such a verdict, a spokesman for Inquest, an organisation monitoring the work of coroners' courts, suggested that the verdict should lead to a 'monumental shakeup in the way immigrants and political refugees ... [are] treated'. It subsequently emerged that Katangole had attempted suicide before and that, had the examining psychiatrist been consulted, she would have strongly advised against the move to Pentonville. According to the JCWI, there were at least half-a-dozen suicide attempts by asylum-seeker detainees during 1987.

How are the abandonment of the normal social conventions of hospitality and the apparent disregard of customary legal rights expected by any UK citizen explained in the case of detained asylum-seekers? One starting point is that the right of asylum has historically firmly belonged to the state that grants it rather than to the individual who claims it (Goodwin-Gill 1983: 104). This places the receiving state and its representatives in an exceedingly powerful position which, it might be surmised, could easily translate into the abuses of state power and administrative discretion.

Second, while individual states are often generous in according asylum to citizens of rival powers or to those who have obvious scientific or technological use-value, they tend to be more resistant to other asylum-seekers. Third, the claims of refugees and asylum-seekers only have limited protection under international law. Their rights are enshrined in the 1951 Convention and a subsequent 1967 Protocol. The Convention stated that the right of asylum would be granted to those who had 'a well-founded fear of being persecuted for reasons of race, religion, nationality, membership of a particular social group or political opinion' (*ibid*: 247 et seq.).

Initial Perceptions Concerning Asylum-seekers

The signing of the Convention and the humanitarian basis of much international law do not, however, necessarily influence the thinking of government officials, politicians and immigration officers (now partly organised in the UK into a self-defensive Immigration Service Union). But these are the people principally responsible for making decisions about admissions, extensions of stay, detentions and deportations.

Officialdom's initial perception of those seeking asylum is likely to be informed by a number of interrelated precognitions which could be contrary to the intent and spirit of the relevant international agreements. Such perceptions may include:

- immigration officers being particularly concerned to exclude those who do not qualify for admission as immigrants, visitors or students. Since the wave of the 1930s, Britain has taken very few refugees, but has admitted (then firmly closed the door on) a significant number of immigrants. This may lead to a presumption that refugees are intending immigrants arriving under a different guise;

- this presumption being strongly reinforced by a popular press seemingly unable to distinguish between immigrants, refugees, visitors or students. This was borne out, for example, when a bizarre report in the *Daily Express* in February 1987, claiming that all visitors from the Asian sub-continent were illegal immigrants, led to a complaint to the Press Council. The Council ruled that the report was 'emotive, exaggerated and liable to appeal to racial prejudice' (*Guardian*, 15 June 1987).

- politicians being under some pressure to honour electoral promises and to respect the force of public opinion to stop all 'immigration'; and

- immigration officers, politicians and the press being equally unable to deal with the rapid population movements (facilitated by quick international transport) which have relatively recently been brought on by a spate of civil wars, natural disasters and other hazards in many parts of the world, with which they are totally, or virtually totally, unfamiliar.

These factors give some indication of what kind of reception and treatment those who arrive at the ports of entry, particularly those who arrive without notice or a significant pressure group acting on their behalf, are likely to receive. The UK government seems able to respond where there is broad sympathy for the refugees' case, where the programme is overseered by the Ministries of State concerned, where the numbers are known and limited and where arrangements for reception and resettlement have been made. Such groups are now termed 'quota refugees'.

Such favourable circumstances, however, rarely apply to an individual or to small cohorts of refugees arriving in Britain and claiming political sanctuary. For such groups, who fail to fit the category of approved or obviously useful refugees, the reception is likely to be much frostier.

There is little doubt that if refugees are black or brown, their case is made more difficult by the prevalence of racial discrimination and prejudice in Britain (and other European countries), by the confusion of their case for asylum with the general hostility to black immigration, and by the belief that black and brown people are likely to remain culturally alienated from the bulk of the British population. The point can perhaps best be made by imagining what kind of reception white South African refugees of British descent would be likely to receive in the event of a black revolution in that country.

After-Entry and On-Entry Detainees

Although this chapter is specifically concerned with the detention of those seeking asylum, it is necessary to observe more generally that there are two principal forms of detention for those held to be violating the Immigration Act of 1971: (a) detention after entry, which is for those accused of having violated the terms under which they were permitted to enter. Here the most common violation is 'illegal entry', but others include 'overstayers' (staying beyond the period stamped on the passport) and working when not permitted to do so; and (b) detention on entry pending a decision to admit, to vary the conditions of admission, to allow 'exceptional leave to remain' or to 'remove'. All these possibilities are discussed below.

Increasing numbers of asylum-seekers are being detained 'on-entry', often because they have been refused 'temporary admission' at the port of entry, sometimes on the grounds that they do not have an address of a relative to go to. It is also possible that 'after-entry' asylum-seekers may be detained. The two most common situations to obtain here are, first, when a 'genuine' asylum-seeker, out of fear, ignorance or even perhaps calculation, gains admittance as (say) a visitor, then later seeks to press a case for asylum (the Home Office treats such applicants as 'illegal entrants' who may be subject to detention on the grounds that they sought entry by deception) and, second, when circumstances in a home country alter adversely, forcing those who were admitted as (say) students or visitors to argue that it is no longer safe for them to return home.

Although relatively small numbers of post-entry asylum-seekers are detained, according to one report (PRT & JCWI n.d.), as a group, they 'spend longer in prison than anyone else held under Immigration Act powers'. Once a decision to treat an asylum-seeker as an illegal entrant has been reached, the full force of the administrative powers of detention granted under the Immigration Act of 1971 can be applied. In 1986 some 1,045 alleged illegal entrants were detained (HO *Statistical Bulletin*, March 1987). This in itself is cause enough for concern, but the extensive use of the powers conferred under the 1971 Immigration Act also raises certain civil liberty questions, particularly over the detainee's restricted access to bail and the frequent denial of their right to a judicial appeal.

In the case of asylum-seekers, there are some additional indications that the Home Office wishes to impede any meaningful access to representation in the pressing of their claims. It is difficult, for example, to interpret the Home Secretary's statement in the House of Commons on 3 March 1987 in any other way. First, he appeared to undermine the hitherto normal expectation that the immigration officer would refer an asylum-seeker to UKIAS ('not all cases ... will be referred'). Second, the representations by MPs to defer deportations pending consideration of the strength of the claim will no longer be allowed 'where early removal is necessary'. Finally, Mr Hurd added, it 'follows that those who wish to seek to challenge in the courts decisions to refuse asylum cannot expect that they will automatically be allowed to stay here until proceedings are completed' (Parliamentary Report, *Guardian*, 4 March 1987).

Though in certain categories of immigration cases it has been common to refuse judicial appeals from inside the country for some time, the comments on notification and MPs' representations signal a new refrain on an old theme. This might be summarised as a ministerial attempt to turn a potentially emotive political and legal matter concerning asylum-seekers' rights into a technical matter best left to an internal decision by the Immigration Service. It remains to be seen whether this attempt will be sustained in law.

Legal Provisions and Issues

Before accepting the British government's right to detain asylum-seekers under the detention provisions of the Immigration Act of 1971 as unproblematic, it is worth making a few references to the issue of detention in international and comparative law. The UN Charter is often seen as the starting point for human rights' law. Article 3 establishes the right to life, liberty and security of person; Article 5 to freedom from torture or cruelty; Article 9 to freedom from arbitrary arrest, detention or exile; and Article 14 to the right to seek asylum. European law on the detention of aliens has been heavily influenced by the European Convention of Human Rights, in which Article 5(1) states that 'No one shall be deprived of his liberty save in [specified] cases and in accordance with a procedure prescribed by law.' The specified cases refer to detention under the criminal law and procedure (normally suspicion of crime); detention as a measure of social protection or control (which refers to the detention of social misfits and minors in compliance with a court order) and, finally, administrative detention (which is the procedure normally evoked by the UK government in the cases considered here). But though the European Convention permits administrative detention as a means of effecting deportation, in the legal testing and application of the Convention, several important provisos have developed to limit the state's power (see ZDWF 1987). These include:

- such detention must not be *unduly prolonged*, as where it can no longer lead to deportation in the reasonably near future (Fawcett 1969: 449);

- while detention for the purposes of deportation can legitimately be made by administrative decision, 'the inability of the detainee to challenge the lawfulness of his detention before a court would be inconsistent with Article 5(4)'(*ibid.*);

- it is possible, though no application in these terms has yet succeeded, that there may be an obligation on contracting states to ensure that no individual suffers treatment forbidden by Article 3 (torture, inhumane punishment) at the hands of a third party;

- another passage in the Convention, Article 5(2), states that 'everyone who is arrested shall be informed promptly, in a language which he understands, of the reason for his arrest and any charge against him'.

A number of restrictions on a state's power to detain have also developed in comparative law. For example, Dutch law has now established beyond dispute that a court may find a detention order unlawful in the case of *détournement de pouvoir* or *abus de pouvoir*. US law is even more protective of the individual about to be deported. There, Goodwin-Gill (1978: 226) comments:

> ... the alien will only normally be arrested where this is in the public interest or if he is likely to abscond. The order to show cause must state the grounds upon which the *prima facie* case of deportability is based in such a way as to enable the alien to meet the allegations against him. Although attempts to introduce the full requirements of the judicial process have generally failed, the statute does provide for the minimum rights essential to a fair hearing'.

In 1925, Justice Anderson of the US district court for the district of Massachusetts made a compelling statement (cited by Grahl-Madsen 1972: 431) regarding the detention of non-criminal aliens: 'There is no power in this court or in any other tribunal in this country to hold indefinitely any sane citizen or alien in imprisonment, except as a punishment for crime. Slavery was abolished by the Thirteenth Amendment. It is elementary that deportation or exclusion proceedings are not punishment for crime.'

Other comparative law from Brazil, Estonia, Belgium, France, Argentina, Canada and Germany, though less strident than that of the US, tend to enunciate similar principles, namely that no taint of criminality should be attached to asylum-seekers, that there should be a definite limit to the length of detention necessary to process the claim for asylum and that some kind of fair hearing should be provided, even if this stops short of full judicial rights (*ibid*: 431–5). Though comparative law provides only a moral, not a binding, force, UK law and practice seems to compare poorly with a number of other countries.

Another legal issue, which emerged in the UK with the arrival of 64 Tamil asylum-seekers in February 1987, was whether non-possession of documents, or the possession of forged or invalid documents, was sufficient reason for the Home Office to detain these passengers pending deportation. The minister then in charge of immigration at the Home Office (David Waddington) strongly upheld the immigration officers' view that 58 of the 64 Tamils were involved in 'an organised attempt by racketeers to secure admission by fraudulent means' and that the absence, or forging, of documents indicated that the Tamils were attempting 'to seek entry through clearly bogus applications for asylum' (*Guardian*, 18 February 1987). The minister's insistence on valid travel documents is in narrow conformity with Article 31(1) of the 1951 Convention which states that 'the contracting states shall not impose penalties, on account of their illegal entry or presence, on refugees who, *coming directly* from a territory where their life and freedom was threatened ... enter or are present in their territories without authorisation, provided they present themselves without delay to the authorities and show good cause for their illegal entry or presence'. (For legal interpretations see Grahl-Madsen 1972: 195–225; and Goodwin-Gill 1986: 143–5.) By emphasising the Tamils' arrival via a third country (India) the minister could give salience to their forged documents, even although the Tamils' case was obviously genuine and the non-authorised documents may well have been an indication of the *strength* rather than the weakness of their claims.

As if to emphasise the legitimacy of the UK government's position, as well as its strict legality, Waddington decided to challenge the view that conditions in Sri Lanka were such as to 'threaten life and freedom' by undertaking a well-publicised visit to the country. However, shortly after his return to the UK, and his reassertion that all was well in Sri Lanka, newspaper reports appeared of serious bombing and communal violence in the Sri Lankan civil war.

The government responded to the Tamil incident by hastily passing the Immigration (Carriers' Liability) Act through parliament. It required airlines to ensure that their passengers carried valid (or apparently valid) travel documents, including visas where necessary. Although the implications of this Act are the subject of a separate study (BRC 1987), three observations are pertinent here: (a) the obligation to admit refugees under Article 31 applies even in the absence of visas or any other form of travel document; (b) the carriers' employees have, in effect, been turned into extension workers for the Immigration Service. Although they are not required to judge the legality of the documents presented to them, they may be placed in iniquitous and unenviable situations, even perhaps having to decide between an applicant's prospects of life or death; and (c) it seems unreal to expect asylum-seekers to obtain travel documents from a government from which they are likely to be alienated and a visa from a British embassy which may be inaccessible or surrounded by government agents or security forces. Indeed, in many circumstances possession of a valid passport and visa is more likely to indicate that the claim to asylum is invalid rather than the reverse.

It is now appropriate to return briefly to the Home Secretary's statement of 3 March 1987. It has already been argued that the inability of the detainee to challenge the lawfulness of his detention before a court is inconsistent with Article 5(4) of the 1951 Convention and that other government's permit a wider challenge than that allowed in the UK. Moreover, the difficulties of interpreting the genuineness of a claim to asylum and the apparent difficulty shown by so experienced an observer as Waddington in judging the conditions obtaining in a country such as Sri Lanka, suggests that other legal remedies should be available to those refused asylum. In particular, access to bail and the right of representation and appeal should be unfettered. Bail is difficult to obtain if an arrivee has been refused leave to enter within seven days. Even after seven days, characteristically sureties of £2,000–£3,000 are required from two people, one of whom has to be a British resident/citizen and the other of whom has to own a home. These conditions are normally insuperable for an asylum-seeker. With respect to the notion that a right of appeal can meaningfully be exercised from abroad, this has been shown to be impractical and seems to undermine established rights in English law for anyone, alien or Briton, to apply for a writ of *habeas corpus* 'calling on those who are detaining him to show that his detention is justified by law', to call witnesses and cross-examine in defence (ADWG 1985: 30). It also appears to violate the entitlement to 'a fair and public hearing', an entitlement which supersedes, so the European Commission of Human Rights argues, the right of a state to control the entry and exit of foreigners (Grahl-Madsen 1972: 276).

Detention Procedures and Conditions

The immigration officer's unusual powers to detain or remove an entrant are mainly derived from a section in the Immigration Act of 1971. In exercising this power he issues form TM2/RLE (Refused Leave to Enter) to detain an entrant under Schedule 2, para. 9. Temporary detention is then confirmed by the issue of form TM3/IS 81 and an interview in a 'secondary examination area', where surprisingly large numbers are held. S. d'Orey (1984: 9–10) estimates that in one year (1981) as many as 20,000 people were detained at Heathrow and perhaps 3,000 in Dover and Folkestone. She suggests that there are serious grounds for concern in the way this temporary detention is organised, but because the individuals refused leave to enter are often unqualified or in transit, their situation, indeed their existence, is barely known, even by concerned voluntary agencies. What remains to be established in the light of the Immigration Service or other sections of the Home Office's apparent concern to bypass the stages of representation and legal appeal, is whether asylum-seeking detainees may be held in temporary detention, then returned to their countries of origin or put onto onward flights without their cases ever having been referred to UKIAS, JCWI or the BRC.

Until the Home Secretary's statement of 3 March, asylum-seekers issued with form IS 91, implying detention for more than a short time, were nearly always referred to a voluntary agency, normally UKIAS, and a more lengthy process of evaluating their status commenced. While the Home Office has no legal obligation to refer asylum cases to UKIAS, in practice, the great majority had been so referred. In March 1983, Waddington argued that there was a 'strong case for formulating arrangements for the notification of asylum cases to an agency ... The Refugee Unit at the Home Office will in future give formal notification to the UKIAS refugee counsellors of all cases when no other agency or Honourable Member has previously intervened and a negative decision has been proposed'. Unfortunately, rather than signal the formulation of a general principle, this very sensible proposal seems to have stemmed from the then minister's reaction to the ire of some Tory backbenchers, furious that a Rumanian was sent back 'behind the Iron Curtain' (*Guardian*, 4 March 1987). The same minister appeared to have abandoned this suggestion in the case of the Tamil asylum-seekers, thus demonstrating the political nature of asylum-related decisions.

Once detained, asylum-seekers then enter, with other 'immigration prisoners', the strange half-world of the immigration detention centres. These are located at Harmondsworth (96 persons), the Queen's Building (Heathrow), the Beehive (Gatwick), Foston Hall (Derbyshire) and the airport and port detention centres at Manchester, Birmingham and the Channel ports. The Ashford and Risley remand centres (the former with a 'deport block' holding 98 prisoners) and any one of the 120 prisons or youth custody centres in Britain may, and often are, also used to hold immigration prisoners for longer than overnight or temporary detention. The majority of women are sent to Holloway. Other facilities have been added at Latchmere House in Richmond, while in 1987 a fresh addition was made to the Home Office's collection of properties in the form of a leased car ferry, the Earl William anchored off Harwich. S. d'Orey's (1984) account on conditions in the detention centres refers to the pre-1983/4 period. While her account remains disturbing (in that there is little to indicate that conditions in those centres have improved), it was thought that some impression of newly-acquired facilities might provide a fairer insight into the Home Office's planned provision for the future.

I accordingly visited the detention facilities aboard the Earl William car ferry in May 1987. At the time there were only two dozen detainees on board; by mid-July the numbers had risen to 70 (including some women). Although the ferry's full capacity was 252, one officer in charge of the facility assured me that it was unlikely to house more than 120 detainees. With some insensitivity, the ferry was opened by the Home Office for its new business in May 1987, shortly after the Zeebrugge ferry disaster.

On the day of the visit the detainees were mainly Tamils, but there were also six Iranians and five Afghani nationals. They were confined to the ferry, but excluded from their cabins during the day. The cafeteria food was adequate, the lounge areas clean, a small shop had been set up on board and a doctor held a regular surgery. If dental attention was required, the detainees would be taken under guard to a dentist in the town. A small deck area had been roped off for a rough-and-ready mosque; table tennis was available on a greasy and gloomy car deck. No adequate exercise facilities were provided; the detainees were not even allowed to walk in an easily-secured dockside area.

The facility's main problem was that it gave the general impression of being under siege from the surrounding town. Adverse comments in the local press about the ferry's health and sanitary arrangements were probably no more than thinly-veiled expressions of racism. Local residents, who had suddenly become enthusiastic defenders of the dubious vistas of the marine environment, had initiated legal proceedings to stop the use of the ferry as a detention centre. Three open demonstrations, apparently inspired mainly from outside the town, also mobilised extreme right-wing opposition to the use of the ferry. The townsfolk tended to regard the detainees as criminals and many saw the ferry's 'offshore' location as an indication that the detainees were 'not really' in Britain. The ferry also took on the air of a hospital ship, with the associated ideas of contagion and disease.

To their credit, the immigration officers, cleaners and privately-contracted Securicor guards seemed conscious of the need to reassure the detainees that they were in safe and non-prejudiced hands. However, one of the detainees spontaneously expressed a strong preference for being guarded by normal prison officers (who, he asserted, knew the difference between criminals and the asylum-seekers 'who shouldn't be in prison'). He thought the Securicor guards inexperienced (they could indeed have been seconded from such mundane tasks as guarding warehouses), unsympathetic and inclined to view the detainees in criminal terms. How far this view was shared is impossible to tell, but an experienced immigration counsellor believed it to be common. This was a view not shared by senior Home Office officials (see below). There was no evidence of brutality or systematic racism, but the general impression gained was that the external conditions surrounding the ferry made this an inappropriate environment to secure individuals who needed sympathetic attention to their needs in a caring, therapeutic environment.

The ferry's use as a detention centre was questioned by a 10-day hunger strike by detainees and constant pressure by voluntary agencies. Its fate was finally sealed, however, by what the leader of the Tamil Action Group, Sinnapur Maharasingham, called 'the furious hand of nature' (*Guardian*, 17 Oct. 1987). The wild storm that struck Southern England on 15-16 October 1987 left Harwich without electricity and holed the Earl William after it burst from its mooring and ran aground on a sandbank. So abashed were the Home Office officials at this apparent reprimand from 'on high' that they released the 35 Tamil detainees on board to their friends and relatives rather than detain them elsewhere.

However, despite this happy case of divine intervention, some of the Tamils were still subject to deportation and detainees from Sri Lanka and other countries remain in other Centres. Two case studies of a Chilean and an Iranian detainee are recorded below.

The Detainees

The following information on two detainees, presented here for illustrative rather than representative purposes, is assembled from agency case notes, personal observation and interview. Some details have been changed to make identification more difficult.

Case 1: Fernando: Fernando arrived from Chile towards the end of 1986 via a third country and has been in detention ever since. He comes from a poor family and left school at 14. As a young man he joined the Young Socialists and became active as a trade unionist in the mining sector. He was a party member and ardent supporter of Allende's Popular Unity government. When that government was overthrown, he fell victim to military and police harassment, torture and brutality. He left Chile in 1976 to join a sister in Argentina. There he was granted refugee status, but became subject to bouts of depression and homesickness and was committed to a mental institution for a time. Believing that the political situation in Chile had changed for the better, he returned home only to be picked up by the civil police, threatened with death and again tortured. His wife was raped by the policemen searching his home and he fell into a disconsolate depression, losing his job as a result.

Hearing of his condition, his sister in England, who herself had been granted refugee status, encouraged him to come to this country and sent him a return ticket to do so. It seems she also indicated that he would find work here with her husband, an independent trader. On arrival, and probably at her suggestion, Fernando told the immigration officer that he was coming to the UK for a short-term visit. His baggage was searched and a letter from his sister was found, indicating that she expected him to stay for a longer period. Later he claimed asylum.

Fernando was immediately sent to the Harmondsworth detention centre, which, a psychiatrist reported, 'reminded him of the places where he had previously been tortured'. One agency concerned with immigration arranged for him to be examined by two psychiatrists, one of whom spoke Spanish. A voluntary charity concerned with the effects of torture arranged another examination. Both reports confirmed that Fernando had been tortured. One referred to the prospect of permanent mental disorder in the event of continued detention; the other mentioned the possibility of suicide.

Fernando's sister elicited the help of a sympathetic MP, who wrote to the Home Office minister on at least six occasions pleading Fernando's case for release, recognition as a political refugee and the withdrawal of his removal order. So far only the last has been achieved. The Home Office insists that Fernando's attempt to mislead the authorities at the original airport interview constitutes sufficient grounds for his removal and continued detention (at the time of completing the data, for over six months). This ostensibly minor detail of the case illustrates how thoroughgoing are the Home Office's attempts to discover inconsistencies in the arrivee's answers and the extraordinary lengths to which the agencies have to go to refute such 'inconsistencies'. According to the Home Office, Fernando's 1976 claim to refugee status was invalid. The department baldly asserted that although Fernando had applied for asylum in Argentina 'this had been refused'. It is interesting to speculate how the department claimed such intimate knowledge of the decisions of the Argentine government seeing that, since the Falklands war, Britain has had no diplomatic relationship with Argentina. The concerned agency had to use the good offices of the UNHCR to establish that Fernando *was* indeed a recognised refugee in Argentina and also managed to find a Uruguayan to make a sworn statement that he knew Fernando in the San Juan refuge in Argentina. The Home Office apparently still did not consider that its erroneous judgement on this issue might put into question its information on other related issues. The department remained unmoved by medical .evidence and was unwilling to consider the simple interim solution of releasing Fernando to the care of his sister pending a decision.

Case 2: Reza: Reza arrived in the UK from France on a fake Dutch passport around Christmas 1986. His journey from his home country, Iran, had been a convoluted one. He had left Iran illegally on foot in October 1985 and spent some nine months in Turkey. In Istanbul he had managed to buy an Iranian passport with which he had travelled to Yugoslavia (where he stayed for over two months) and thence to Greece (where he had stayed for three months). There he had obtained his false Dutch papers and travelled to Britain via Italy, Switzerland and France. In that the 1951 Convention permits the receiving country to download cases to the country of first asylum, the question of his recognition in Britain was much complicated by this prior history. Negotiations with the Turkish, Yugoslavian and Greek governments ensued, but none of them would accept any responsibility for Reza's fate. Although Reza was only in

France for one night en route to the UK, the Home Office decided to 'try' removal to France, but this backfired, as the French authorities detained him, accused him of being a terrorist (apparently a sure-fire way of not having to recognise an asylum-seeker), broke his spectacles and returned him to Britain.

Apart from his European and Asian journeys, Reza had once been a student in the US, where he had married, produced a child and also established a close relationship with another woman. Unfortunately for Reza, neither of these women were prepared to vouch for him. As far as they were concerned, their relationships were over and they did not wish to persuade the US authorities to intervene on Reza's behalf. Why then did he leave the US? According to Reza, he felt compelled to return to Iran to search for a missing and loved brother. The Home Office official reviewing Reza's case did not take this story seriously. 'Paragraphs 41 and 205 of the UN Handbook put great store on an assessment of credibility, but this is a feature notably lacking in this case', he opined. Far from being involved in a quest for a missing brother, as he claimed, it seemed evident to the official that Reza had 'abandoned his wife in the US to avoid domestic responsibilities'.

As with Fernando, the agency concerned had to go to great lengths to establish, in this case from a former college roommate of Reza's in the US, that there was indeed a missing brother. A sworn testimonial from the roommate, now a respectable computer systems engineer working for a leading US aeroplane manufacturer, established beyond doubt that many urgent family telephone calls were received and made regarding Reza's brother and that he was indeed agitated and preoccupied with his fate when leaving the US for Iran. Officials at the Home Office also disbelieved other statements about Reza's political activities in Iran, but, as in the previous case, they do not apparently regard the refutation of one of their most damaging accusations (the missing brother issue) as questioning their Olympian certainty about the supposed lack of credibility of Reza's other statements.

Although we have included details of only two cases, other client histories and the comments of case workers for the responsible agencies suggest that there are a number of disturbing features about Home Office evaluations. First, great credence is placed on the judgement of the immigration officer at the initial interview. Little or no account is taken of the difficult situation genuine applicants face in justifying themselves (in a second or third language) to an overworked or unsympathetic official after a long journey and possibly also after a recent loss of family lives, careers or property. Second, any inconsistency in the arrivees' statements are minutely recorded and used against them. Any positive evidence produced in favour of the applicant is rarely acknowledged in correspondence and does not lead to a reassessment of other negative judgements, often made after the event by desk officers who have not seen the applicant. Third, very little advice is given on the limited rights an asylum-seeking detainee does possess. And fourth, official communications are distant and superior in tone, held not to be challengeable by asylum-seekers. Although perhaps expected in view of the common precognitions of the Immigration Service, several case workers have been surprised to find representations by lawyers, MPs and medical practitioners dismissed with similar insouciance.

Home Office Perceptions

Three senior Home Office officials kindly agreed to be interviewed in connection with this study. As there were no significant disagreements between them, their views on a number of issues have been recorded below, as if with a collective voice.

The Home Office agreed that the current pattern of asylum-seeking had changed and that the majority now sought asylum on-entry rather than after-entry, which had previously been more common. The officials did not, however, feel that this change in pattern implied that any changes to current procedures or to the discretionary powers of immigration officers were needed.

The officials maintained that there is a clear distinction between asylum applicants and 'third country cases'. Whereas those arriving directly would be, and are, treated fairly under the 1951 Convention (which the government strongly upheld), those arriving via a third country (with whom genuine applicants are often confused) would be regarded in a different light.

The officials also felt that the emphasis on (and agency concern with) the *detention* of asylum-seekers gave a false impression, as 'the great majority' of them are given temporary admission. Although the exact figures were not at hand, the officials estimated that about nine arrivees were given temporary admission for every one detained. (Based on the minister's figure cited earlier, this would yield a total of 1,170 temporarily admitted compared to 130 asylum-seekers detained.)

Given that many of the arrivees were carrying false documents obtained in a third country after they had left their natal home, the Home Office officials did not think that too much weight was being attached to the initial interview. On the matter of false documentation presented on entry, they held a far more open position than that contained in the statement by Waddington cited earlier. They were careful to indicate that documentation was only one of many items considered in the decision to grant immigration status and that the guidelines in the UNHCR Handbook were generally followed. They agreed that in some circumstances the possession of false documents could be grounds for suspicion. Equally, in other cases, the opposite applied. They insisted, however, that false documentation was normally obtained in third countries, which did not indicate a hasty departure under an immediate threat from within the applicant's original country.

With respect to notifying the voluntary agencies, the officials were unable to provide the kind of assurances that UKIAS, in particular, were seeking. They confirmed the minister's statement that it was uncertain whether UKIAS would be notified at all, let alone within a particular period. They also averred that failure to notify was 'not inadvertent', but a deliberate decision reflecting internal discussion of a particular case.

They were, in principle, opposed to the idea of detention and very much preferred to make decisions that did not necessitate such action. The Home Office's Refugee Unit was automatically notified of all detentions and there were regular reviews of cases, both at the port of entry and at Immigration Service headquarters. It was confirmed that desk officers at Lunar House would be unlikely ever to interview a detainee or an asylum-seeker personally. When questioned again about whether this placed undue reliance on the port of entry interview, this was denied. On the contrary, it was argued, all representations, from agencies, lawyers, medical practitioners and MPs were given careful consideration.

The officials held that a long detention usually reflected an applicant exhausting the processes of judicial appeal and review rather than undue delays at the Home Office (although resources in the Refugee Unit were somewhat stretched and a quicker result could no doubt be achieved with more staff). Lengthy delays on some cases also had to be set in context. With the exclusion of asylum-seekers, the turn-round time for most detainees was two and a half days and it was difficult to imagine doing much better than that. No conclusive comment emerged as to whether it would be in the interests of all parties to put an absolute limit on the period of detention, though I gained the impression that some such proposal might be seriously considered.

The discussion about legal representation turned on whether asylum-seeking detainees should acquire rights akin to those of British residents or should have the same as those granted to arrivees under the 1971 Immigration Act. They inclined to the latter view. They felt that an appropriate safeguard against abuse was provided by the possibility of challenging the act of detention through presentation of a writ of *habeas corpus* when there was a failure to serve a notice properly under the terms of the Immigration Act of 1971. They could envisage no circumstances of wider legal challenge other than the improper serving of this notice. This view contrasts markedly with that of a leading refugee lawyer. Goodwin-Gill (1986: 149–50) writes: 'Detention, it is submitted, must not only be shown to be legally authorised, but also to be necessary: and if the criminally accused are so protected, no less can be due to non-nationals not so affected, or to those in search of refuge and protection'.

On the conditions of detention, no-one pretended that the facilities provided were luxurious, but it was asserted that they 'compared favourably' to other similar detention centres. (It was not established what the comparator was.) It was not thought that improving the system of recording arrivals, transfers and departures of detainees was worth the effort, though there was an expressed willingness to entertain a specific proposal on this question. The argument presented that there seemed to be a lot of unnecessary transfers was vigorously denied. Detainees were not capriciously moved around. They had to be moved from some places (such as Harmondsworth) where an absolute limit of five days applied. Other reasons for transfer included the fact that ordinary prisons did not admit people over the weekend, whereas Harmondsworth did. Phones were provided, so relatives and lawyers could be advised of the movements of detainees (though it was agreed that, except in one case, phone cards and coins were not provided). The officials were not, in any case, aware of any significant number of complaints by relatives or lawyers trying to locate detainees.

In responding to a suggestion that the authorities should adopt a more relaxed posture, given the small numbers of refugees and asylum-seekers arriving in the UK, the respondents agreed that UK numbers are small by international, especially German, standards. By way of parenthesis, it can be noted that asylum applications in the UK rose from 2,352 in 1980 to 5,444 in 1985. The figure for 1986 was only 3,900. Asylum-seekers in other European countries during 1986 included 15,000 in Sweden, 26,300 in France and 99,700 in West Germany (HO *Statistical Bulletin*, 19 May 1987; BRC figures). Statistical evidence such as this was of little interest to the interviewed officials, however, who felt that tough measures were necessary for preventive reasons and as a public indication of the difficulty of getting into the UK. It would be much worse if, like Canada, they had to 'push the door shut' after a more liberal practice had become institutionalised.

Conclusions and Recommendations

This chapter was first written as a commissioned report for the BRC and other agencies as a means of influencing public policy. As such, the conclusions took a more schematic and practical form than is usual in an academic work. I have retained a summary of these recommendations in this version to indicate the lines of possible reform.

At the level of political and administrative reform, I recommended that a statement be issued at ministerial level reaffirming the UK's commitment to the spirit and purpose of the Conventions relating to the treatment of asylum-seekers from all countries. This would create a positive atmosphere of goodwill. Immigration officers should be provided with regular briefings integrated into their normal training in respect of the legal provisions pertaining to refugees and the conditions obtaining in selected countries. These briefings should be led by independent legal and academic tutors and addressed from time to time by representatives of the UNHCR, UKIAS, JCWI, the BRC and other relevant agencies. The normal reviews of cases within the Home Office should include interviews of applicants by desk officers from Lunar House. Such interviews should be given more credence than those conducted at the port of entry where factors associated with psychological stress may have produced distortions. Except in exceptional cases, asylum-seekers at the port of entry should be given temporary admission pending a decision on their status, particularly where they can be released to the care of relatives or to an accredited voluntary agency. Asylum-seeker detainees should be clearly distinguished from other Immigration Act detainees. Separate statistics should be routinely made available each month to the agencies concerned and on request to other interested parties. This information should appear in the Home Office statistics at least every quarter and in the prison statistics at least once a year. A daily log of all asylum-seekers should be computer-generated and stored by the Refugee Unit of the Immigration & Nationality Department of the Home Office. Access via terminals and modems located at the ports of entry, the places of detention and at recognised agencies should be freely available.

At the legal level, I recommended there should be a clear maximum period (seven days) during which the provisions for administrative detention under the Immigration Act of 1971 apply. In the small number of cases where there is a need to hold on-entry asylum-seekers to establish *bona fides* and to evaluate complex claims for asylum, there should be a fixed limit to how long this process can be continued before release. A period of 90 days is recommended, at which time the status of 'refugee' or 'exceptional leave to remain' must be granted. During the period of detention the detainee should be allowed untrammelled access to legal consultation and representation. Applications for bail under the Bail Act of 1976 should be permitted and the current restrictions discontinued. Applications for the release from detention from day 8 to day 90 should be permitted on three grounds (i) that the state has abused its power, (ii) that the state is held to be detaining the individual with no reasonable prospect of returning him other than to a country where he might suffer torture or danger and (iii) that the period of detention has been unduly prolonged in view of the medical condition of the detainee. A clear written statement of the grounds for detention should be available to the detainee in his own language, to his legal representative and to any other interested party. Until a computer-generated list can be accessed (see above), the Immigration Service should be obliged to notify a recognised agency of all asylum-seekers presenting themselves at a port of entry within 48 hours. Appeal rights should be made unambiguous. The administrative appeals system should be reformed to allow opportunities for cross examination. Adjudicators and tribunal members should be obliged to call expert testimony concerning the country of origin in all asylum cases. There should be no question that the appellant has a right to remain in this country pending the outcome of his case. The quick processing of claims should not be at the expense of natural justice, or the rights to representation and advice.

I further recommended that the conditions under which asylum-seekers (and all Immigration Act detainees) are held should in no way imply that they are being convicted of a criminal offence. Ideally, there should be purpose-built reception centres, including desks staffed by legal aid practices, the Home Office and relevant voluntary agencies. In no sense should the atmosphere resemble a prison. Instead, a therapeutic, counselling and caring environment should be fostered with minimal (preferably only perimeter) security. Apart from access to telephones, a list of immigration advisory bodies and suitable lawyers should be provided in a manner comprehensible to the detainee. Visits from relatives in this country should be freely allowed and facilitated. The detainee and his relatives should be provided with a clear map of the place of detention in relation to the surrounding transport. The practice of moving detainees without serious cause (see below) should cease. Detainees should have full rights to educational and recreational facilities. In addition to medical and dental attention, personal counselling and suitable clothing should be provided. The detainee should have the right to independent medical advice. Alternatives to detention centres, such as a refugee hostel run by the agencies, should be actively encouraged. Pending such provision, a detainee should be held in a Home Office facility (to be known as a 'reception centre') not more than 20 miles from the three major ports of entry (Gatwick, Heathrow and Manchester airports). The lease on the Earl William facility should be allowed to expire. (This recommendation turned out to have been unnecessary. As explained earlier the facility was shut after suffering storm damage.) Other than in the cases of riot or civil emergency, no-one shall be moved from their original place of detention (except in conditions of severe overcrowding) and only when the detainee, his legal representative and relatives (if any) are provided with at least 24 hours' notice and a clear indication of the alternative place of detention.

Acknowledgements: Thanks for advice and help to: Helen Bamber, Martin Barber, Ken Browne, Steve Cohen, Jeff Crisp, Ann Dummett, Selina Goulbourne (for legal advice), Mr A. Holton, Mr N. Montgomery-Pott, Mr R. P. Morris, Clive Nettleton, Abdul Paliwala, Thea Rogers, Philip Rudge, Sally Verity Smith and Barry Stoyle.

12 ASYLUM AND XENOPHOBIA IN WEST GERMANY

Robin Schneider

Auschwitz is only the ultimate consequence of racism (I say of racism and not of anti-semitism because, as is well known, Sinti and Roma were killed just like the Jews), and racism is just one form of xenophobia. What Auschwitz should have taught us and what we can observe everywhere today, is that murder and mass murder is the natural and ultimate consequence of xenophobia... Now xenophobia exists in our midst today in a form which, by and large, reproduces the anti-semitic syndrome.

(Tugendhat 1987: 22)

Is Racism a Daily Event?

The above quote by Ernst Tugendhat, the philosopher and Jew living in Berlin who was forced to flee from the Nazis, represents part of his intervention in a highly sensitive so-called 'Historiker debatte'. He provocatively focuses his attack on a point shared by both sides in the controversy (equally obsessed with the role of the National Socialists) who confine their arguments only to the 'ultimate' effects of racism. According to Tugendhat, the position in support of the German people's right to defend themselves against the 'Asiatic threat' (held by Nolte) and the supposed alternative, of anchoring West Germany firmly 'in the west' (held by Habermas), invariably overlook the actual alternatives at our disposal today. As a result, the end effects of their arguments are very similar.

Some may feel it is an exaggeration to speak of racism in Germany as a daily event, but what memories must the 'new camps' in Germany re-evoke (or still evoke) among the German people? What new ethnic boundaries are constituted and internalised when Arabs, Kurds and, above all, Palestinians are deported from West Germany into the civil war in Lebanon - even if they are deserters from the Syrian army (which incidentally controls Beirut airport)?

'Refugees become Victims of the Summer Break'

Thus read the headline of a left-wing Berlin newspaper in launching a frontal attack on the West German government for opportunistically taking advantage of the summer break of 1986 to twist the arms of voters in the pre–election campaign. The general election was scheduled to take place in mid–January 1987 after the Christian Social Union (CSU) had managed to force the political opposition, plus the liberal wing of the governing coalition, onto the defensive during the Bavarian state elections in mid–October. What had happened?

After many years of disagreement over whether or not legislation pertaining to asylum and the rights of alien citizens should be tightened up, the coalition parties (the Christian Democratic Union (CDU) and the CSU) and the Free Democratic Party (FDP) eventually agreed in late June 1986, only a few days before parliament's summer recess, to introduce some quite substantial changes to the existing asylum procedures. Although these changes were considered unconstitutional by some critics and merely ineffective by others, Burkhard Hirsch from the liberal wing of the FDP felt that while the agreed measures would be of little use, they would also be fairly harmless. The FDP, he felt, had at least stood by its agreements within the governing coalition and, most importantly, had prevented the sensitive subject of asylum from becoming an election issue. At a meeting a few days earlier, Chancellor Kohl had issued his first warning that attempts to prevent the 'misuse of asylum' could seriously undermine the constitution. Less than a week later, speaking on behalf of the CSU, the Minister for the Interior, Mr Zimmermann, went so far as openly to insist that paragraph 16.2.2 of the Constitution, which stated that 'politically persecuted persons had the right to asylum', be annulled.

Lively discussions followed over the next few weeks, with every politician remaining in Bonn, even if only for a short time, joining in the protest against 'asylants' (as refugees in present–day Germany are called) 'flooding' and 'swamping' West Germany and 'pushing back the Germans'. The tabloids and popular press wrote of the 'millions waiting at the door' and, for months on end, every political broadcast, radio and television programme saw politicians agitating against refugees. Even liberal newspapers, such as the *Süddeutsche*, began to use phrases like 'the flood of asylants' and the *Zeit* even went so far as to carry a caricature on its front page of a sewer washing asylants over the wall from East to West Berlin.

Meanwhile, the opposition and the FDP, together with some members of the CDU (such as Hanne Laurien and Ernst Benda) argued that the right to seek asylum was a basic constitutional right which, in a democracy, may not and cannot be changed. (In fact paragraph 19 of the Constitution specifically states that its main provisions are not subject to change.) However, changes were introduced at another, lower level. First, negotiations with East German leaders resulted (in autumn 1986) in the Berlin wall acting as an effective barrier to refugees. And second, 'intimidation measures' were introduced which went way beyond anything the socialist/liberal coalition had introduced in 1982.

A debate in the Bundestag in March 1986 over new legislation to govern asylum procedures revealed that the intimidation measures introduced in 1982 had already begun to take effect against the refugees in West Germany. For example the prohibition against working for a period of two years had made refugees heavily dependent on social welfare, xenophobia had increased and camps were once again being built. The UNHCR representative, René van Rooyen, felt that, taken as a whole and considering the duration of the asylum procedures, measures to control entry were becoming more and more unbearable for the people concerned. As he put it, they in effect 'violate the human dignity of those who seek refuge in our country' and he went on to call for their reversal as a 'basic precondition for the improvement of the general climate' in Germany (van Rooyen 1987). But the situation only became worse. In fact it became so bad that the Commissioner for Refugees in the European Parliament, Heinz-Oskar Vetter, in his report of February 1987, went so far as to accuse West Germany of being 'partially devoid of human dignity' in the way it cared for its refugees. The German government had actually admitted that various measures, such as forcing refugees to lodge in collective hostels, not allowing them to work, restricting their movement, not allowing them to cook, reducing their entitlement to social assistance and then insisting on paying it in kind rather than cash, were all deliberately made as unpleasant as possible in an attempt to deter the asylum-seekers from coming into the country in the first place (Vetter 1987: 17).

Making it Impossible to Use a Basic Right

In addition to the measures described above, government policy has shifted away from that of trying to prevent misuse of the constitutional right to asylum towards that of making the legitimate use of this basic right impossible. It was with this in mind that new negotiations with East Germany were entered into at the beginning of 1986. These led to East Berlin's position becoming somewhat unreliable in that the so-called inter-German 'credit swing' was increased and the status of Berlin turned into a saleable commodity. Since then no Tamils have been able to flee to West Berlin. In addition, secret negotiations have been conducted with other west European governments to standardise visa regulations for citizens from the main refugee countries and to introduce further restrictions in the transit zones, thus constructing a legal basis whereby the West Berlin police can turn back refuge seekers at the border.

A new law governing asylum procedures, in force since 1 January 1987, has virtually demolished any chances of persecuted people finding refuge in West Germany (see Pfaff 1987; Rittstieg 1986). Under the terms of this law the following criteria now pertain.

- Any political action by refugees against injustices in their home countries is forbidden; grounds arising after leaving the home country (the so-called *Nachfluchtgründe*) are no longer taken into consideration in the granting of asylum.

- Even the German police are now entitled to turn asylum-seekers back at the border. (The Frankfurt Legal Assistance Committee has described some of the effects of this legislation during the first months after the law came into force in 1987).

- 'General emergencies', such as the civil wars in Sri Lanka or Lebanon, are no longer regarded as sufficient grounds for granting asylum. In the first half of 1987 alone, this measure enabled the West German authority in charge of foreign refugees in Zirndorf to reduce the number of successful claimants to less than 10 per cent.

- Even those refugees whose freedoms or even lives are threatened can now be deported - repeated applications and the submission of further evidence no longer having a postponing effect.

- And finally, the former two-year ban on asylum-seekers applying for work has been extended to five years and a one-year ban introduced for 'East bloc' refugees, who were previously exempted from any form of work ban whatsoever.

According to the West German human rights organisations and various welfare associations involved with assisting refugees, these measures are blatant violations of the Constitution, especially of its basic rights to asylum, human dignity and equality. But how, one might ask, can these rights be enforced and who is entitled to press claims before the Constitutional Court?

The West German borders have been made more or less impermeable to refugees through visa regulations. Many other western European countries had introduced these requirements some years earlier, which was what made West Berlin such a useful loophole. Now the few who still succeed in getting in are evicted, usually in direct contravention of the 1951 Geneva Convention for Refugees, by which West Germany is supposed to be bound. According to its terms, there is *de jure* protection against deportation for anyone with 'a well-founded fear of being persecuted for reasons of race, religion, nationality, membership of a particular social group or political opinion' (UNHCR 1979: 84). West Germany is presently in the process of dismantling the constitutional right to asylum in a highly ruthless manner and in apparent violation of international law.

Apropos the new legislation on asylum procedures, Heinz-Oskar Vetter argues that not only are armed struggles and internal conflicts worldwide phenomena, they are also the reason why most refugees become homeless. 'People are fleeing from senseless brutality, from the grave deterioration of social, economic and physical conditions which have been caused by military and other forms of violence: armed conflicts are nothing but a form of violation of human rights' (Vetter 1987: 36). In the long term, he continues, development aid must be redirected. It must contribute to the solution of problems and prevent the streams of refugees from arising (*ibid:* 49).

Asked why development aid has so far failed to prevent the streams of refugees, the Secretary of State, Volkmar Köhler answered, on behalf of the West German government, that streams of refugees could not be stopped with development aid – now or in the future – but that German development policy, as part of a world policy for peace and stability, is likely to keep them out. He thus manages to divert attention away from the inevitable consequences.

Refugees in a Foreign Country: the State and Asylum

Wilhelm Emil Mühlmann saw the state as 'rooted in the right to sanctuary' and believed that it was through its ability to offer protection and thereby establish this right that one could recognise whether or not it was powerful (1961: 55). Mühlmann, the sage of German ethno-sociology, even went so far as to argue that asylum formed the basis of 'ethnogenesis'. He spoke in much the same vein as Thomas Paine had done, when he fled to France from his native England after publishing his works on human rights. In France, Paine was elected to the National Convention before Robespierre had him thrown into prison. Then, in 1802, he made his second journey to North America, where 20 years earlier he had joined the struggle of the colonies for independence: 'O! ye that love mankind! Ye that dare oppose not only the tyranny but the tyrant, stand forth! Every spot of the old world is overrun with oppression. Freedom has been hunted round the globe. ... O! receive the fugitive, and prepare in time an asylum for mankind' (Paine 1969: 30–31).

These words still hold true today, but the functions, mechanisms and implementation of power seem to have changed so much that we find it paradoxical to trace the roots of state power back to the idea of asylum. It seems paradoxical, however, precisely because our present-day asylum legislation has been blatantly and perversely distorted (cf. Schneider 1986).

In the transatlantic industrialised states, as well as in the neo-colonial nationalist states of the third world, power relationships are no longer seen in terms of Mühlmann's (1962: 55) adage that 'a man of power who cannot offer protection loses his power [and] a protégé who does not exercise fidelity loses his protection'. Because of the state's monopoly on weapons almost everywhere, power now has to be demonstrated differently. Whether it be exercised by ethnic or economic clans, military elites or parliamentary democracies in search of legitimacy, the principle of reciprocity is no longer very meaningful. This is true even if, in the final analysis, the state manages to reproduce itself through power rather than legality, which is exactly what happens when a national uprising is suppressed.

'A foreign place is desolate. It has, so to say, no soul for the newly arrived' (Sombart 1919: 886). These sad but beautiful words come from a short chapter in Werner Sombart's monumental portrayal of capitalism in which he looks into what proportion of aliens (emigrants, exiles or refugees) are involved in the development of capitalism. The terror of national socialism has for a long time blinded us to the fact that our world has been built up by foreigners. For the emigrant, as Sombart (*ibid.*) put it shortly before the Nazis unleashed their pogroms against the Jews, there is 'no past ... no present ... only a future'. The aliens, which even the German Jews had become, had been robbed of their present. Now we simply rob aliens of their future. Those who come to Germany as foreigners are simply not allowed to harbour hopes of a future in the country. This is why there are new camps in Germany and why *Abschreckung* (meaning intimidation or deterrence) is also being adopted by our European neighbours.

The important contribution aliens have traditionally made to commerce is now supposed to cease. As Georg Simmel (1968: 64) points out, traders have always been aliens. According to Sombart, this is because it is impossible for aliens to engage in other professions. Being excluded from participating in public life because their surroundings have no meaning for them, aliens can, at best, use their environment as a way of earning a living and this, says Sombart (*ibid.*), might well be at the root of capitalistic commercial thinking.

This is rather similar to Max Weber's 'spirit of capitalism', except that instead of a 'Protestant ethic', Sombart (*ibid*: 890) refers directly to the 'representatives of the capitalistic spirit', namely the Scottish reformers who came to East Prussia and Posen in the 17th and 18th centuries, the refugees from the old German empire and Holland, the reformers and Mennonites who built up the silk industry at Krefeld, the 25,000 Huguenots who fled from France in the 17th and 18th centuries, the founders of industry in the old Austrian and German empires (of which 10,000 came to Berlin alone), the Italians who went to Germany and England, and the English who went to Holland. As Sombart (*ibid.*) put it, 'we can clearly perceive that the transition to capitalist organisation can always be traced back to the influence of the immigrants'. But even as early as 1795, the presence of aliens created a certain amount of uneasiness, in that Friedrich Wilhelm II considered it necessary to introduce a so-called 'act of mercy':

> In order to limit the continual surge of French and Dutch emigrants ... our Chief War Council ... the governors and commanders ... in the surrounding provinces ... and because of the invasions from Saxony, and also in the Mark Electorate, have ordered that all emigrants, who do not possess a special permit, be rejected and turned out right at the gates of the cities.

In his appendix to *Sociology*, Georg Simmel (1909), reflecting on his own experiences, comments on the strangeness of our relations with aliens, especially refugees:

> Here [in the aliens] the unity of closeness and farness contained in every human relationship has reached a constellation which we can describe as follows: the distance within the relationship means that that which is near, is far away; strangeness or foreigness, however, means that that which is far away, is near. The quality of being foreign is, of course, very positive in a relationship, it means a special interdependence; the inhabitants of Sirius are not really foreign to us ... they simply do not exist for us, they are neither near nor far. The alien is an element of the group

> itself, not unlike the poor and the manifold internal enemies, an element whose position in the group at once includes a position outside of and vis-à-vis the group.

Once again the alien, the fugitive, becomes the evil enemy so necessary in helping us overlook the real distances between ourselves and our neighbours. As Kirchheimer (1985: 564) so aptly put it, 'politically asylum ... has its weaknesses; often it becomes effective only because people have not totally lost the ability to be ashamed'.

REPORTS AND DOCUMENTS

I THE RECEPTION AND RESETTLEMENT OF REFUGEES IN PORTUGAL

Ana Maria Silva

This document includes a historical view of Portugal's relations with other people and the work that has been carried out with refugees in the last decade.

Historical Introduction

Throughout its history Portugal has benefited enormously from its contacts with various populations all over the world and their unique cultures. Whether by natural inclination, as some claim, or through necessity, the Portuguese are generally open-minded towards aliens and capable of overcoming cultural and ethnic barriers when relating to them.

There were Portuguese carvels sailing the seas between Europe and the west coast of Africa as far back as the 14th century. By the early 16th century, King Manuel of Portugal had signed a treaty of alliance and friendship with the King of the Congo (a kingdom situated on the southern banks of the River Zaire). As a result, Congolese noblemen travelled to Portugal to study at the University of Coimbra and Christian missionaries, masons and blacksmiths sailed from Portugal to settle in West Africa, where trade flourished. It was another three centuries before Livingstone arrived, but, in the meanwhile, although Portugal had been predominantly Christian for centuries, Muslims and Jews coexisted peacefully alongside the Christians in Portugal, especially in Lisbon.

The spillover effects of the intolerance of the Spanish Inquisition put an end to this situation. From then onwards, and for the good part of three centuries, the banner of tolerance was hauled down in Portugal and hoisted in the Netherlands, to where a sizeable number of Portuguese Jews moved and settled. By 1820, the decaying Inquisition was formally abolished and gradually Portugal returned to its former tradition of tolerance and acceptance of all races and religious beliefs.

A more recent example of Portuguese tolerance took place during the Second World War when a number of Jews fleeing from the Nazis found shelter and refuge in Portugal. Here, non-governmental organistions played an important part in setting up schemes for sheltering children whose families had been broken up and many middle-class Portuguese families brought up children as if they were their own.

Policies of the New Regime

In 1974, new democratic institutions were set up to address the world refugee problem. A number of Portuguese politicians had themselves been political refugees abroad and had drawn on their own experiences when they promulgated laws, by-laws and regulations in an attempt to make a positive contribution to international solidarity and to safeguard human rights.

What in 1974 amounted only to formal recognition of those subjected to undue persecution or discrimination in their own countries on political, ethnic or religious grounds, suddenly became a national issue and a major source of social concern. This change was sparked off by the exodus of Portuguese settlers from the former Portuguese colonies in Africa. With Angola, Mozambique, Guinea, Sao Tomé, and the Cape Verde Islands becoming independent virtually overnight and their new rulers showing little sympathy for the plight of the Portugese settlers, over the next two years approximately 600,000 settlers fled back to Portugal. To meet the sudden and somewhat unforseen influx, the Portuguese government reserved dozens of hotel rooms all over the country and set up a government organisation to provide the 'refugees' with immediate shelter and future resettlement. The initial task group, to which I belonged, was quickly enlarged as the numbers fleeing from Africa grew, but after a peak between 1975 and 1977, was again reduced as resettlement was being achieved.

This was a difficult task, but one from which a considerable amount was learnt about the reception and resettlement of shifting populations. By the time the initial task group had been replaced by another government organisation in 1978, a valuable body of experience and professional know-how had been acquired from having dealt with the first wave of asylum-seekers from the former Portuguese colonies. It should be noted, however, that just after the overthrow of the undemocratic regime in 1974, Portugal was selected as a country of asylum by certain Latin American refugees, especially from Brazil, Chile and Uruguay. These were mainly exiled politicians and intellectuals who came in small numbers. This and the fact that they shared a rather similar culture to the Portuguese meant that they were not too visible After Brazil's return to democracy, their numbers were considerably reduced.

The introduction of new Portuguese nationality laws meant that by 1975 many of those coming from Portugal's former colonies had lost their Portuguese nationality. The majority, however, chose to stay in Portugal and to seek asylum.

Despite its rather low profile, the government did in fact try to establish a legal framework within which to deal with these asylum-seekers and refugees. The 1951 Convention and the 1967 Protocol played an important part in helping to formulate such legislation.

Initial Reception and Resettlement

After 1980, the Direcçao de Apoio e Reinstalaçao/Divisao de Apoio a Refugiados (DSAR), a special branch within the Centro Regional de Segurança Social de Lisboa (the Ministry for Labour & Social Security (CRSS)) was to deal with the refugees' social and sometimes legal problems, working in close collaboration with the UNHCR office in Portugal.

The DSAR does everything associated with both the initial support of individuals or groups and their permanent settlement.

Apart from the secretarial staff, everyone working in the DSAR has some sort of social science training and those in charge of the initial reception are also conversant in English and/or French.

With help from the CRSS, the UNHCR and the Resettlement Fund of the Council of Europe (FRCE), it became possible to purchase a large house and a farm where refugees and asylum-seekers could obtain shelter when they first arrived. CARITAS, the non-governamental Catholic organisation, is presently running this institution by agreement with the CRSS with the aim of creating a humane family atmosphere. All expenses are met by the Portuguese government. The institution offers the refugees intensive and free courses in Portuguese language, agricultural techniques and craftsmanship. If the refugees decide against accepting this offer of accommodation and training at the Wellcome Centre, they are granted a monthly sum of money roughly equivalent to the unemployment benefit.

Refugees qualify for assistance in education, professional training, cheap housing (outside the expensive urban areas) and for setting up small individual or family businesses. It is worth mentioning that in Portugal refugees and asylum-seekers are free to settle wherever they wish. Nevertheless, over 90 per cent have chosen to live within the Greater Lisbon area. It is also important to note that those awaiting recognition of refugee status are given certain benefits usually only offered to recognised refugees, namely Portuguese language courses, professional training and assistance, with all expenses covered by the Portuguese government. Refugees and asylum-seekers also have exactly the same access to medical aid as national citizens.

The Refugee Problem

The DSAR aims to foster any valid initiatives directed towards achieving self-sufficiency and freedom from public assistance. This is often made difficult by the refugees' poor or non existent knowledge of the Portuguese language, religious taboos, broken family ties, different socio-cultural roots, fear of persecution, poor schooling, lack of confidence in their own capabilities, ignorance of their rights as refugees and, frequently, an unwillingness to adapt to local work and social conditions. Finally, refugees from underdeveloped countries tend to have rather high expectations. When they find themselves in a relatively poor country, in which everyone is expected to make a contribution, they can become dissatisfied and apathetic.

The Integration of Refugees

In an attempt to integrate their refugees, Portugal has been signing annual agreements with the UNHCR, which has essentially agreed to support various schooling and training programmes to facilitate professional and residential integration. One of the most difficult problems has been to locate cheap houses or apartments to buy or rent.

Another agreement, intended as a transitional measure to prevent the refugees from becoming marginalised, concentrates on providing a favourable climate for their social and professional integration. Apart from meeting immediate economic needs, it also provides professional psychological and psychiatric support should this become necessary.

Resettlement

Legal provisions for the resettlement of refugees were drafted only in 1983, allowing insufficient time to elapse in which to evaluate their impact. So far, however, they seem to have presented no real problems. Seventeen resettlement authorisations have been granted to date – fifteen from Sao Tomé, one from Tanzania and one from Angola. All of these were to people coming to Portugal, not by choice, but as a last resort. It is worth noting that governments allowing refugees into their countries bear a greater responsibility when the arrivals have previously been authorised, for these are not asylum-seekers but legal refugees, for whom the administrative authorities should, athough unfortunately they seldom do, organise their files more hastily given that the risk of violating the immigration laws has been ruled out.

The Portuguese government has agreed to accept a total of 70 people for resettlement each year. Although this number is small by the standards of other countries, the total has never yet been reached, for the selection of candidates is very strict. All applications are submitted via the UNHCR and prospective candidates carefully selected on a case-by-case basis with a view to assessing their suitability for a true and meaningful resettlement.

So far cooperation between the UNHCR office in Lisbon and the Portuguese government agency, CRSS, has been fruitful, with a lot of mutual consultation, and there seems every reason to believe that this will continue in the future.

Conclusion

Since the numbers are relatively small, Portugal is able to give its refugees individual help and emotional support in the difficult transition towards integration. Hopefully, in that the refugee is given not only initial financial help but also opportunities to learn the language and to become gainfully employed, the help will be of lasting benefit in ensuring the refugee's eventual financial independence.

The problems associated with resettlement can undoubtedly be reduced if the Portuguese government and the UNHCR work together at an early stage to create the right conditions for successful integration.

II SPANISH RESETTLEMENT PROGRAMMES

Maria Cruz Jordana and Lorenzo Sanchez Pardo

Introduction

Before examining the Spanish government's programme for the resettlement of asylum-seekers and refugees, it would be helpful to take a brief look at the legal and social provisions which have been made available to this group over the past few years.

These fall into two definite stages, marked by the Law Regulating the Right to Asylum and Conditions of Refugees which was passed on 26 March 1984.

The Pre-Law Situation

For many years Spain generated large numbers of refugees, but, until very recently, there were no legal provisions in the country for protecting refugee interests.

Then, in 1978, Spain eventually signed the 1951 Convention and the 1967 Protocol on Refugees. This act coincided with the re-establishment of democratic freedoms in Spain.

Although from the beginning of the 1960s Spain began to receive large numbers of refugees from Cuba and other Latin American countries, the first legal regulation on this matter only came into force in 1979. Spain's tradition as a country of asylum is still, therefore, very short.

It is important to point out that, throughout this period, the Spanish state never even contemplated setting up programmes to attend to the refugees' social needs. The responsibility for financing schemes to help these people was shouldered by the UNHCR with the cooperation of various non-governmental organisations. Apart from providing a few specific services, such as dining halls, until 1984 the role of the Spanish state was basically confined to financing 25 per cent of the costs of programmes undertaken by the UNHCR. In 1979/80, it did, however, implement a programme for taking in refugees from South East Asia (covered elsewhere in this book in the contribution by Maria Jose Santa Cruz Robles).

The Post-Law Situation

The approval of this law by the Spanish parliament (on 26 March 1984) and the specific rules and regulations pertaining to it (of 20 February

1985) represent a real milestone in the management of asylum and refuge. In its defence of the interests of refugees choosing Spain as their country of asylum, it is considered to be one of the most progressive laws in Europe.

Without going into the details of its content, two important aspects of this law should be noted:

> It makes a clear distinction between refugees and asylum-seekers. The former comprise those solely in need of legal protection, whereas the latter are those who, in addition to requiring legal protection, have expressed a desire to settle in Spain. The practical consequence of this is that while refugees must apply for their residence and work permits, asylum-seekers are automatically granted work permits on the grounds that holding a job is considered indispensable to their social integration. It entitles applicants of both refugee and asylum status, as well as recognised refugees and asylum-seekers, to apply for state social welfare.

As a consequence of applying the said law, as from 1984 the Spanish government took over complete responsibility for financing social service programmes to help refugees and asylum-seekers. The budget earmarked for this purpose has been increased each year and, in 1987, reached 739,000,000 pesetas. This finance is, however, discretionary and always subject to budgetary availability.

General Characteristics of Refugees

Before proceeding, it would be helpful to look at some figures on the numbers and origins of the people who arrive in Spain requesting refugee or asylum status, for both these features are important in determining the resettlement process.

The total number of settler and transit refugees recognised as such on 30 June 1987 came to 1,225 and 2,757 respectively, as can be seen in Table II.1. These data show that their number is relatively low in comparison with other European countries, making their integration into Spanish society relatively trouble free.

If to this we add that 35.31 per cent of recognised refugees and 20.7 per cent of recognised asylum-seekers are Spanish speaking (see Table II.2), it becomes evident that resettlement is a relatively easy process.

Table II.1: Numbers and Status of Refugees and Asylum–Seekers in Spain on 30 June 1987

Refugees		*Asylum–Seekers*	
Recognised	2,757	Recognised	1,225
Refused	1,145	Refused	367
Deregistered*	3,504	Deregistered	369
Applications being processed	3,916	Applications being processed	3,267

Source: Ministry of the Interior

* A high proportion of people who were recognised as refugees but lost this status through voluntary waiver or because democracy was restored in their country of origin, thus enabling them to return, are included in the deregistered figure.

Table II.2: Distribution by Nationality of Recognised Spanish–Speaking Refugees and Asylum–Seekers (1 October 1986)

Refugees

Nationality	*No. of Persons*	*% of Total Recognised*
Argentinian	167	6.5
Bolivian	4	0.15
Colombian	6	0.23
Cuban	547	21.3
Chilian	112	4.3
El Salvadorian	25	0.9
Guatemalan	7	0.27
Equatorial Guinean	21	0.8
Mexican	1	0.03
Nicaraguan	21	0.8
Saharan	1	0.03
Total Spanish–Speaking Refugees	**912**	**35.3**

Nationality	*No. of Persons*	*% of Total Recognised*
Cuban	94	12.00
Chilian	52	6.7
El Salvadorian	2	0.3
Equatorial Guinean	9	1.1
Nicaraguan	4	0.6
Total Spanish–Speaking Asylum–Seekers	**161**	**20.7**

Source: Ministry of the Interior

Care of Refugees and Asylum–Seekers in Spain

The Spanish model has three basic features:

Public Responsibility

Since 1984, the financing of programmes for refugees and asylum–seekers has been wholly borne by the Ministry of Labour & Social Security, although it must be pointed out that in order to ensure greater independence in dealing with this group of people, the programmes are implemented and managed by non–governmental organisations (such as the Spanish Red Cross and the Spanish Commission for Refugee Aid (CEAR)). In Spain, therefore, all the social welfare programmes undertaken by non–governmental organisations are state–financed.

The Ministry of Labour & Social Security has created a specific centre, the State Refugee Social Service Centre (CESSAR), which is responsible for the planning and follow–up of social services for refugees and asylum–seekers.

Open, Non–Institutionalised Approach

Unlike other European countries, in Spain applicants for refugee or asylum status do not have to live in closed institutions (such as refugee camps or accommodation centres) until they have received a reply to their application for protection. The Spanish model is based on granting the recently arrived a monthly payment sufficient to cover their board and lodging requirements. This obliges them, from the very beginning, to face the problems of day–to–day life on their own and, therefore, has the advantage of making their social integration more dynamic, for they are forced to gain a rapid, in–depth knowledge of the receiving country and to avoid becoming dependent on institutions, although they do have professional guidance and support from the various non-governmental organisations.

Specialist Social Services

Specialist social services, rather than the general municipal social services, are assigned to take care of the refugees' needs. There are two reasons for this:
First, refugees are faced with specific language, cultural and psychological obstacles which require far more specialised attention than a general service would be able to provide.

Second, the country's general social services are still relatively underdeveloped and do not cover all existing areas of requirement. Such deficiencies are more serious for a highly vulnerable group such as refugees, who frequently lack family or social backing in the country of asylum.

Refugee Care Programmes

Refugee care programmes are designed to cater to the refugees' needs from the moment of their arrival in Spain until the settling-in and integration process is complete. These needs fall into three basic categories, namely economic, juridico-legal and health. The latter category also includes all aspects of mental health and therefore calls on the help of multi-disciplined teams (including social workers, psychologists, sociologists, doctors and economists).

Initial Insertion Programme

The purpose of this programme is to attend to the material needs of those applying for refugee or asylum status when they first arrive in Spain, as well as to plan and initiate a subsequent integration process for those who lack their own resources.

The first stage covers meeting the refugees at the airport or border (where necessary), providing emergency accommodation, distributing aid for clothing, processing documents and supplying information and guidance about the status for which they are applying.

Once the initial emergency or urgent period has passed, a second stage begins in which the refugee and his or her relatives are prepared for integration into the society and economic self-sufficiency. During this stage, the refugees are given Spanish language and general education classes, their academic qualifications are ratified and they are given access to various training and occupational re-education workshops.

Throughout this period, monthly payments are made to cover individual or family subsistence requirements. The amounts, which vary according to the size of the family, are calculated to give an independent adult 75 per cent of the minimum professional wage.

Wage–Scholarship Programme

This is earmarked mainly for young refugees who wish to regard Spain as their country of permanent asylum. The object is to give a technological and occupational training to those who were too young to benefit from such facilities in their country of origin.

The programme is thus conceived as an instrument for medium–term integration, for its aim is to give the refugees the kind of training that will enable them to gain access to the labour market under the best conditions possible both in Spain and in their own country should there exist any possibility of their returning.

To qualify for a place on the Wage–Scholarship Programme, refugees must have demonstrated their desire to remain in Spain by applying to the Spanish government for asylum. Transit refugees are excluded on the grounds that they do not fulfil this requirement.

Scholarships are initially awarded for one year, but are renewable if the beneficiaries can be shown to have taken reasonable advantage of them. These technical or occupational training courses generally last for approximately three years, with most of the subjects studied being pitched at the middle level.

The holders of these scholarships receive a monthly grant equal to that provided by the Initial Insertion Programme. In addition, they also get a supplementary benefit for the purchase of books, enrolments and, in some cases, transport. In 1987 the scholarship programme was able to provide places for 250 students.

Resettlement Programme

This programme, which is directed towards achieving the refugees' economic self–sufficiency, provides a one–off grant to enable them to set up some form of self–employment or business activity.

To become a beneficiary of this aid, the maximum amount of which is 850,000 pesetas, it is necessary, as in the case of the scholarship programme, to have demonstrated a wish to remain in Spain by applying for asylum. Transit refugees are therefore likewise excluded.

Resettlement plans are submitted to the CEAR, which administers the various integration programmes. Its function is to appraise the feasibility of the plans submitted, to orient refugees towards the activities and regions in Spain offering the best prospects and to give general advice on Spanish legislation and other such matters.

In the course of 1986 alone, as many as 245 plans were approved. The types of activities chosen were highly varied and included such things as goods haulage, small grocery businesses, craft, electrical and mechanical workshops, and Vietnamese and Laotian restaurants.

Since 1987, all applicants for the resettlement programme who live in Madrid have had to attend a 30–hour business adaptation course for instruction on various aspects of the business world. This ranges from how to choose what kind of business to enter into, to the various methods of marketing, finance, accountancy and the relevant legislation.

Return Programme

As its name implies, this programme is directed towards those refugees who can and want to return to their countries of origin but lack the means to do so. All the applicants so far have been from Latin America.

It began in 1983 by giving aid to returning Argentinian and Uruguyan refugees, but subsequently, as from 1985, all the applicants have been Chileans.

The financial aid provided by the Spanish government is basically directed towards occupational resettlement, housing and other emergency help. The maximum amount for a family unit would be in the region of 750,000 pesetas.

Candidates are selected by a commission made up of representatives from the Spanish administration, the UNHCR and the non-governmental organisations working with refugees.

More recently a study has been carried out to evaluate the feasibility of changing the programme from one that basically involves providing financial assistance to one that tries to coordinate its efforts with those of institutions involved in similar work in Chile, with a view to improving the chances of integrating returned refugees.

Periodic Assistance Benefit Programme

The aim of this programme is to help refugees and asylum-seekers who, through age or some chronic handicap, are unable to become financially self-sufficient. It basically involves distributing monthly benefit payments, which are equivalent to the assistance benefits received by Spanish citizens who have no income of their own.

Barriers to Social Integration

If one were to attempt to make a general appraisal of how well the refugees adapted to and became integrated into Spanish society, it would probably be very positive. The closeness in language and cultural identity of a large proportion of the refugees and asylum-seekers living in Spain, their low number in relation to the total population and the availability of adequate financial provisions or the capacity of the local integration programmes (wage and resettlement scholarships) are all plus factors.

Nevertheless, it is a mistake to be too satisfied with the way in which this group are resettling, for there are still some barriers to be overcome which require thought and research. Some attempt has been made to set up a programme of sociological research in this area, which, when completed, will hopefully cast some light on the problems involved in the integration process and how these are affected by the state-financed programmes. The results of the research so far seem to be pointing to the following problems:

Delays in Processing Applications

Although the authorities are legally required to come to a decision on refugee and asylum applications within six months, in practice this period is in many cases considerably longer. This is an important problem, common to most European countries, and it seriously hinders the resettlement process in that applicants are denied access to the most basic instruments for achieving their social integration (such as residence permits, work permits and access to general public services) during the period their status is being dealt with.

Apart from the considerable psychological stress it creates at a personal level, this situation has immediate effects on the resettlement process.

– It makes the period during which applicants are in the Initial Insertion Programme unnecessarily long and consequently uses up funds that could be more profitably used during the integration phase.

– It prevents people who would benefit from joining the local integration programmes from gaining access to them, for only those with the status of an already recognised refugee or asylum–seeker, or at least with favourable expectations of achieving such status, qualify for a place.

– It tends to foster the habit of living off 'unearned income' by creating a dependency on governmental aid, which hinders the development of the refugee's own potential and resources.

Difficulty Gaining Access to the Social Services

Earlier in this chapter I referred to and justified the existence of specialist social services. However, while aware that these people need to receive special treatment when they first arrive and are adapting to the receiver country, once this phase is over, they would probably become more quickly integrated socially if their needs were met by the ordinary social services.

To this effect it should be stated that, although the law does not in general differentiate between refugees and other Spanish citizens, it also gives no specific indication that refugees are entitled to benefit from the public services. As a result, in practice, it is frequently difficult for them to gain access to these services, particularly in areas such as housing and employment, where there is strong competition from Spanish citizens. In others areas, like education, for instance, there is usually no problem of access.

Attempts are currently being made to rectify the existing anomalies so as to achieve a degree of standardisation of access to the public services for this group of people.

As far as the social services are concerned, there is no legal impediment to their use by refugees. The problem arises because, in the light of the country's recent history of economic crisis and because there are relatively few refugees, it is felt that the needs of the refugees should not be allowed to take precedence over those of Spanish nationals.

To end, I would at least like to mention the serious difficulties being experienced by the so-called 'illegals', who are recognised neither as refugees nor asylum-seekers and who far too frequently live in appallingly squalid conditions. For them, the path to integration is truly difficult, they have no social security and, in the majority of cases, survive on the fringes of the underworld. For these people, the setting up of separate programmes to those existing for legal refugees is an urgent priority.

A Note on Terminology: Following the 1951 Geneva Convention on Refugees' Statute, Spanish law distinguishes between refugees and asylum-seekers. The former are people who may be considered, under the terms of the Geneva Convention, to be entitled to apply for the juridical protection of the country of arrival. The latter are those who, besides applying for juridical protection, have also expressed a definite wish to remain in and become integrated into the country of arrival. According to Spanish law, they are entitled not only to special juridical status but also to residence and work permits.

III COOPERATION AND CONFLICT BETWEEN VOLUNTARY AGENCIES AND GOVERNMENT IN SWITZERLAND

Walter Stöckli

Introduction

In Switzerland, seven voluntary agencies are held responsible for the integration and general assistance of recognised refugees. These are CARITAS (based in Lucerne and caring for approximately 40 per cent of the refugees), the Swiss Red Cross (based in Berne and caring for about 25 per cent), the voluntary agency attached to the Protestant churches (caring for 15 per cent), the Swiss workers' voluntary agency in Zurich (10 per cent), the Christian peace services in Berne (5 per cent), the Swiss ecumenical voluntary agency (3 per cent), and the Jewish voluntary agency in Zurich (2 per cent).

The Swiss central office for aid to refugees, OSAR, is the umbrella organisation under which these seven voluntary agencies unite, together with ISAR (OSAR's international equivalent) and the Lichtenstein Red Cross. Most of the voluntary agencies have responsibilities other than helping refugees, but OSAR's task is to coordinate this part of their activities. One of ISAR's tasks consists of building a consensus around what kind of work is carried out in the refugee and asylum-seeker sector, another is to cooperate with outside bodies, especially the federal authorities.

The diagram overleaf indicates the structure of the federal authorities with respect to refugee aid.

The refugee delegate, DAR (Délégué aux Réfugiés), refers to both the person who holds the office and the office itself, of which he is the head. (In this document, 'DAR' will normally refer to the office and 'delegate' to the person.) DAR is the office with which OSAR has its most important dealings in structural, contractual and personal matters.

The Federal Department for Justice & Police is the second most important in that it is responsible for judging appeals against the DAR's asylum decisions. The appeals are made directly to the Minister for Justice & Police rather than to the Minister of the Council or the Federal Council itself, which is the supreme *political* authority.

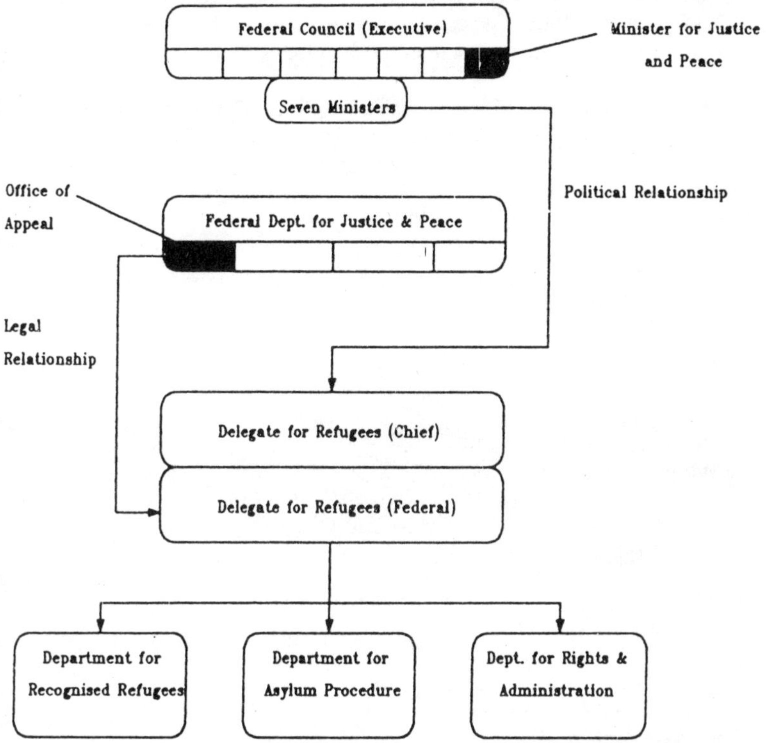

The following groups operate alongside and in cooperation with the DAR and the OSAR:

(1) *The executive board of OSAR*, which is made up of seven representatives of the voluntary agencies plus the delegate, who does not hold a right to vote.

(2) *The Confederate Commission for Questions Concerning Refugees*, which was constituted in accordance with the laws on asylum and which advises the various ministers and other federal authorities concerned with asylum. The members of this group, who are politicians and members of DAR or one or other of the voluntary agencies, usually meet about once or twice a year.

(3) *The Commission on Asylum Law*, which is an OSAR advisory committee dealing mainly with legal questions. It consists of experts in jurisprudence and representatives from the voluntary agencies, the UNHCR and the DAR (including the delegate himself), as well as one representative from the aliens' division of the cantonal police force.

(4) A strategy group, recently initiated by the minister (at the request of the delegate) to develop ideas, perspectives and strategies for refugee policy in the 1990s. The group consists of the heads of various federal authorities and one representative from OSAR.

There are a number of other established groups, including a group for the welfare of recognised refugees, several which are engaged in studying the various countries of origin, one for the study of Tamil problems, another on the Tamils in Berne, as well as one working for the return of Chileans.

Apart from all these permanently established bodies and *ad hoc* committees, there is also a close network of contacts between different people at different levels, as the following diagram indicates:

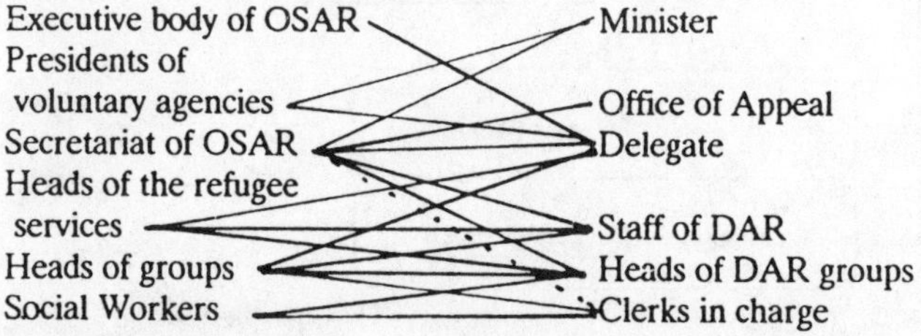

In this network of cooperation, personal relationships obviously play an important part.

Dealing with Different Levels of Conflict

Low-level conflict

Most of the voluntary agencies carry out the tasks requested of them by the federal authorities without ever feeling the need to question their content. Helping elderly Swiss nationals, for example, or giving aid to handicapped people or to smallholders, or even promoting development, are all free of any controversy and, until some years ago, so too were refugees.

Whereas the government ultimately controls and partially finances this voluntary work, its role is none the less restricted to stipulating the general framework within which the voluntary activities are carried out. This places the voluntary agencies in a strong position in the event of low-level conflict, for it means that they have a higher authority to turn to should this be necessary and yet they remain relatively independent of it.

High-level conflict

The relationship between the voluntary agencies and the federal authorities becomes seriously strained, however, when the authorities' interests and intentions collide with the voluntary agencies' aims. The question of granting aid to Switzerland's refugees has experienced just such a shift in recent years. The conflict is less about how much the government spends on helping refugees as it is about the effect this has on Switzerland's internal political climate as witnessed, for example, by the rise in xenophobia, the loss of popularity for politicians who support the refugees and the critical situation which has arisen in the labour market.

Whenever there is a serious conflict over some crucial aspect of the work, the question invariably arises of whether such close cooperation with the federal authorities is still justified. The problem is similar to that faced by the leader of a political party who wonders whether to keep going with the coalition or to change to the opposition.

Conflict-free situations

Apart from the low and high-level conflict situations mentioned above, there are certain areas in which the voluntary agencies can work on their own in a more or less independent manner. These areas, which are not financed by government money, are of special importance to the voluntary agencies because they allow them to innovate and creatively shape their work according to their own aims and ethics.

Legal Tasks and Contracts

Assistance to recognised refugees

According to Article 31 of the asylum law, all recognised voluntary agencies, namely those under the OSAR umbrella, must offer some form of relief to recognised refugees. The aim of the welfare is to guide the refugees towards independence. This is done through providing counselling, practical support and financial aid. Refugees are assisted in this way for five years after their arrival in Switzerland, after which the responsibility for their welfare is taken over by the government, which offers various forms of financial support. These include a monthly financial supplement for people on low salaries, financial aid for schooling or additional education, the insurance on a loan, travel costs for family reunions, and repatriation and resettlement allowances for those wishing to return to their countries of origin. The amounts and conditions under which financial aid is granted are set out in various contracts in which the directives and rates are clearly stipulated. The confederation reimburses 100 per cent of what the voluntary agencies spend on giving financial support to the needy and the initial 'starting' payment to the refugees, 70 per cent of the integration aid, 100 per cent of the repatriation and resettlement allowances, as well as 75 per cent of the voluntary agencies' overheads.

Even more important than the financial assistance the voluntary agencies give to recognised refugees is the counselling and other work they do to help the newcomers to deal independently with their own integration problems. The social workers will, if necessary, also act as mediators in conflicts between the different ethnic groups, help resolve problems that may arise with landlords or neighbours and give practical help in looking for jobs and accommodation.

Apart from this individual help, the voluntary agencies sometimes develop projects for integrating groups of refugees. The government does, however, insist on negotiating separate financial arrangements for each project.

There is very little day-to-day conflict between the voluntary agencies and the individual refugees in their care. It is rare for a refugee to express dissatisfaction about the amount of support being given by a voluntary agency, but if support is withheld, the refugee can appeal to the DAR, although even if the DAR decides in the refugee's favour, there is still rarely a reason for conflict.

The main source of tension between the DAR and the voluntary agencies is usually over how much money is going to be allocated to a particular project. This tends to be played out between the social workers and the clerks in charge of making the financial decisions.

Voluntary Agencies and Asylum Procedures

According to Article 15 of the asylum law, every interview with an asylum-seeker, both on the cantonal and the federal level, has to be attended by a representative of one of Switzerland's seven voluntary agencies. This is to ensure that the procedure takes place according to the rules and that the asylum-seeker is given ample opportunity to state all his or her reasons for seeking asylum. This role is mainly that of a guarantor (rather than an attorney) who makes sure that each asylum-seeker is heard and that everyone who fits the category of a refugee according to the 1951 Convention and to Swiss asylum law does receive asylum in Switzerland.

Nevertheless, despite this observer status, the voluntary agency representative is in a rather weak legal position vis-à-vis the asylum procedures. He or she may ask questions and intervene in the event of incorrect behaviour on the part of the official, but has no rights to legal action or even the rights of a party.

It is obvious that this is an area in which there is a lot of conflict. The people who work for voluntary agencies tend as a rule to be generous towards granting asylum. They are different to the 'alien' police officials in a number of ways, in personality as well as the way in which they communicate with 'aliens'. Although there are some structural reasons for these difficulties, many of the problems and quarrels in this area are more personal in their nature. The voluntary agencies tend to find many of the police officials unfriendly, restrictive and uncommunicative; the officials, on their part, feel that too many of the voluntary agencies' representatives are totally undiscriminating in their support for asylum-seekers and many insist on unnecessarily thorough and extensive interviews. Most of these conflicts are taken no further than the officials and representatives concerned, but if there are a number of criticisms about a particular person or authority, or if the incident is particularly serious, the head of one of the groups will be asked to intervene.

Under the terms of a new law (which came into force on 1 January 1988) the federal government will finance the full costs of the interviews, of which there are expected to be about 12,000 per year. The voluntary agencies are determined that the financing of these costs will in no way interfere with their independence or influence who they appoint as their representatives. Should the authorities attempt to exert too strong an influence over them, the voluntary agencies would immediately have to reconsider their participation in this area.

Further Forms of Cooperation

Support for asylum-seekers

While their applications for asylum are being processed, the prospective refugees are supported by the individual canton's welfare office (which is later reimbursed by the federal government). The federal authorities have, however, given local mandates to voluntary agencies in several Swiss cantons to run reception centres for the asylum-seekers; in other places the voluntary agencies and cantonal authorities run the reception centres together.

In the running of a reception centre conflicts are bound to arise from time to time, especially between the centre's managers or social workers on the one hand and the alien police or welfare office on the other. Questions arise, for example, over how open or restricted the centre should be, over whether the police should be allowed to enter the centre and if so, under what circumstances, over what efforts should be made to help the asylum-seekers find accommodation and jobs, or over how to react in the event of a hunger strike or other such protest. Sometimes, of course, the centres need to turn to the police for assistance as, for example, if a riot breaks out in the centre or there is a fight between asylum-seekers.

Whenever any unexpected problem arises with a particular group of asylum-seekers (such as the psychological traumas suffered by the Tamils, or the presence of unaccompanied minors) the voluntary agencies are normally the first to recognise it and will spontaneously assume responsibility for dealing with it independently of the authorities. Cooperation at a later stage (usually with respect to financing by the authorities) may follow.

Legal aid for asylum-seekers

In recent years the voluntary agencies have become more strongly committed to the idea of giving legal aid to asylum-seekers. In Switzerland there are more than 20 counselling offices for asylum-seekers, which are used mostly by those who have already had their requests for asylum turned down in the first instance. These offices offer counselling in procedural and legal questions and even grant legal representation during the appeal procedure. This activity is closely associated with the presence of a voluntary agency representative during the initial interview; if the voluntary agency representative recommends granting asylum but the request for asylum is turned down, then the voluntary agency responsible for the counselling office will step in to help the asylum-seeker.

OSAR itself only provides legal representation for a few important cases. Although it does intervene in individual cases, more often than not it merely critises a general practice. The same applies to the UNHCR. The initiative to intervene generally comes from the lawyer who works for OSAR, but the costs of the case are usually borne by the UNHCR.

This is a very conflict-ridden area, which is hardly surprising considering that it is about something as open to interpretation as a person's reasons for having to leave their country.

Future Development

Under the terms of the new law, the voluntary agencies are entitled to apply for the partial or complete financing of projects for integrating whole groups of refugees. The voluntary agencies do not expect any major conflicts in this area, for it is of interest to all parties concerned that the most disadvantaged groups are properly integrated.

The new law also provides for repatriation in the form of counselling, relief and resettlement aid for any asylum-seekers who are willing to return to their country of origin. Although both the voluntary agencies and the cantonal authorities will be entitled to administer these provisions, it is easy to foresee that they will have very different approaches to the task in that they have such different aims and expectations. While the cantonal and federal authorities' main interests lie in having the rejected asylum-seekers leave the country with as little fuss or publicity as possible, the voluntary agencies are far more interested in what happens to the asylum-seekers once they return home and in ensuring their reintegration and their motivation to assume responsibility for themselves, although without giving them privileges that are denied to those who have stayed behind in their home country. The voluntary agencies are also concerned with reducing the causes for flight and with making links between refugee-aid and development-aid projects. These issues are bound to lead to some quite serious conflict if the voluntary agencies are to avoid becoming the authorities' lackeys.

Political Disputes

Revision of the law

In 1986, despite bitter opposition from a powerful minority, the Swiss parliament passed a second revision of the seven-year old asylum law. During the preparation stage, when the various propositions were being deliberated and commented upon and MPs were being lobbied, the voluntary agencies did all they could to oppose what they knew would create considerable aggravation. The conflict became even more intense, however, when 60,000 citizens started demanding that the law be put to a referendum.

Over a period of several months the representatives of voluntary agencies and the federal authorities faced one another over the media and on various public platforms. Despite the sometimes vociferous discussions, which have hurt a number of self-help groups and militant circles and left a great residue of mistrust, the cooperation and trust between the voluntary agencies and the federal authorities has been affected only marginally and their partnership has remained basically in tact.

The question of legitimacy

There is no real consensus among the legal departments of the different voluntary agencies over what they regard as legitimate practice by the federal authorities. In fact the differences among them are sometimes so great that they go well beyond the realm of the purely legal and become full-blown political issues. The public dispute over the Tamils which has been waged in the Swiss press over the past few years is one such example.

At the beginning of 1986, OSAR started publishing a specialist journal in which questions about asylum law and asylum policy are discussed at length and in which some of the federal authorities' decisions and practices have been criticised from a legal point of view. There are a number of cantonal and federal officials among its subscribers.

Everyday Politics: Closing the Borders

The following incidents, taken from a Swiss newspaper, are fairly typical examples of what has been happening on Switzerland's borders:

- The city of Zurich's welfare office has been closed down due to an immense influx of Lebanese asylum-seekers. These Lebanese, who came to Switzerland from Italy, were subsequently returned to Italy without legal grounds. This was done before they had been given a chance to file a request for asylum.

- A Turk has died of exhaustion after having crossed the green border in southern Switzerland.

- A Sikh has been returned to India for the second time, despite having claimed that he had been tortured after his first return. Even although he was able to submit new evidence of persecution, his second request for asylum was not accepted.

- Two Lebanese who lost their way when crossing the green border in southern Switzerland had to be rescued by helicopter from a vertical mountain cliff.

Reports such as these bring a regular stream of protests from the voluntary agencies against the harsh treatment meted out to asylum-seekers by the federal authorities. What they object to most are the rigorous border controls, the punishment of asylum-seekers who enter the country illegally, the unscrupulous way in which people are turned back at the borders, and the extremely restrictive conditions under which asylum-seekers who have registered officially at a border-post are allowed to enter the country. Now that the new law has come into force, the controls have become even tighter, with far fewer 'border-gates' at which requests for asylum can be filed. Anyone picked up elsewhere risks being sent straight back to the neighbouring state, which may or may not agree to their return depending on whether it has signed a bilateral agreement with Switzerland. Only those in possession of a passport and, if required, visa, or who claim to have been persecuted in the neighbouring state, are entitled to enter Switzerland. Genuine refugees, who have fled directly to the Swiss border from their country of origin have no entry rights and are only likely to be allowed in if the Swiss authorities are unable to prove that they have ever stayed in any one of the neighbouring countries. The same applies to asylum-seekers who claim to have lost or destroyed their passports. Those who cannot be turned back at the border are directed to one of the four reception posts and, after a short interview to establish their identities and details about their journey, are placed in one of the 60 centres for asylum-seekers. This new procedure, designed to deter potential asylum-seekers and to disperse those already in Switzerland, is bound to create a considerable amount of conflict in years to come between the voluntary agencies and the federal authorities.

State/OSAR Relations with International Organisations

Because the UNHCR's headquarters are in Geneva and its High Commissioner is a Swiss citizen, there is quite a lot of close personal contact between the UNHCR and various important Swiss government officials. Nevertheless, this contact tends to be rather informal and, although there is a legal provision for the UNHCR's opinion to be heard in doubtful cases, it has no real role to play in the Swiss asylum procedure. Since 1982, however, the UNHCR has paid for a legal advisor to work for OSAR and this has meant that there has been a certain amount of prompt and accurate feedback on the legal and political aspects of the various asylum issues.

The Amnesty International office in Switzerland keeps in close contact with OSAR. Its approach to the Swiss authorities is more aggressive than that of the voluntary agencies, which play a more supplementary role, but which are none the less grateful for the existence of Amnesty's independent voice.

State/OSAR Relations with Self-help Groups

In several Swiss cities there are private groups concerned with helping asylum-seekers in some way or another. The sanctuary movement, for example, has been active since the mid 1980s in trying to prevent 25 Chileans from being sent back to Chile. After sheltering in a church in the canton of Zurich for almost a month and a 20-day hunger strike, the Chileans succeeded in persuading the Swiss authorities to re-examine their case, with the result that, although several still had to leave Switzerland, not one of them was returned to Chile. In 1986, under the auspices of the church, 18 Tamils, who were due to be deported to Sri Lanka, were hidden in the homes of private people. This action was also successful in so far as the Tamils were granted permission to remain 'for the time being' and are, in fact, still there. OSAR and the recognised voluntary agencies have mixed feelings about these groups and their actions. Although they are often pleased by the way in which such actions bring publicity to a special problem, they also feel that these militant groups frequently focus attention on the wrong issues and in an unacceptable manner. By taking such extreme positions, however, they do allow the voluntary agencies space for their own more moderate approach through negotiation and attempting to build up public sympathy and understanding.

Conflict and Cooperation

In the build-up to the vote for the revised asylum law, which took place on 5 April 1987, there was daily media coverage of the constant arguments and controversies which were being waged between the voluntary agencies and the federal authorities.

In the head-on confrontation between the federal authorities and OSAR (representing the voluntary agencies), the people involved remained relatively fair, despite their severe disagreements. In fact only two-and-a-half months after the vote had been carried, a senior government minister, Mrs Kopp, proclaimed the Swiss 'day of the refugee', which was to be organised and carried out by the voluntary agencies.

The voluntary agencies have, however, been locked in an ongoing battle with the federal authorities since 1984 over whether or not the Tamils should be returned to Sri Lanka. When the federal government ordered the return of 18 Tamils in 1986, the official in charge of the canton of Berne refused to carry out the order and the sanctuary movement took the Tamils into hiding. The situation has subsequently been defused through the creation of a working group in which the federal government, the cantons, OSAR and the sanctuary movement are all represented.

This has led to a situation in which many high-ranking federal government officials have developed close relationships with the heads of voluntary agencies. They meet privately to exchange ideas and sometimes to discuss confidential documents even before these are circulated among the members of their own party. It goes without saying, however, that important documents are also sometimes kept away from the enquiring eyes of the voluntary agencies.

Conclusion

It is sometimes difficult to establish exactly when and where the voluntary agencies agree or disagree with the authorities. Their position is definitely 'pro' recognised refugees, 'pro' any *bona fide* refugees (in other words, anyone they are convinced would be in danger were they sent home) and 'pro' the humane and fair treatment of anyone who asks for asylum. But although this does not necessarily mean that they automatically oppose the federal authorities, this position does create antagonisms with them. The voluntary agencies are not, however, in favour of giving refugees or asylum-seekers more than they deserve and they too have been affected by changes in the refugee climate and by the more restrictive asylum practices of recent years. The difference in OSAR's position now and in 1968, when the Czechoslovakians came, is probably just as great as the difference between OSAR and the federal authorities in 1988.

V REFUGEES IN WEST GERMANY: A RESEARCH REPORT

Andreas Germershausen

Introduction

The scientific study of worldwide forced migration and refugee movements is internationally a new field in which West German social scientists have yet to establish an independent area of research. The social sciences in West Germany did, however, have a tradition of research on refugees, from a human rights' and charity perspective, during the period of the Weimar Republic, but this was interrupted in 1933. When the more pragmatically–oriented sciences renewed the tradition in 1945, it was only in a very limited way, with the focus solely on the needs of expelled, displaced and predominantly East European refugees, who at that time were being integrated into West German society. The political focus of refugee work and research was recognised, even at the time, as being too national in focus (Frings 1951: 9). More worldwide problems were considered only at the beginning of the 1970s. This coincided with an increased interest in developing countries which, although not explicitly concerned with refugees, did have a considerable impact on studies into the causes of refugee problems worldwide.

Immediately after the Second World War, as well as in the 1950s and 1960s, most of the research on refugees was approached from a legal or social work perspective.

Legal and Social Work Studies

The legal profession has tended to concentrate on the status of the main groups of refugees who have immigrated to West Germany (or have been staying there as displaced persons) since the West German republic was founded in 1949. Most of these were from Eastern Europe. The legal profession has also shown an interest in problems associated with adapting international agreements ratified by West Germany to national jurisdiction, as well as in the significance of constitutional law for basic human rights, of which the right to asylum had been included since 1949.

Social work studies have looked mainly at everyday social problems (housing, the situation in the camps, schooling); problems associated with integrating the refugees into the economy, especially into agriculture; the authorities' role in this integration process, which included special legislation for expelled or displaced persons; and the setting up of associations for such people.

The new resettlement programme is in some ways a 'large social experiment' which, for several reasons, needs to be properly researched. Stockholm University's Centre for Research in International Migration & Ethnic Relations (CEIFO) has consequently initiated a research project to run from 1 July 1986 until June 1989.

This research project, which we shall briefly present here, should not be regarded in the same light as an experiment with a controlled set of background factors. There were several significant changes in the system during the first four years and these, along with a simultaneous and rapid increase in the number of asylum-seekers, have substantially altered the basic conditions of the resettlement reform. CEIFO's study is therefore best seen as an analysis of the resettlement programme as it is being implemented on behalf of three different ethnic groups of refugees and asylum-seekers (the Chileans, Kurds and Poles) in six selected municipalities during the period between 1984 and 1988.

These three particular groups of recently-arrived refugees have been selected because they represent such diverse and contrasting cultures. An attempt is made in the project to examine both the 'reform' and the integration process from three different perspectives, namely that of the refugees themselves, that of the municipalities (in this case looking at the attitudes of both the public and of the politicians and administrators responsible for implementing the policy) and, finally, that of the historical and political context of the reform at the national level. Each of these three perspectives constitutes a separate study within the overall project.

Three Selected Refugee Groups

How well refugees integrate into Swedish society may depend, among other factors, on their cultural and socio-political background in their country of origin, their subjective evaluations of these, their personal characteristics, their hopes and plans for the future and their chances of returning.

This part of the project may be said to have two aims. The first is to study the different ways in which refugees become integrated into the various aspects of Swedish society, such as work, education, politics and religion. The second is to study how this integration process is affected by the psycho-social and cultural 'baggage' the refugees bring from their home countries and to observe how their intentions, expectations and future plans change over time.

Six Municipalities

Different municipalities, or local units, possess different qualifications or pre-conditions for refugee work, determined by social, economic and political contexts and by how much or little previous experience they have had with immigration and immigrants. Some municipalities can offer good housing but no work opportunities; others, such as the more popular ones within the larger city areas, try to take fewer refugees than they had previously been receiving. Although most of the municipalities have set up local refugee programmes, some are more ambitious than others in the way in which they implement them. In most respects the municipalities are free to administer their refugee programmes as they see fit and to give as much or as little attention as they wish to, for example, ethnic interests or the psycho-social consequences of a life in exile.

The National Context

Even before the reform had been decided upon, a first draft had been prepared by a working group within the Ministry of Labour. Suggestions had come from the National Labour Market Board (which wanted to rid itself of this particular responsibility), from municipalities (which were asking the state for money to pay for their expenditure on refugees) and from the National Board of Immigration (which by then had already taken on the responsibility of organising the systematic transfer to Sweden each year of about 1,250 quota-refugees from international refugee camps).

The somewhat apolitical decision-making process will be analysed, as will the impact of the reform on the central administration of Swedish refugee policy, especially within the National Board of Immigration. Before embarking on this, however, we would like to give a slightly more detailed description of the three sub-projects mentioned above.

Refugee Immigration to Sweden

Between 1944 and 1988 immigration is estimated to have increased Sweden's population by approximately one million people (roughly 8 per cent of the population as a whole). This figure includes the immigrants themselves and any children born to them in Sweden (SOU 1974). The peak years of immigration were 1969 and 1970. In 1970 alone, 73,500 people immigrated to Sweden while 21,300 emigrated. Up to 1967, Sweden allowed spontaneous labour immigration and, until 1972, organised recruitment of foreign workers to some big companies. Family immigration has been encouraged all along and, from the beginning, Sweden's immigration policy has upheld the principle of permanent immigration, in other words, immigrants who have obtained residence permits will normally have them extended if they choose to stay in the country.

As a result of post-war immigration, Sweden has acquired a considerable number of linguistic minorities. Before this it had been extremely homogeneous both linguistically and culturally in comparison with other European countries, with the only long-established native linguistic minorities being the 10,000 Lapps and 30,000 Tornedal Finns living in the northernmost parts of the country.

Table V.1 Refugee Immigration in Sweden 1950-1986*

	1950-67	1968-77	1978-84	1985	1986	1987	Total
Poland	400	4,700	4,200	400	400	300	10,400
Czechoslovakia	300	3,100	600	100	100	100	4,300
Hungary	8,200	4,700	1,200	100	100	200	14,500
Other E. Europe	1,200	500	1,000	200	600	700	4,200
Greece	-	5,000	100	-	-	-	5,100
Yugoslavia	6,300	700	-	-	100	-	7,100
Iran	-	-	2,900	2,600	4,700	6,600	16,800
Iraq	-	-	2,000	1,000	1,100	500	4,600
Lebanon	200	1,200	100	200	500	300	2,500
Turkey	-	4,700	1,400	200	300	300	6,900
Uganda	-	600	100	-	-	100	800
Vietnam	-	-	3,800	100	300	400	4,600
Chile	-	6,500	3,800	500	1,500	1,600	13,900
Other L. America	-	-	4,300	-	200	300	4,800
Other Countries	7,400	6,300	2,500	1,200	2,300	2,600	22,300
Total	24,000	38,000	28,000	6,600	12,200	14,000	122,800
Average per year	1,300	3,800	4,000	6,600	12,200	2,900	3,200

Note:* Excludes all children under 16

Recent figures, however, show that immigration is once again on an upward path. In 1986, 25,100 non-Nordic citizens were registered as immigrants in Sweden, which was the highest figure for any year since the peak period in the early 1970s, when immigration was running at almost 50,000 per year as against less than 9,000 in the mid-1970s. A radical change has taken place in the composition of immigration to Sweden, with increasingly large numbers coming from countries outside Europe (over half of all foreign immigration in 1986) and much of this increase being due to the high level of refugee immigration. In 1987, a large proportion of the 14,000 asylum-seekers arriving in Sweden came from countries such as Iran, Iraq, Chile and Poland. From Table V.1 showing refugee immigration from 1950 (a yearly average has been calculated), we can see that the most recent refugee numbers far exceed the average for previous periods.

The total number of refugees received is different from the total number of refugees now living in Sweden. Refugees who arrived in Sweden a long time ago have usually, in one way or another, changed their refugee status since then. Some have left Sweden, others have died and many have become naturalised Swedish citizens. The exact number of people who still have refugee status is unknown but at a rough guess was probably somewhere between 20,000 and 30,000 in 1985.

The Refugee Study

Although this is to some extent a longitudinal study (its duration is from June 1986 to July 1989), it should be pointed out that the period of actual data collection was only a little over one year – the fieldwork started in February 1987 and ended in the spring of 1988. As we mentioned earlier, the study looks at three refugee groups in six of Sweden's 284 municipalities (of which 247 have agreed to take part in the refugee resettlement programme in 1988). Apart from what kind of refugee resettlement programme they offered, other criteria taken into account in selecting the six municipalities for the project included size, geographical position, economic opportunities, previous experience of immigration and motivation.

With few exceptions, all the subjects who were interviewed arrived in Sweden after January 1985. Table V.2 shows how many people were interviewed in each of the refugee groups and their distribution in the municipalities.

The interviews, which were conducted by immigrants who came from the same ethnic backgrounds as those who were being interviewed, combined semi-structured interviews with a series of questionnaires which the interviewees filled in.

Table IV.2: Number of Refugees Interviewed up to January 1988

Municip-ality	*Chileans*	*Kurds*	*Poles*	*Total*
Bollnas	--	15	4	19
Finspang	--	--	44	44
Jarfalla	16	1	15	32
Lessebo	16	--	--	16
Sundsvall	20	15	--*	35
Uppsala	14	15	17	46
No. in Group	66**	46***	80	192

Notes:

* *Six more families hoped for*

** *More Chilean women to be interviewed*

*** *More Kurdish women to be interviewed (at the time of the first interview there was no Kurdish female interviewer). It is unacceptable according to Muslim culture for a man to interview a woman.*

The interviews usually lasted for about three and-a-half or four hours, but there were some which took considerably longer. The Kurdish interviewer spoke of one case in which an interview had started at 10 a.m., broken at 1 p.m. (because the interviewee had to attend an Immigrant Association meeting), was resumed again at 4 o'clock in the afternoon and went on until 1 o'clock the next morning, with only one break for an evening meal. In total, it had gone on for at least 10 hours, which is an illustration of the semi-structured nature of the interview. Although the interviewer is equipped with a standard set of questions which are laid out in an interview guide, if the answers to these questions are interesting enough the interviewer is free to pick up points and ask follow-up questions. All the interviews were recorded so that they could be closely analysed at a later date.

The interview guide is divided into six main sections containing questions under the following headings:

1. Subjective biography
2. Socio-political background i.e:
   Social network in home country
   Family in home country
   Leisure activities in home country
   Political attitudes and activities

Childhood socio-economic situation
Education, profession and social mobility
Current class affiliation

3. Period before flight
4. The flight
5. First period in Sweden
6. Reception into the municipality

The different questionnaires each subject was required to fill in were as follows:

1. A general background questionnaire
2. Some special questions from the interview guide
3. A social network questionnaire
4. A self report depression scale (CES-D)
5. A perceived cultural distance measure
6. A housing questionnaire

The interviewers also record their own observations of the subjects and of the subjects' general home situations. In fact the interview and the various questionnaires are designed to gather as much information as possible. The method is, however, very time consuming and requires a close and good relationship between interviewer and interviewees.

To get some idea of the scale of the project, it is important to remember that it includes two other areas of study - on the setting up and administering of refugee reception in six municipalities and on the nature and implementation of the 'reform'. The aim is to look at the problems from as many perspectives as possible and thus to be able to discuss the reform from several complementary perspectives. The two sub-projects are discussed in brief below.

The Study of Six Municipalities

Among the six selected municipalities, Jarfalla (partly a suburb and partly a city with its own industry) is within commuting distance of Stockholm, while another, the old university city of Uppsala, is some 12 miles north of it. Both these municipalities have taken in refugees in the past and both want to reduce their quotas in the future. The four other municipalities have had less previous experience of refugees. Two of these are about 300 miles north of Stockholm, in a region to which almost no refugees had come before 1985. Sundsvall, which is a regional centre with a population of about 90,000, has a thriving industry, busy trade and excellent communications. Bollnas is the centre of a large rural area, with forests, some industry, a railway station and a population of 28,000. The fifth municipality is an old town in the south of Sweden called Finspang, which was known for having recruited immigrants to its weapons industry in the 17th century and had also had some experience of labour immigration in the 1960s, but had had few refugees before 1985. It has a population of around 24,000. And finally, Lessebo, a small place but well-known internationally for its fine-paper industry, is even further to the south. It has a population of 9,000 and no previous experience of refugees.

A series of interviews have been carried out with local civil servants in all branches of the administration that in one way or another come into contact with the refugees. To gather material on how local programmes are being implemented at the grassroots' level, interviews have also been held with those who meet the refugees directly in their daily work, as well as with the leaders of political parties in the municipal councils and with politicians in charge of local refugee policy.

Descriptions will be given of the local services available to refugees for various aspects of their lives, including basic information, work and vocational training, housing, education, language, culture and leisure. An attempt will be made to analyse the various administrative styles and forms of organisation, as well as ethnic considerations, adopted by the local resettlement programmes. The report will be comparative (it will be drawn from all six municipalities) and will use some of the statistical data the municipalities in question have collected on the refugee programmes and on how they are being implemented.

The Study of the Reform

The aim of this part of the project is to provide a general introduction to the reform – as it was first envisaged, later elaborated and eventually decided upon and implemented. Swedish refugee policy will be described both historically and from an international perspective. A short presentation will be included on the refugee resettlement programme before 1985.

Former ministers in the Ministry of Immigration and general directors of the National Board of Immigration are interviewed, as are other leading officials in these two national immigration agencies. The members of two working groups, which have been studying refugee resettlement in anticipation of proposals for a reform, will also be questioned. A bill to parliament was long delayed. Several actors and several interests were involved. The National Federation of Local Municipalities represented some but not all local interests. The main characteristics of the 1985 reform will be described and analysed.

The reform of 1985 was in many ways quite different from the early ideas about how it should be designed and the programme being implemented in 1988 is different again from the reform decisions taken in 1985. The amendments made in the first four years will be discussed, as will also the implications of the heavy increase in the number of asylum-seekers and the line-up of people waiting in refugee camps for asylum decisions or placement in a municipality. As we mentioned earlier, the National Board of Immigration is responsible for the national administration of the reform programme. Some of the implications of the new system for the internal organisation of the Board, for its relations to local units and for its immigration policy at large, will be discussed. And finally, the report will also include an analysis of the political debate about refugee resettlement.

Financing and Staff

This project is co-financed by the Swedish Research Board for Social Sciences & Humanities, the Swedish Building Research Council, and the Ministry of Immigration. Furthermore, every year the Tercentenary Foundation of the Swedish National Bank pays the salary of one full-time researcher. The budget, which has been earmarked for three years, is approximately 1.3 million Swedish kroner (£110,000 sterling) per year.

The project coordinators are Tomas Hammar, Anders Lange and Charles Westin.

Anders Lange, together with Orlando Mella (on the Chileans), Omar Sheikmous (Kurds), and Halina Vigerson (Poles) are responsible for refugee studies.

Matti Simila and Maritta Soininen are responsible for the studies of the six municipalities' refugee programmes.

Tomas Hammar is responsible for the study on the reform and its implementation at the national level.

V REFUGEES IN WEST GERMANY: A RESEARCH REPORT

Andreas Germershausen

Introduction

The scientific study of worldwide forced migration and refugee movements is internationally a new field in which West German social scientists have yet to establish an independent area of research. The social sciences in West Germany did, however, have a tradition of research on refugees, from a human rights' and charity perspective, during the period of the Weimar Republic, but this was interrupted in 1933. When the more pragmatically-oriented sciences renewed the tradition in 1945, it was only in a very limited way, with the focus solely on the needs of expelled, displaced and predominantly East European refugees, who at that time were being integrated into West German society. The political focus of refugee work and research was recognised, even at the time, as being too national in focus (Frings 1951: 9). More worldwide problems were considered only at the beginning of the 1970s. This coincided with an increased interest in developing countries which, although not explicitly concerned with refugees, did have a considerable impact on studies into the causes of refugee problems worldwide.

Immediately after the Second World War, as well as in the 1950s and 1960s, most of the research on refugees was approached from a legal or social work perspective.

Legal and Social Work Studies

The legal profession has tended to concentrate on the status of the main groups of refugees who have immigrated to West Germany (or have been staying there as displaced persons) since the West German republic was founded in 1949. Most of these were from Eastern Europe. The legal profession has also shown an interest in problems associated with adapting international agreements ratified by West Germany to national jurisdiction, as well as in the significance of constitutional law for basic human rights, of which the right to asylum had been included since 1949.

Social work studies have looked mainly at everyday social problems (housing, the situation in the camps, schooling); problems associated with integrating the refugees into the economy, especially into agriculture; the authorities' role in this integration process, which included special legislation for expelled or displaced persons; and the setting up of associations for such people.

Although refugee research is still largely dominated by these two disciplines, more and more interdisciplinary exchanges are now taking place. Law, with its tradition of more sophisticated research, has started to look at problems that are relevant to the other social sciences (Beitz & Wollenschläger 1980; Köfner & Nicolaus 1986; Marx, R 1978, 1984; Otto et al. 1987). These are located in three main areas:

First, because of the increase in the numbers of refugees from third world countries, the courts of justice are being forced to learn about non-European legal and political institutions, for these are directly relevant to the asylum proceedings. Legal research is being undertaken to systematise the results of individual proceedings. The reasons for flight given by asylum applicants from various countries and the legal outcome of the proceedings are being summarised for each of the countries in question (Marx, R 1978). In the field of comparative national law, for example, important statements are being made about how different governments use political power. These are operationalised in the asylum proceedings and also often result in lively controversies. One such debate, which looks at torture as a cause of asylum and as an instrument of executive action and repression in the political systems of non-European societies, directly challenges many of the social scientists' assumptions (Frankenberg, 1978).

Second, is the legal controversy over the international definition of a refugee (determined by the Geneva Convention) and over how it should be interpreted from the point of view of national jurisdiction and legislation on asylum. The question rests on whether the reasons for leaving, as stated in the Convention, are always valid or whether they are valid only if it can be proved that a state has a specific interest in exactly those characteristics which are in accordance with the reasons for protection enumerated by the Convention. There is no question, however, that the indications of pursuit acknowledged by the Geneva Convention are characteristics of collective entities, which have to be ascertained individually in the course of acknowledging a refugee (Köfner & Nicolaus 1986). In this respect, legal studies have been published that place information about individual decisions to flee in the context of collective flight situations. Several social science studies on the processes of marginalisation of ethnic and religious groups are referred to in the legal debate.

And third, lawyers are investigating problems arising from the different statuses of the various groups of refugees. Especially significant in social science research in recent years have been studies in which the determination of the status of so-called 'contingent' or 'quota' refugees has been looked at in relation to individually-recognised refugees. These studies have been particularly useful for projects dealing with the integration of South East Asian refugees, which will be discussed later in this report.

Social Science Research

Research on refugees in the social sciences is generally fairly varied, but on the actual topic of worldwide refugee problems, it has to be admitted that very little has been published. Attempts are, however, being made to persuade German social scientists to provide more detailed background information on this subject, but so far they have hesitated to comply with the request.

Nowadays social work oriented refugee research is becoming more prevalent in the social sciences (see Ronge 1984: 11ff). Some of the studies are on the same groups that were being looked at in the 1950s, though with the added advantage of historical distance. Included among these are studies on the integration of expelled and displaced persons, as well as on exiled groups, such as the former inhabitants of the Baltic provinces and of the Soviet Union after 1945.

Slightly more attention is paid to the problems of new groups of refugees, especially refugees from South East Asia. Although some of the studies are dissertations, many are specially commissioned to supplement pilot projects which, from a social work perspective, are designed to integrate refugees and their families. These projects are usually financed by the relief organisations responsible for housing the refugees (see Treuheit & Otten 1986).

From a social science standpoint, the research on integration processes contains some basic weaknesses, the main criticism being that there is no systematic analysis of research carried out in circumscribed areas. Regional and local histories tend to be insufficiently related to more general issues. In this respect, there is a real need for extensive historiographical research (Steinert 1986).

Individual Studies

A research project is presently being set up to examine migrant movements to and from Germany during the 19th and 20th centuries. In this, as Bade (1987:5) convincingly puts it, 'determining factors, circumstances of development, and resulting phenomena of migration regarding the history of the population and its economic and social history' play an important part, 'as well as political problems and those relating to national and international law, which go with flight and forced migration movements'.

Much of the literature on the third world contains descriptions of conditions in the refugees' countries of origin which are helpful to refugee studies, as are the labour migration studies which were first published in the 1960s. But far too little attention is paid to the questions that are really important to refugee research, which on the whole tends to lack any real systematic analysis. Yet, in recent years scholars working in the field of development studies have been doing some very good social science research on refugees (including work on refugees from Afghanistan and Namibia) for which these criticisms are invalid (see e.g. Nuscheler 1984).

Some important studies, which attracted a considerable amount of attention among German social scientists in the 1960s, were undertaken by the Frankfurt Institute for Social Research on prejudice, racism and exile. Although the conditions leading to flight and exile were important in the research findings of these studies, they were not, however, set against the contemporary background of worldwide refugee movements.

Evaluating the Research

Scholars of all fields agree that there are weaknesses in the way in which refugee movements have been documented in the social sciences, for there is a definite absence of any accurate and detailed recording of either historical or contemporary worldwide mobilisations of population segments. This lack of proper documentation is also evident in non-scientific work on refugees. The founding of a documentation centre in 1980 (by the relief organisations working with refugees) has, however, gone some way towards improving the situation (Bueren & Wolken 1987; ZDWF 1987). The material in the centre, which is at the disposal of lawyers, independent groups and the interested public, is mainly on the legal and political aspects of asylum.

Some of the research social scientists should be doing on refugees is being taken over by journalists and people working in relief and human rights' organisations. Much of this is of a high-quality, some of it better than the current university output (Amnesty International 1986; Kauffmann 1986; Spaich 1982).

There is at present surprisingly little privately-sponsored research on refugees in the German social sciences. The only case, of which I am aware, is a small quantitative study, sponsored by the UNHCR, on some new settlements in Ethiopia and Central America.

Research Bias

When considering refugee and asylum problems, it is impossible to distinguish clearly between an expert judgment and a political opinion. There is nothing new about this; but what is new, however, is that this is now recognised both by representatives of local political action committees (who stand up for the rights of refugees in their communities) and by those who basically control national politics in the non-governmental organisations.

This also holds true for social scientists and lawyers, who also participate in the political debate. For example, they defend a notion of 'protection from pursuit' based on ethical and constitutional grounds, which makes no allowance for quantitative restrictions of refugees, and yet, both because of their historical experience of European refugees and because they acknowledge that European states have a responsibility for worldwide refugee movements, these same experts are drawn into an active engagement in day-to-day politics.

Suggestions for Future Research

First, there is a general need for systematic research into the reasons for the present world refugee crisis. We know that refugee movements mainly occur when ethnic, religious or political aspirations come into conflict with the various authorities of the state, often leaving the population in question with no alternative but to flee, especially if the conflict has got out of control. We also know that antagonisms between relatively small social segments can lead to broader conflicts if the authorities step in to support one or other of the adversaries and that at this point the escalating spiral of conflict can be reduced only by the exodus of part of the population. But it is important in this context to have more sociological, political and social-anthropological studies on the actual development of such conflicts in these countries. It is also necessary to ensure that the origins of the refugee movements are looked at in a more systematic manner in these studies than has been the pattern so far in the social sciences in West Germany.

Second, the causes of refugee movements need to be analysed within a wider historical perspective. This is also important for ascertaining which countries are most likely to grant asylum to refugees. Among the indicators of a country's willingness to accept refugees are how many institutions or related agencies, charities, human rights' organisations and federations of lawyers or social workers are specifically set up to work with the refugees. Processes leading to the drafting of national legislation especially applicable to refugees, as well as the development of authorities with a corresponding mandate, should also be brought into the research.

Third, the worldwide refugee crisis should be understood within the context of general worldwide population movements. Political repression in the countries of origin is sometimes a factor in other forms of mass mobilisations and emigration, even although not necessarily acknowledged as such. One such example is the phenomenon of the so-called migrant workers who often emigrated for political reasons. In this regard, the formation of refugee colonies has to be understood within the context of the formation of ethnic communities in general. More research needs to be done on the ability of refugee groups to reestablish traditional institutions in exile. Relations between refugees and other migrants of the same ethnic groups should be analysed and an investigation made of what kinds of positions refugees are able to take up in immigrant communities.

And finally, various political proposals have been put forward at an international level in an attempt to find solutions to the present world refugee crisis. These have to be evaluated in terms of how they fit in with national political attitudes (including xenophobic reactions) and with the various models set up by different countries to accommodate immigrating refugees. Historical and cross-national comparisons would also be useful.

VI THE COPENHAGEN REHABILITATION CENTRE FOR TORTURE VICTIMS

Erik Karup Pedersen

Background

Victims of torture have existed throughout history, but it was not until the aftermath of the Second World War and the atrocities of the German concentration camps that the medical profession began to conduct any serious research into the effects of torture. In 1949/50, the first articles appeared in the scientific journals identifying the so-called KZ-syndrome, whereby it was noted that torture victims suffered from 'lack of concentration, nightmares, sleep disturbances, headaches, sexual difficulties, and an inability to adapt socially'.

A group of lawyers working to obtain an amnesty for prisoners of conscience and people imprisoned or detained on political, religious or racial grounds, founded Amnesty International in London in 1961 and, in 1973, Amnesty International launched a campaign against torture at its annual meeting in Paris. This campaign, together with the clinical findings on the KZ-syndrome, encouraged 12 medical practitioners interested in the effects of torture to hold a meeting in Copenhagen in 1974.

What these doctors had in common was a belief that people who had been exposed to torture had as much claim to medical attention as battered or abused children or people who had suffered the traumas of industrial or road accidents. Torture, they argued, did not only concern the press, the police and the military, it was also a medical matter.

Thus, in the same year, 1974, these 12 Copenhagen doctors started to examine people who had been exposed to torture. Their first patients included a group of about 30 Greeks and approximately the same number of Chilean refugees in Copenhagen, who had also been exposed to torture.

Between 1974 and 1982, medical groups, usually working under the auspices of Amnesty International, carried out similar examinations in several countries all over the world, in Canada, France, the Netherlands, the USA, Italy, Sweden, Great Britain and the Argentine. To coordinate this work, Amnesty International set up a medical advisory board and later established a permanent post for a medical adviser at its headquarters in London.

As a result of these medical examinations in various parts of the world, the idea that torture victims were entitled to and required medical attention became very much more widely accepted. The doctors' next step was to make the move from diagnosis to treatment and to this effect the medical groups working under the auspices of Amnesty International approached its medical advisory board which, in turn, put the proposal to

Amnesty International's executive committee. Although interested in the proposal and in the work the doctors had been doing, Amnesty International felt that, as an organisation, it could not engage in the task of providing medical treatment for the sick. It was at this point, then, that the Copenhagen doctors decided to establish an independent centre in Copenhagen for the treatment and rehabilitation of torture victims and this was how the RCT (Rehabilitation Centre for Torture Victims) came into being.

Objectives

The RCT's basic objectives are as follows: to run a centre for rehabilitating people who have been subjected to torture and their families; to instruct Danish and foreign health personnel in how to examine and treat people who have been subjected to torture; to engage in research on torture and on the nature and extent of its effects with a view to improving the treatment of its victims and its eventual abolition; and to set up an international documentation centre for the purposes of disseminating information about torture, studying the consequences of torture and rehabilitating people who have been subjected to torture.

Structure

The RCT was opened in Copenhagen in 1982. There is an interdisciplinary approach to the treatment within a standard treatment programme, consisting of psychotherapy, based on the victim's torture-situation, physiotherapy, general somatic treatment and social counselling, plus the treatment of the victim's spouse and/or children. In both examinations and treatment, special care is taken to avoid any situation that might remind the victims of their torture.

In its early phase, from 1982 to 1984, the RCT was able to treat about 20 victims per year, but since then has acquired the capacity to treat double that number. There are about 20 people on its staff, which includes several doctors, physiotherapists, social workers, secretaries, interpreters and librarians, as well as a business manager, a bookkeeper and some special consultants such as dentists.

The annual budget was around £750,000 in 1986 and £1 million in 1988. Of this, half comes from the Danish state and the Nordic Council and the other half from private sources.

The RCT has also set up an International Rehabilitation and Research Centre for Torture Victims (the IRCT) to coordinate work between similar centres and to establish new centres in other countries, especially in the less industrialised parts of the world such as the Philippines and Africa.

Evaluation of Results

The members of the treatment team are generally satisfied with the progress of their patients, but are cautious about making claims about a torture victim's recovery until they have had an opportunity to observe the patient for at least five years after treatment has been completed.

The RCT's address is:

Juliane Maries Vej 34
DK–2100, Copanhagen 0,
Denmark.

VII EUROPEAN INITIATIVES ON ASYLUM

Philip Rudge

Introduction

The current evaluation of the member organisations of the European Consultation on Refugees & Exiles (ECRE) has led us to four basic conclusions:

- The nature and scale of the asylum question in Europe is seriously misunderstood and badly misrepresented;
- Consequently the response of some governments is inappropriate and excessive in terms of restriction and deterrent policies;
- There is a very real risk of the abandonment of humanitarian values and commitments established over recent decades and codified in many international conventions relating to refugees and human rights;
- The inward-looking preoccupations of many European states are blocking action urgently needed for the long-term resolution of problems leading to refugee movements.

In short, we are heading in the wrong direction, motivated by a fortress mentality, and distracted from developing an appropriate response to the global dimensions of the problem. Yet European states expect poorer countries, often beset by grave economic and social problems, to continue to carry the overwhelming responsibility for the world's refugees.

The evidence of the restrictive policies in Europe has been detailed in numerous reports by human rights and non-governmental organisations and the Council of Europe in recent years. Such policies refer to the prevention of access by asylum-seekers, notably from third world states, to the refugee determination procedures and inadequate provision in the fields of housing, employment, accommodation and social welfare benefits. Of particular concern more recently is an increase in the use of detention of asylum-seekers and measures to prevent the actual flight of asylum-seekers to Europe from refugee generating states through the imposition of visas and punitive legislation against airlines carrying 'undocumented aliens'. In a very real sense there is an attempt by some European states to move their immigration controls from points of entry in Europe and to replace them in third world states themselves.

To an alarming degree decision making in the area of asylum is moving away from the traditional human rights and humanitarian field of policy-making. It is increasingly the subject of fora dealing with terrorism, drug trafficking and policing on the one hand, and with economic streamlining on the other. Policy-making is proceeding at an accelerated pace in order to reach some decisions of very profound importance for the future of refugees and asylum-seekers in Europe. Some of the initiatives are public, some are very confidential; some have UNHCR and NGO input, some have none; some include all western European countries, some include very few. All are in their different ways important.

Council of Europe

CAHAR is an ad hoc committee of experts on the legal aspects of territorial asylum, refugees and stateless persons, on which all 21 of the Council of Europe countries are represented, usually by officials of the Ministry of the Interior or Justice. CAHAR has failed to produce an agreement over who is responsible for examining an asylum request. A new initiative was launched at the end of 1986 to finalise an agreement following political pressure, particularly from West Germany. The UNHCR attends CAHAR's meetings, but in general NGOs have no right to be present and the proceedings of this committee are strictly confidential.

The Parliamentary Committee on Refugees, Migration and Demography

This committee consists of representatives of national parliaments and is an advisory committee for the parliamentary assembly of the Council of Europe. Its agenda includes many refugee and migration issues of concern to European countries, as well as analyses of refugee and migration questions outside Europe. A recent important report published by this committee and endorsed by the parliamentary assembly was the so-called Bohm report (1985) on the living and working conditions of refugees in Europe.

Human Rights Division

A recent initiative, which has been strongly supported by the Human Rights Division of the Council of Europe, is to formulate a new article on the subjective right of asylum to be added to the other articles in the European Convention on Human Rights and Fundamental Freedoms.

UNHCR/Governmental Consultations

These started after the European consultations on the arrival of asylum-seekers in Europe which took place in Geneva in May 1985. A number of European governments and the UNHCR have since met in Stockholm, the Hague, and Gerzensee (Switzerland) and a fourth meeting was held in Norway in early 1988. The governments and the UNHCR have established 'problem-oriented' working groups which meet more often and which have dealt specifically with the question of Iranian and Tamil refugees in Europe. UNHCR staff attend these meetings; so far NGOs may not attend and the discussions are confidential. Observers from the United States and Canada have attended some of the meetings.

The Trevi Group

At the end of 1986, the 12 governments of the EEC established a consultative process under the control of Ministers of the Interior or Justice to examine questions of terrorism, drug abuse and illegal immigration. Officials from the 12 countries meet frequently and, from time to time, their proposals are discussed by ministers. The recommendations have no legal force in themselves, but government ministers in a number of European states are explaining new national measures by reference to these agreed European practices. (One example is the introduction of legislation controlling airlines.)

The European Parliament

The European Parliament approved the so-called Vetter Report in March 1987. The Vetter Report was a product of the European Parliament's Committee on Legal Affairs & Citizens' Rights and was prepared after research in a number of European countries by Mr Heinz Oskar Vetter, a socialist member of the committee from the Federal Republic of Germany. This report made a great many recommendations which referred to the better treatment of asylum-seekers in Europe and commented on the need for harmonisation at a high level rather than the level of the lowest common denominator. The Vetter recommendations will be examined in due course by the European Commission and by the European Parliament.

The European Commission

The European Commission has recently been preparing a directive on the harmonisation of asylum practice for the 12 countries of the EEC. This directive is the responsibility of Directorate D of the Directorate-General III. It was being prepared as a matter of great urgency because of the pressures to harmonise the EEC's internal market mechanisms before the target date of 1992. The European Commission's mandate is specifically related to the abolition of internal frontiers and the safeguarding of the external frontiers of the 12 EEC countries. This means that the principal motivation of the process is the economic dynamic of a unified market. Consultation was strictly limited until the directive was completed (at the end of 1987) and presented to the Council of Europe and to the European Parliament. No non-governmental input is envisaged, although there is a level of consultation with the UNHCR.

The Schengen Group

This group consists of the countries of Benelux plus West Germany and France. It has met at official and ministerial level to discuss harmonisation of visa requirements and an agreement on which country is responsible for examining an asylum request. No UNHCR or non-governmental participation has been permitted. The Schengen countries published a draft conclusion of their work in December 1987.

Airlines

Consultations continue between national governments and individual airlines, the International Air Transport Association (IATA) and the International Civil Aviation Organisation (ICAO). IATA invited governments to a meeting in Geneva in June 1987 to discuss developments in airline policies, including measures taken by governments to punish airlines for transporting undocumented aliens. It is believed that there is very grave disquiet amongst many pilots' associations and airline staff bodies about the increasing responsibility being given to them by governments to control the movement of undocumented aliens or potential refugees.

European Consultation on Refugees and Exiles

Public opinion is deeply polarised about the asylum issue; many people have indeed been sensitised to the human rights context of the refugee phenomenon by the presence of refugees from many parts of the world in their countries. But many other people have manifest racist and xenophobic attitudes which are encouraged by extremist political parties and are not sufficiently combatted by national authorities. The NGOs participating in the ECRE have, in recent months, consulted extensively to formulate a package of proposals which constitute an alternative to the present deteriorating situation and aim to uphold the principal of asylum in Europe and to respond to the global refugee problem. A policy document containing these initiatives has now been circulated to governments and experts. It is reproduced as Document VIII *A Refugee Policy for Europe* in this volume.

The ECRE non-governmental agencies have also circulated this set of suggestions for the widest public debate and we hope that the UNHCR and sympathetic governments in both Europe and the third world will consider this package of measures as being the basis for a more open and honest debate on these very complex issues.

VIII A REFUGEE POLICY FOR EUROPE
The European Consultation on Refugees & Exiles

Introduction

In the past few years European Governments have begun to work together in a number of different forums to develop methods of limiting the numbers of asylum applications. This is mainly in reaction to recent increases in the number of applications made by national of Third World States. These discussions are expected to culminate in plans which would unify the policies and practice of the European Community in relation to asylum-seekers by 1992. This in turn can be expected to have a major impact on other European States.

Voluntary agencies in Europe concerned with refugees have become increasingly alarmed by the progress of these Governmental discussions. They appear to be motivated by the intention to restrict access to the asylum procedures of European countries. Many of the meetings are taking place in secret and policies are being developed which do not result from consultation with concerned agencies. Parliamentary scrutiny of the process has been minimal. Considerations relating to the needs of individual refugees and to the need for a global approach to the world refugee problem do not appear to be taken into account.

Voluntary agencies believe that the refugee problem in Europe cannot be looked at as one of immigration control. This document puts forward a refugee policy for European Governments which is comprehensive and practical. The voluntary agencies hope that it can provide a basis for informed discussions between Governments, inter-governmental and non-governmental organisations.

Objective of the Policy

To reach a situation in which Europe upholds the principle of asylum, fulfills its obligations under the 1951 Convention Relating to the Status of Refugees, the 1967 Protocol and other Related Conventions and Agreements, and responds adequately to the global refugee problem.

Need for the Policy

Although all European countries consider that they fulfill their obligations to those in need of international protection under the 1951 Convention and 1967 Protocol, it is clear that neither part of the policy objective is being fulfilled at present in most European countries. The right to asylum is threatened by measures being taken in many countries, which are intended both to deny access to asylum-seekers and to encourage restrictive interpretations of the Convention and Protocol.

Voluntary agencies are aware of the views of European Governments and of the need to put forward practical proposals for solving contemporary refugee problems while fulfilling the overall policy objective. The agencies believe that the proposals set out below meet this requirement. Taken together they constitute a package of measures intended to ensure a fair and orderly policy, while safeguarding the right of asylum and tackling the questions posed by the spontaneous arrival of asylum-seekers in Europe from other continents.

Essential Elements of the Policy

A comprehensive refugee policy requires a commitment to a range of measures introduced simultaneously. No single measure among those outlined below will solve the problems. Taken together they would have a major impact.

1. Responsibility for Examining Asylum Requests

In spite of intensive discussions lasting several years, European Governments have failed to reach an agreement defining the notion of the 'country of first asylum', i.e. the country which would be responsible for examining asylum requests. Such an agreement is essential if asylum applications in Europe are to be dealt with in a fair and orderly way, in accordance with Article 31, and not to result in endless diversion of asylum-seekers from one country to another. It is understood that the Council of Europe's Ad Hoc Committee of Experts on the Legal Aspects of Territorial Asylum, Refugees and Statelessness (CAHAR) is involved in a renewed effort to draw up an agreement on this issue. Expert opinion, both within and outside Governments, however, remains pessimistic about the likelihood of European Governments being able to reach agreement on a text. The ECRE has appointed an *Expert Group* to examine this problem and make proposals for public discussion.

2. Geographic Limitation to the 1951 Convention and 1967 Protocol

The withdrawal of the geographic limitation (Article 1B(1)(a) of the Convention) still maintained by Italy and Turkey would be an important element of an effective, harmonised european refugee policy. These countries are unlikely to agree to such a withdrawal unless they are convinced that this will not leave them to cope with disproportionate numbers of refugees from outside Europe.

3. Measures to Improve the Availability of Durable Solutions for Asylum-seekers

The fact that some refugees of a particular group manage to reach Europe without adequate documentation while others are obliged to remain in precarious circumstances without access to any satisfactory durable solution creates an obviously unacceptable situation. It is therefore proposed that an orderly resettlement procedure should be established whenever possible in situations where large numbers of refugees are trying to reach Europe from a country of first arrival. This procedure would require that certain conditions (set out below) be fulfilled in the country of first arrival. Where these conditions are indeed fulfilled refugees who have made their way spontaneously to Europe could reasonably be asked to return to the country of first arrival and enter the procedure.

3.1 Situation in the Country to Which an Asylum Seeker May Be Returned

The following conditions must exist in a country to which an asylum seeker is to be returned:

- Basic protection (including specifically protection against refoulement) and assistance during a waiting period. These minimum conditions have been spelt out by the Executive Committee of the High Commissioner's Programme in their Conclusion No.22 (XXXII), Section II.
- Effective access to a local procedure for the determination of refugee status (wherever possible countries should be parties to the Convention).
- Effective access to an efficient and adequate resettlement machinery.
- Facilities for temporary local settlement which have regard for the conditions of life of the local population.
- Facilities for voluntary return to the country of origin, when this is possible and specifically requested by the asylum seeker.

These conditions are intended to generate confidence among refugees that they have access to genuine opportunities, including the opportunity to apply for resettlement in a European country. Where these conditions apply and where refugees nevertheless seek to bypass the procedures and travel to Europe directly, Governments are entitled to ask them to return to the country of first arrival and enter the procedures, provided that that country is willing to readmit them without penalty and to provide access to the facilities described above. Where an asylum seeker expresses a fear of persecution or a fear that his/her physical safety or freedom are endangered in the country of first arrival, the authorities of the European country concerned should give favourable consideration to his/her asylum request (cf Conclusion 15 (XXX) of the UNHCR Executive Committee, paragraph k, XXX Session).

Where the essential conditions described above do not exist, it is unacceptable that refugees seeking asylum in Europe be returned to a country of first arrival.

3.2 The Return of Recognised Refugees to Countries of First Arrival where no Resettlement Opportunities are Available

In some cases, refugees who have received Convention status or broadly equivalent treatment in a Third World country seek to enter Europe as asylum-seekers. While there is a need for resettlement opportunities in Europe for some of these persons, particularly close family reunion cases, most agencies would accept that such people can be returned to their country of asylum provided that adequate protection and a 'durable solution' are indeed available. This would mean voluntary repatriation, local settlement, or temporary local settlement. A clear definition of what constitutes adequate facilities in such situations needs to be developed through consultations between Governments, inter-governmental organisations and NGOs.

3.3 Resettlement Criteria

In establishing resettlement mechanisms for refugees in countries of first arrival Governments and UNHCR will need to agree on the criteria for deciding which refugees have priority. These criteria will naturally be influenced by the specific situation, but some general points can be made:

- First priority should be given in all cases to people who are at risk, and to reunification of families.
- Governments of resettlement countries should also consider giving a high priority to those with established links in their country.
- 'Ability to integrate successfully' should not be a criterion for resettlement to the detriment of refugees at risk.

3.4 Conclusion

The proposals in these first three sections constitute the core of the ways in which agencies feel that a system satisfactory to all concerned could be evolved. It should be stressed again that in the absence of such procedures forcible return of asylum-seekers to a country of first arrival or transit outside Europe will normally be a violation of Article 31 of the Convention and may also be a violation of Article 33.

4. Policy towards Asylum-seekers who, after a full and fair Status Determination Procedure, are not Recognised as Refugees in the Country where they Applied for Asylum and who are Denied Permission to Remain in that Country

The number of asylum-seekers forced to return to their countries of origin by European Governments in recent years, after rejection of their applications, has been relatively small. In those cases where this has happened, however, the process can be devastatingly traumatic. Some asylum-seekers have committed suicide rather than return. There is an urgent need for a clear and humane policy in this area.

Forcible return of a rejected asylum seeker to the country of origin should not be contemplated before the opportunity has been offered to seek entry into another country when this is possible within a reasonable time. Governments should in any case set a time limit beyond which they will not normally insist on return even if the asylum application is rejected. Governments should establish agreed procedures for doing this.

Where an asylum seeker is indeed to be returned, governments should make arrangements for the following facilities:

- Access to counselling from suitable NGOs experienced in this field;

– Respect for the asylum seeker's wishes as regards the method of return;
– Appropriate assistance towards reintegration.

5. Visas and Airline Policies
Although it is clearly the established right of States to impose visa requirements when they so decide, it is contrary to international legal principles to impose entry visa requirements exclusively in order to prevent people from leaving their own country or country of first arrival in order to seek asylum. The rapid extension of visa requirements by many European States in recent years has made it considerably more difficult for refugees from certain countries to seek and obtain asylum in Europe. It is to be feared that by 1992 visas will be required by nationals of all countries outside Western Europe who wish to enter any European country. In order to reinforce the impact of their visa requirements a number of European Governments have introduced legislation to fine airlines for transporting passengers who do not have adequate documentation. This imposes responsibilities on airline staff which they are not mandated or qualified to fulfill, while in many cases making it impossible for genuine refugees to leave their countries.

This process seems to be motivated by the concept of Fortress Europe 1992, protected from undesired immigration by a comprehensive visa policy. It is the view of the voluntary agencies that this policy is unworkable in the ways intended, undesirable, and is being developed without public consultation in the countries concerned.

The agencies accept that European Governments probably fear that substantial numbers of people may suddenly seek to leave a non-European country affected by violence and unrest and fly direct to European countries to seek asylum. It is the agencies' view that this type of situation can be dealt with in a planned and appropriate way in consultation with other countries in the region concerned. The fear of this possibility can in no way justify the range of restrictive measures now being introduced.

6. Promote the Analysis of Root Causes of Refugee Movements and Take Action to Avert New Flows of Refugees
A comprehensive solution to the global refugee problem 'includes the need to address the causes of movements of refugees and asylum-seekers from their countries of origin' (Resolution 41/124 adopted by the General Assembly of the United Nations on 16 December 1986). The General Assembly also adopted at its 41st Session in December 1986 Resolution 41/70 on International co-operation to avert new flows of refugees by which it endorsed the conclusions and recommendations in the Report on this subject prepared by the Group of Governmental Experts. The study on Human Rights and Massive Exoduses which Prince Sadruddin Aga Khan made at the request of the United Nations has been a considerable contribution to the general understanding of what the root causes of refugee problems are. These studies give a detailed analysis of the links

between the global economic and political order and the creation of refugee movements.

An international consensus exists therefore on these questions and we propose that European Governments should take the lead in launching the difficult and prolonged international action required to avert new flows of refugees.

7. Define Ways in which Europe can Contribute to Ensuring the Protection and Assistance of Refugees Outside Europe, and Promote Situations in which People do not Need to Flee and in which those who have Fled are able to Return

Just as Europe needs to harmonise its internal protection and assistance policies for refugees, so it also needs to develop clear policies towards the protection and assistance of refugees outside Europe. These obligations to provide support to countries which host large numbers of refugees are clearly spelt out in Conclusion 15 of the UNHCR Executive Committee. Many countries are able to disregard their international responsibility to protect and assist refugees from neighbouring countries, because they face no sanctions if they do so and because they receive inadequate support from the international community. In such cases this situation may lead directly to the diversion of the refugee movement towards Europe. European Governments therefore have a political interest as well as a humanitarian duty to ensure that all countries with which they have political, diplomatic and economic relations are able to fulfill responsibilities when faced with the arrival of large numbers of refugees.

This responsibility of European Governments to help safeguard the rights of refugees outside Europe naturally also extends to the prevention of the expulsion of nationals and to the facilitation of voluntary repatriation. In recent years too many States have been able either to expel groups of their nationals, to refuse to allow their nationals to return home, or to refuse to allow refugees settled in their country to return home voluntarily, without attracting significant international condemnation or sanctions. European Governments need to be aware of the totally interconnected nature of the global refugee problem. A failure to insist on the norms of internationally accepted behaviour or to provide poor countries with the resources to tackle a problem may have direct or indirect repercussions for Europe itself.

8. Projecting Positive Images of Refugees

Some Government officials and politicians at present project negative images of refugees and asylum-seekers to the public. They also frequently give the impression that the number of people seeking asylum in Europe or likely to seek asylum here is far greater than it in fact is. A number of measures are therefore proposed which would help to project more positive and accurate images of refugees and asylum-seekers in the public mind:

– Words such as 'floods', 'influxes', 'waves', 'torrents', 'streams', 'bogus' 'swamped', 'abusive', etc. should be avoided.
– Government information offices in each European country should publish booklets describing the situation of refugees, the refugee policy of the Government and including recent detailed statistics. These booklets could be drafted in cooperation with NGOs.
– Specific ideas and programmes should be introduced, such as:
* *National refugee documentation centres;*
* *Special events such as Refugee Day or Refugee Friendship Week;*
* *Training seminars for judges, officials and others involved in refugee decision–making;*
* *Study of refugees in curricula of schools, colleges and universities, particularly in courses on law, contemporary history, social sciences and international relations;*
* *Cultural, historical and political information about countries of origin.*
– Governments should publicise regulations and advisory guidelines given to Government officials dealing with asylum–seekers.
– Governments should work with NGOs to promote positive images of refugees.
– Governments and NGOs should promote a detailed understanding of refugee issues in the Press.
– Governments and NGOs should promote research into public attitudes towards refugees and into the source of public perceptions of refugees. The research should measure how far public perceptions differ from objective reality and the extent to which government policy is shaped by its analysis of public perceptions rather than by an analysis of the actual situation.

Conclusion: Harmonisation of Asylum and Assistance Policies

Moves towards the harmonisation of asylum policies are taking place in a number of European governmental forums. No comparable work appears to be taking place at the European level on the harmonisation of protection, assistance and resettlement policies in Europe, nor on a concerted European response to refugee situations outside Europe. Parliamentary committees of the Council of Europe and the European Parliament have made a series of positive proposals to safeguard the standards contained in the 1951 Convention and in the European Convention for the Protection of Human Rights and Fundamental Freedoms within the asylum policies of European States. At the same time however Ministers and officials of Interior and Justice Departments are meeting under a series of ad hoc arrangements to elaborate measures aimed uniquely at the exclusion of undocumented aliens including those wishing to claim asylum. The agenda for these secret discussions which are taking place without parliamentary scrutiny include terrorism and drug–trafficking. Such discussions appear to threaten the human rights standards established by the parliamentary process of the Council of

Europe. In order to ensure proper consideration of issues of great public importance the voluntary agencies call on the Council of Europe and national parliaments to guarantee that all those with experience and knowledge of the issues are able to contribute to the formulation of harmonised procedures.

Note: This official ECRE document is reproduced by the kind permission of Philip Rudge, the Secretary to this body. He asks us to add that in his view 'it is extraordinary that there is no long-term governmental strategy for a European asylum policy. The ECRE document therefore stands as an attempt by the concerned non-governmental agencies to develop the basis for a strategy in the long-term. Further detailed work will be necessary on each section of the proposal' – *DJ & RC.*

REFERENCES

ADWG [Anti-Deportation Working Group] (1985) *The Right to be Here*, London, ADWG

Amnesty International (1986) *Schutz für politisch Verfolgte: Verwirklicht das Grundrecht auf Asyl*, Bonn

Amnesty International (1987) *Annual Report*

Angell, A. & S. Carstairs (1987) 'The Exile Question in Chilean Politics', *Third World Quarterly*, vol. 9, no. 1, pp. 148–67

Ashby, Lord E. (1977) *Einstein was a Refugee*, World University Service

Bade, Klaus J. (1987) 'Sozialhistorische Migrationsforschung und Flüchtlingsintegration', in Rainer Schulze, Doris von der Brelie-Lewien and Helga Grebing (eds) (1987) *Flüchtlinge und Vertriebene in der westdeutschen Nachkriegsgeschichte*, Hildesheim

Bambirra, V. (1971) 'La Mujer Chilena en la Transición al Socialismo', *Punto Final*, Santiago de Chile, no. 133, pp. 1–8

Bambirra, V. (1972) 'Liberación de la Mujer y Lucha de Clases', *Punto Final*, Santiago de Chile, no. 151, pp. 10–15

Barker, M. (1981) *The New Racism: Conservatives and the Ideology of the Tribe*, London, Junction Books

Barth, Frederick (1969) *Ethnic Groups and Boundaries,* Boston, Little, Brown and Co.

Beitz, Wolfgang G. & Michael Wollenschläger (eds) (1980) *Handbuch des Asylrechts,* Baden-Baden, Zwei Bände

Bettati (1987) *L'asile politique en question: Un statut por les réfugiés,* Paris, Presses Universitaries de France

Blaschke, Jochen (1984) 'Islam und Politik unter türkischen Arbeitdmigranten' in ders. (co-ed) *Islam und Politik in der Türkei* (Jahrbuch zur Geschichte und Gesellschaft des Vorderen und Mittleren Orients), pp. 255–94

Blaschke, Jochen & Birgit Ammann (1988) 'Kurden in der Bundesrepublik Deutschlands: Ihre soziale und kulturelle Situation' in Y. Mönch-Bucak (ed) *Kurden: Alltag und Widerstand,* Bremen, pp. 90–9

Blaschke, Jochen & Jangiskhan Hasso (1988) 'Yezidi in Exil: Chacen für das Uberleben einer religiösen Minderheit' in Andreas Germershausen & Wolf-Dieter Narr (eds) *Flucht und Asyl: Berichte über Flüchtlingsgruppen,* Berlin, Edition Parabolis

Bo, B.P. (1986) 'Usynliggjoring, spredning og seleksjon: Tendenser i dagens innvandringskontroll', in Swedin (ed.) 7. *Nordiske Migrations Forskerseminariet*, Sigtuna, Naut-rapport 1987: 2

Bohm Report (1985) 'Living and Working Conditions of Refugees in Europe', *Council of Europe*, Parliamentary Committee on Refugees, Migration and Demography

Brand, Robina (1981) 'A Happy Place to Be, *Community Care*, 22 October, pp. 22–4

Bravo, R. & R. Todaro (1985) 'Chilean Women and the UN Decade for Women', *Women's Studies International Forum*, vol. 8, no. 2, pp. 111–16

BRCa [British Refugee Council] (1987), *Tamil Asylum-seekers: Implications for a British Asylum Policy and Carriers' Liability*, London: BRC

BRCb [British Refugee Council] (1987) 'Settling for a Future', *Policy Report*, April, London, BRC

Browne, A. (1979) 'Latin American Refugees: British Government Policy and Practice', *Britain and Latin America, An Annual Review of British-Latin American Relations 1979*, London, Latin American Bureau

Bueren, Ilse & Simone Wolken (1987) 'Rechtssprechungsübersicht zur Anerkennungspraxis der Verwaltungsgerichtsbarkeit mit Hinweisen auf die Spruchpraxis des Bundesamtes für die Anerkennung ausländischer Flüchtlinge', *ZDWF-Schriftenreihe*, no. 19, Bonn

Chaney, E.M. (1973) 'The Mobilization of Women in Allende's Chile' in Jaquette, J. (ed.) *Women in Politics*, New York, John Wiley

Change Reports (1981) *Military Ideology and the Dissolution of Democracy - Women in Chile*, London, Change International Reports, no. 4

Cohen, Robin (1987) *The New Helots: Migrants in the International Division of Labour*, Aldershot, Gower

Commission Européenne (1988) *Avant-Projet de Directive du Conseil relative au rapprochement des règles concernant le droit d'asile et le statut des réfugiés*, Brussels, The Commisssion

Costa Lascoux, J. (1988) 'Réfugiés et demandeurs d'asile en Europe', *Revue Européenne de Migrations Internationales*, vol. 3, no. 1, pp. 239–66

Council of Europe (1975) *Report on the Situation of de facto refugees*, Parliamentary Assembly Document 3642, 5 August, Strasbourg, The Council.

Cuny, Frederick C. (1979) 'Viewpoints', in *Disasters*, vol. 3, no. 4

Dalglish, Carol (1980) 'Occupational Background of the refugees from Vietnam in Great Britain', *New Community*, vol. 8, no. 3, pp. 344–6

de los Angeles Crummett, M. (1977) 'El Poder Femenino: The Mobilization of Women against Socialism in Chile', *Latin American Perspectives*, issue 15, vol. 14, no. 4, pp. 103–14

d' Orey, S. (1984) *Immigration Prisoners: a Forgotten Minority*, London, the Runnymede Trust

ECRE (1987) *A Refugee Policy for Europe*, Policy document, September

Edholm, Felicity, Helen Roberts and Judith Sayer (1983) *Vietnamese Refugees in Britain*, London, Commission for Racial Equality

European Programme to Combat Poverty (1986) 'Problems arising from Migrating Movements of Refugees, Migrants and Ethnic Minorities', A round table, October

European Seminar (1987) *Training and Employment of Refugees in Europe*, British Refugee Council, September

FASIC (1981) *A Socio-Psychological Study of 25 Returning Families (1980)*, London, World University Service (UK) 1981, pp. 35-40

Fawcett, J.E.S. (1969) *The Application of the European Convention on Human Rights*, Oxford, Clarendon Press

Field, S. (1985) 'Settling Refugees: The Lessons of Research', Home Office Research Study No. 87

Finlay, Ros & Jill Reynolds (1985) *Better Social Services for Refugees*, Leeds, Refugee Action

Frankenberg, Günter (1987) 'Politisches Asyl - ein Menschenrecht? Versuch, den Schutz vor Folter auszuweiten', *Kritische Justiz*, no. 1

Frings, Paul (1951) *Das internationale Flüchtlingsproblem 1919-1950*, Frankfurt

Gallissot, R. (1985-86) Seminaire *Migrations et Pluralisme*, Université de Paris II, Unité Migrations et Society, CNRS

Garrett, P. (1978) 'Growing Apart: The Experiences of Rural Men and Women in the Central Valley of Chile', Madison, *University of Wisconsin*, unpublished Ph.D. thesis

Goodwin-Gill, G.S. (1978) *International Law and the Movement of Persons between States*, Oxford, Clarendon Press

Goodwin-Gill, G.S. (1983) *The Refugee in International Law*, Oxford, Clarendon Press

Goodwin-Gill, G.S. (1986) 'The Detention of Non-nationals with Particular Reference to Refugees and Asylum-seekers', *In Defence of the Alien*, Vol. 9. pp. 138-51

Greenberg, Stanley (1981) *Race and State in Capitalist Development*, New Haven, Yale University Press

Grahl-Madsen, A. (1972) *The Status of Refugees in International Law, Vol.2, Asylum Entry and Sojourn*, Leiden, A.W Sijthoff

Guillon, Claude (1988) 'Les SSAEL soixante ans d'accueil de réfugiés', *Revue Européenne de Migrations Internationales*, vol. 4, nos. 1&2, pp. 115-25

Home Office (1987) [UK Government] *Statistical Bulletin*, Various months, London, The Home Office

ICIHI [Independent Commission on International Humanitarian Issues] (1986) *Refugees: Dynamics of Displacement*, London, Zed Books

Igonet-Fastinger (1983) 'Approche socio-anthropologique et socio-historique de l'identité', *Revue de Recherches Sociologiques*, Louvain, vol. 15, no. 2/3

International Migration Review (1984), special issue, 'Women in Migration', *International Migration Review*, vol. 18, no. 4, pp. 881-1314

Jaquette, J. (ed.) (1973) *Women in Politics*, New York, John Wiley

Joint Working Group for Refugees from Chile (1975) *Refugees from Chile*, London, Joint Working Group for Refugees from Chile

Joint Working Group for Refugees from Latin America (1979) *Refugees and Political Prisoners in Latin America*, London, Joint Working Group for Refugees from Latin America

Joly, D. (1988) *Refugees in Britain: An Annotated Bibliography*, Centre for Research in Ethnic Relations, bibliography no. 9

Jones, P. (1982) 'Vietnamese Refugees', Home Office Research & Planning Unit, Paper no. 13

Kardam, Ahmet (1988) 'Hintergrund und Perspektiven der Fluchtbewegung aus der Türkei' in Andreas Germershausen & Wolf-Dieter Narr (eds) *Flucht und Asyl: Berichte über Flüchtlingsgruppen*, Berlin, Edition Parabolis

Kauffmann, Heiko (ed.) (1986) *Kein Asyl bei den Deutschen: Anschlag auf ein Grundrecht*, Hamburg

Kay, D. (1987) *Chileans in Exile: Private Struggles, Public Lives*, Basingstoke, Macmillan

Kirchheimer, Otto (1985, 1961) *Politische Justiz: Verwendung juristischer Verfahrensmöglichkeiten zu politischen Zwecken*, Frankfurt am Main, Fischer

Köfner, Gottfried and Peter Nicolaus (1986) *Grundlagen des Asylrechts in der Bundesrepublik Deutschland*, Mainz und München, Zwei Bände

Kunz, E F. (1973) 'The Refugees in Flight: Kinetic Models and Forms of Displacement', *International Migration Review* vol. 7, no. 2, pp. 125–46

Lam, Emily (1980) 'Health Visiting Vietnamese Refugees in Britain', *Health Visitor*, vol. 53, July, pp. 254–5

Levin, Michael (1981) *What Welcome? Reception and Resettlement of Refugees in Britain*, London, Acton Society Trust

Marx, R. (1978) *Asylrecht: Rechhts-sprechungsübersicht mit Erläuterungen: Gesetzessammlungen*, Baden-Baden, Zwei Bände

Marx, R. (1984) *Eine menschenrechtliche Begründung des Asylrechts*, Baden-Baden

Mattelart, M. (1976) 'Chile: The Feminine Version of the Coup d'Etat' in Nash, J. and Safa, H.I. (eds) (1976), pp. 279–301

Micksch, Jürgen (ed.) (1987) *Flüchtlingsinitiativen – eine Reaktion auf zunehmende Ausländerfeindlichkeit*, Berichte von 'Pro Asyl' Gruppen, Texte zur Lage, Frankfurt am Main, epd-Dokumentation, no. 14 (Evangelischer Pressedienst, Friedrichstraße 2–6, D-6000 Frankfurt am Main 17)

Morokvasic, M. (1983) 'Women in Migration: Beyond the Reductionist Outlook' in Phizacklea, A. (ed.) (1983), pp. 13–31

Mougne, Chris (1985) *Vietnamese Children's Home: a Special Case for Care?*, London, SCF

Mühlmann, Wilhelm Emil (1961) *Homo Creator*, Abhandlungen zur Soziologie, Anthropologie und Ethnologie, Wiesbaden (Harrassowitz)

Naess, Ragnar (1986) 'Norsk statlig rasisme', *Materialisten*, no. 4

Nash, J. & H.I. Safa (1976) *Sex and Class in Latin America*, New York, Praeger

Nettleton, C. (1984) 'The UK as a Country of Resettlement for Third World Refugees', *Refugee Report, 1984* London, British Refugee Council

Nettleton, C. & N. Simcock (1987) *Asylum Seekers in the UK: Essential Statistics*, British Refugee Council, September

Neves-Xavier de Brito, A. (1986) 'Brazilian Women in Exile: The Quest for an Identity', *Latin American Perspectives*, issue 49, vol. 13, no. 12, pp. 58-80

Nuscheler, Franz (1984) *Nirgendwo zu Hause: Menschen auf der Flucht*, Baden-Baden

Oliveira da Costa, A., Porciuncula de Moraes, M.T., Marzola, N. and da Rocha Lima, V. (1980) *Memorias - das Mulheres - do Exilio*, Rio de Janeiro, Paz e Tierra, Projecto Memorias do Exilio (II)

Otto, J. et al (eds) (1987) *Asylnovelle 1987 und Schutz der De-facto-Flüchtlinge*, Baden-Baden

Paine, Thomas (1969) '(1776): Common Sense and the Crisis', in Paine, Thomas (1969) *The Complete Writings of Thomas Paine*, Foner, Philip S. (ed.), vol. 1, New York, Citadel Press

Palma, C. (1984) *Women in Chile, Yesterday and Today*, London, Chile Solidarity Campaign

Pearson, Rachel (1982) 'Understanding the Vietnamese in Britain. Part One: Background and Family Life', *Health Visitor*, vol. 55, August, pp. 426-30

Pescatello, A. (ed.) (1976) *Female and Male in Latin America*, Pittsburgh, University of Pittsburgh Press

Phillips, A & J. Hartley (1977) *Education for Refugees*, London, World University Service

Phillips, Simon and Pearson, Rachel J. (1981) 'Dealing with Vietnamese Refugees', *British Medical Journal*, 21 February, vol. 282, pp. 613-16

Phizacklea, A. (ed.) (1983) *One Way Ticket, Migration and Female Labour*, London, Routledge & Kegan Paul

PRT & JCWI [Prison Reform Trust & Joint Council for the Welfare of Immigrants] (n.d.) *Immigration Prisoners Project. Last Among Equals: Immigration Act Prisoners and the Remand Population,* Paper no. 3, London, The Trust and The Council

Reid, Jeanice & Timothy Strong (1987) *Torture and Trauma*, Sydney, Cumberland College of Health Sciences

Rittstieg, Helmut (1986) 'Asylrecht gegen Flüchtlinge', *Informationsdienst Ausländerrecht*, no. 11-12, pp. 322-8

Ronge, Volker (ed.) (1984) *Berufliche Integration ausländischer Flüchtlinge*, Wuppertal

Rooyen, René van (1987) 'Die Asyldiskussion in der Bundesrepublik Deutschland', in Micksch 1987, pp. 13-28

Rudge, P, (1986) 'Fortress Europes' in US Committee for Refugees *World Refugee Survey, 1986* New York, The Committee

Safa, H.I. (1977) 'The Changing Class Composition of the Female Labour Force in Latin America', *Latin American Perspectives*, issue 15, vol. 4, no. 4, pp. 126-36

Schneider, Robin (1986) 'Flucht: Bemerkungen zum Welt-flüchtlingsproblem und der Negation unseres Asylrechts', *AWR Bulletin*, vol. 24 no. 4, pp. 179–185

Schneider, Robin (1988) 'Kurden: Flüchtlinge vor Folter und Krieg' in Andreas Germershausen & Wolf–Dieter Narr (eds) *Flucht und Asyl: Berichte über Flüchtlingsgruppen,* Berlin, Edition Parabolis

Silva–Labarca, M. (1981) 'Mujeres Chilenas Exiliadas: Procesos de Transformación Ideológica y de Comportamiento', *Chile–América*, Rome, nos. 74–5

Simmel, Georg (1968) 'Das individuelle Gesetz: Philosophische Exkurse' in Landmann, M. (ed.) Frankfurt am Main, Suhrkamp

Sombart, Werner (1919) *Der moderne Kapitalismus: Historischsystematische Darstellung des gesamteuropäischen Wirtschaftlebens von seinen Anfängen bis zur Gegenwart*, vol. 1, no. 2, München & Leipzig, Duncker & Humblot

Soulier, Gérard (1987) 'Le respect du droit d'asile, preuve et garant du droit démocratique' , *France Terre d'Asile: La lettre d'Information,* no. 65, Juin, pp. 8–18

Spaich, Herbert (ed.) (1982) *Asyl bei den Deutschen: Beiträge zu einem gefährdeten Grundrecht*, Hamburg

Stein, B.N. (1980) *Refugee Resettlement Programmes and Technics*, Report to the US Select Committee on Immigration & Refugee Policy, Michigan State University, Resource Center for Refugee Resettlement

Stein, B.N. (1981) 'The Refugee Experience: Defining the Parameters of a Field of Study', *International Migration Review,* vol. 15, no. 1, pp 320–30

Steinert, Johannes–Dieter (1986) *Flüchtlinge, Vertriebene und Aussiedler in Niedersachsen: Eine annotierte Bibliographie*, Osnabrück

Stevens, E.P. (1973) 'Marianismo: The Other Face of Machismo' in Pescatello, A. (ed.) *Female and Male in Latin America*, Pittsburgh, University of Pittsburgh Press

Thränhardt, Dietrich (1984) 'Im Dickicht der Verbände...' in R. Bauer and H. Dieβenbacher (eds) *Organisierte Nächstenliebe: Wohlfahrtsverbände in der Krise des Sozialstaats,* Opladen, pp. 55–66

Treuheit, Werner & Hendrik Otten (1986) *Akkulturation junger Ausländer in der Bundesrepublik Deutschland: Probleme und Konzepte*, Opladen

Tugendhat, Ernst (1987) 'Wie weit sind die Positionen von Nolte und Habermas voneinander entfernt?', *Niemandsland*, vol. 1, no. 2, pp. 21–23

UNHCR [United Nations High Commission for Refugees] (1979) *Handbuch über Verfahren und Kriterien zur Feststellung der Flüchtlingseigenschaft gemäβ dem Abkommen von 1961 und dem Protokoll von 1979 über die Rechtssstellung der Flüchtlinge*, Geneva, UNHCR

Vasquez, A. (1982) 'Mujeres en el Exilio: La Percepción del Exilio de las Mujeres Exiliadas en Francia', *Mensaje*, Santiago de Chile, no. 314, pp. 618–34

Vernant, Jacques (1953) *The Refugee in the Post-war World*, London, Allen & Unwin

Vetter, Heinz Oskar (1987) *Bericht im Namen des Ausschusses für Recht und Bürgerrechte zu den Fragen des Asylrechts* Tl. B.: B. Begründungen, Anlagen, Europäisches Parlament: Sitzungs-dokumente, Ser. A. Dok. A2-227/86/B. February 23 1987 (PE 107 655/B/endg) English version titled *Draft Report on the Right of Asylum*

ZDWF [Zentrale Dokumentationsstelle der Frien Wohlfahrtspflege für Flüchtlinge] (1987) *European Lawyers Workshop on Detention, Choice of Residence and Freedom of Movement of Asylum-seekers and Refugees*, Bonn, ZDWF

INDEX

This index includes all voluntary and international agencies, but government departments are not listed separately: see the country concerned for a general entry.